THE FAITH OF GIRLS

Exploring the spirituality and faith of girls on the verge of adolescence, this book presents fresh insights into children's spirituality and their transition to adulthood. Phillips has listened to girls' voices speaking in depth on the themes of self, God, church, and world, and reflected on their experiences and understandings in the light of current psychological, philosophical and sociological thinking, all placed into dialogue with a feminist approach to contemporary theology and bible. Phillips offers 'wombing' as a metaphor for their transition to young adulthood, and suggests strategies faith communities might adopt to companion girls more effectively through the fragility of puberty. This book will appeal to all those exploring areas of youth ministry, pastoral care, Christian education, nurture and childhood studies, psychology and theology.

This is a landmark text which breaks new ground in the study of the faith of girls. It deserves to be widely read and reflected upon. Grounded in nuanced biblical readings of neglected texts about girls, an impressive range of diverse theoretical perspectives from theology, gender studies, psychology and sociology, and offering original qualitative field work, Anne Phillips skilfully works all this together into a powerful text which will excite feminist scholars and practical theologians alike, while being of immense value to practitioners. Both church and academy should welcome and honour this text.

Nicola Slee, The Queen's Foundation for Ecumenical Theological Education, Birmingham, UK

Explorations in Practical, Pastoral and Empirical Theology

Series Editors: Leslie J. Francis, University of Warwick, UK,
Jeff Astley, North of England Institute for Christian Education, UK
Martyn Percy, Ripon College Cuddesdon and
The Oxford Ministry Course, Oxford, UK

Theological reflection on the church's practice is now recognised as a significant element in theological studies in the academy and seminary. Ashgate's new series in practical, pastoral and empirical theology seeks to foster this resurgence of interest and encourage new developments in practical and applied aspects of theology worldwide. This timely series draws together a wide range of disciplinary approaches and empirical studies to embrace contemporary developments including: the expansion of research in empirical theology, psychological theology, ministry studies, public theology, Christian education and faith development; key issues of contemporary society such as health, ethics and the environment; and more traditional areas of concern such as pastoral care and counselling.

Other titles in the series include:

Theological Foundations for Collaborative Ministry
Stephen Pickard
978-0-7546-6829-9

Shaping the Church
The Promise of Implicit Theology
Martyn Percy
978-0-7546-6600-4

Testimony in the Spirit
Rescripting Ordinary Pentecostal Theology
Mark J. Cartledge
978-0-7546-6352-2

Theological Perspectives on a Surveillance Society
Watching and Being Watched
Eric Stoddart
978-0-7546-6797-1

The Faith of Girls

Children's Spirituality and Transition to Adulthood

ANNE PHILLIPS

Northern Baptist Learning Community, Manchester, UK

ASHGATE

Published by
Ashgate Publishing Limited
Wey Court East
Union Road
Farnham
Surrey, GU9 7PT
England

Ashgate Publishing Company
Suite 420
101 Cherry Street
Burlington
VT 05401-4405
USA

www.ashgate.com

British Library Cataloguing in Publication Data
Phillips, Anne.
  The faith of girls : children's spirituality and transition
  to adulthood. -- (Explorations in practical, pastoral and
  empirical theology)
  1. Girls--Religious life. 2. Faith development.
  I. Title II. Series
  234.2'3'08342-dc22

Library of Congress Cataloging-in-Publication Data
Phillips, Anne, 1947-
  The faith of girls : children's spirituality and transition to adulthood / Anne Phillips.
    p. cm. -- (Explorations in practical, pastoral, and empirical
theology)
  Includes bibliographical references and index.
  ISBN 978-1-4094-2198-6 (hardcover) -- ISBN 978-1-4094-2199-3 (ebook)
  1. Girls--Religious life. 2. Christian education of girls. 3.
Preteens--Religious life. 4. Christian education of preteens. I. Title.
  BV1577.P55 2011
  259'.22--dc22

                                                                    2011005553
ISBN 9781409421986 (hbk)
ISBN 9781409421993 (ebk)

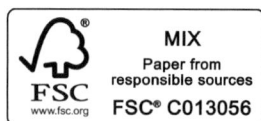

MIX
Paper from
responsible sources
FSC
www.fsc.org   FSC® C013056

Printed and bound in Great Britain by
TJ International Ltd, Padstow, Cornwall.

To
James and Clare

Contents

List of Tables

Preface

A writer dreams of coming across an area of study grossly under-researched, one which as yet commands little library shelf-space, into which to speak. I stumbled across such a lacuna in my work as theological educator and ordained minister. Involved for many years in writing on children in the church and promoting a theological base on which to build good practice in their pastoral and spiritual care and nurture, I had a real 'penny dropping' moment when I looked for gender based qualitative studies on girls, following through an increasing awareness of their 'loss of voice' as they grow towards their teens. I found none of any serious nature. 'Children' are of both the genders, a fact which the collective noun hides. Most of the literature on children is written by men who, however open to gender issues, cannot help but write from their own standpoint, and biblical material which stimulates theological reflection most commonly features the male child. Another conspicuous gap in the literature was of girls passing through the age of transition to adolescence. Most books on 'childhood', especially those on spirituality, end at age 11 when children begin secondary school; those on young people commonly start at 14 when the first flush of puberty is over and they are well into their teen years.

I chose, therefore, to focus this research project on 11–13-year-old girls who regularly attend church, so who are in some measure on a faith journey. My aim was to study their faith through their early negotiation of many of the changes puberty brings. This book is the fruit. Over a ten-year period I read, talked, interviewed, wrote, discussed and lectured so that I might have something substantial to say to church and academy and, I hope, to all those interested in girls' spirituality from whatever context. As so many women do, I had to fit it around a full-time ministry, family commitments and personal difficulties, and had to maintain motivation when my research was marginalised by those for whom the combination of children (especially girls), a qualitative methodology, and a contextual approach to theology erroneously signalled triviality. I hope readers will find this to be far from the case.

All this meant that I have depended along the way for support from many people, for which I am profoundly grateful. Through most of the long research period, Nicola Slee has been a critical friend as she has supervised, guided and encouraged my work. Nicola is a constant source of inspiration to many scholars for her personal warmth and courage, as well as her rigorous scholarship, theological insights and creative writing. Her interest in exploring feminist research as a form of spiritual practice resonates with my own experience. As I have travelled this journey with and about girls, my own faith has been enormously enriched.

To my staff colleagues at Northern Baptist College (now Learning Community) at Luther King House in Manchester, I owe a huge debt, as I do to the College for the financial support of my doctoral studies. Among these colleagues, I pay special tribute to Rachel Jenkins who was friend, adviser, teacher and confidante until her untimely death in 2006. Richard Kidd, with whom I now share the role of Co-Principal, has also been a wise counsellor and friend, and the sharer of many a theological debate. Ecumenical colleagues from the other colleges in the Partnership for Theological Education, and members of its research community, have also played their part.

I am fortunate to belong to a group of fine women in and around Manchester who are all also engaged in theological research. Meeting regularly, we read and comment on each other's work, toss ideas around, share one another's joys and struggles, all of which makes the research pathway less lonely. To Kim Wasey, Jan Berry, Clare McBeath, Ann Peart, Jo Harding and Alison Woolley, my thanks for companionship, loan of books, insightful feedback and the challenge of creative conversation. Alison Peacock too belongs to that circle of supporters and encouragers; additionally her skill of careful proofreading has been a gift to me. Conversations with Margaret Garner helped resource my imaginative journey into the structure of the womb in pregnancy as she shared her medical expertise with me.

The research could not have been undertaken without girls to interview, and to them also I'm grateful, for all that they shared of themselves. They appear in the book under pseudonyms, and they and their locations will not be identified. With the passage of time since the interviews many may not remember their participation, certainly not what they said to me, but it is upon the frankness and openness of their responses at that moment in their lives that my findings are based. I have tried to remain faithful to their words and their meanings as I have analysed and interpreted them; I see my role as one of advocacy for them, so that through my reflections their voices might be heard, and workers with future generations of girls might be enabled to pay attention to their inchoate thoughts and their struggles towards womanhood, that their spiritual nurture may be more informed. So my thanks to them, and to the ministers of their churches: Anne, Andy, Mark, Clare, Matt and Tim acted as gatekeepers and it was through them the interviews were arranged.

Without access to resources, and special places of quiet to study I could not have carried out my research. Special acknowledgement and thanks therefore go to the people and places offering those, particularly Rachel Eichhorn, Learning Resources Tutor at Luther King House, and staff at St Deiniol's (Gladstone's) Library and The Queens Foundation, Birmingham where I have done much of the writing in Reading Weeks and on Study Leave.

Finally, my thanks to my family for their forbearance while I have been buried in this seemingly interminable enterprise. To James and Liz, Clare and Reuben, I can now be a 'proper' mother again, while to Silas and Samuel I hope to give quality time so that I can learn from them about being a grandmother.

Anne Phillips
Luther King House
Manchester

Chapter 1
Introduction

Naming Girls

She conceived again and bore a daughter. Then the Lord said to him, 'Name her Lo-ruhamah, for I will no longer have pity on the house of Israel or forgive them' ... When she had weaned Lo-ruhamah, she conceived and bore him a son.[1]

This exploration of the faith of girls in this book opens with scripture, and begins with a girl who, unusually for one of both her age and gender, has a place in biblical theology.

Hosea and Gomer had three children. Biblical scholars have paid a great deal of critical attention to Gomer's story, and feminist study is redeeming her reputation and that of the original author, assigning the unbridled patriarchy of the final text to later redactors. The couple's two sons, Jezreel and Lo-ammi, have had the significance of their names for Israel subjected to detailed comment and analysis, but Lo-ruhamah is rarely accorded more than a passing mention on the way to her younger brother's story with which hers is closely linked. The middle child of three often struggles with identity. That Lo-ruhamah is a girl has not been noted as of any significance even in feminist exegesis, the children's birth and the sequence of their naming being accepted as a naturally and arbitrarily occurring order (boy-girl-boy).[2] However, Lo-ruhamah is almost alone in scripture as a named pre-pubescent girl. More usually, girls are identified by their connection with a male relative or adult figure: so sister and daughters 'belong' to Moses, Jairus and the Syro-Phoenician woman respectively, while both Naaman's wife and her slave girl are anonymous.[3]

I bring Lo-ruhamah to the foreground of attention as her treatment represents for me the fate of girls, from birth to puberty both in the bible and in the church:

---

[1] Hosea 1.6, 8. All biblical quotations are from the New Revised Standard Version.

[2] For example, Yvonne Sherwood, 'The Prostitute and the Prophet: Hosea's Marriage in Literary-Theoretical Perspective', *Journal for the Study of the Old Testament* (*JSOT*) *Supplement* 212 (Sheffield, 1996), pp. 116–18; Alice A. Keefe, 'Woman's Body and the Social Body in Hosea', *JSOT Supplement* 338 (Sheffield, 2001), pp. 190ff. Despite their focus on female imagery in Hosea, neither finds any significance in the gender of the second child in relation to the message it conveys.

[3] Also in the New Testament are the servant girl Rhoda (Acts 12.13–15) and the girl who danced for Herod (Mark 6.17–29 and Matthew 14.1–12), who is probably in her early teens.

her distinctive characteristics, history and identity are fused with those of more dominant males, and so the unique part she has to play in the story goes unrecognised. She is named by her father in response to YHWH's command. The control that biblical fathers have over their daughters is absolute: even at an older age, two daughters, Leah and Rachel, submit to their father Jacob's duplicity, while for Jephthah, a vow to YHWH takes precedence over his daughter's life.[4]

Lo-ruhamah means 'not pitied' or 'not loved'. Many commentators deny that the naming of Hosea and Gomer's children has any personal reference to them as individuals, that this is merely a rhetorical device to convey a strong message to Israel. Sherwood argues strongly against such a dismissal, as it contradicts the normative connection between a name and the meaning it is intended to convey, either for the individual or for a community. The force of this is summed up by Bal who points out that names have a 'specific meaning that integrates character into (its) life' to which she adds that it 'can also imprison it there'.[5] Happily, Lo-ruhamah is released from such imprisonment when she is re-named Ruhamah.[6]

Her names have a root connection with the Hebrew *rechem*, meaning 'womb';[7] its negative form therefore denotes something deeper and more unnatural than the English translations suggest. It signifies a complete rejection both of the parental bonding at birth and of any loving or caring instinct, which is a denial of moral living. That not only the individual but also the nation was formed 'in the womb' becomes a theme of worship and hope in the exilic period, and YHWH's remembrance of the child she bore is proclaimed by Deutero-Isaiah to be immutable even where a human mother's may fail.[8] The text of Hosea in its redacted form is part of this exilic and post-exilic corpus of prophetic and wisdom literature, so while there is no reason to doubt the veracity of Hosea's family history (Gomer's name has no other symbolic significance, and the name of the older son, Jezreel, is best understood in the context of pre-exilic history), Lo-ruhamah's name does carry these resonances. Israel's story is founded on call and covenant, re-call and new covenant, not once but many times. Integral to that story is Israel's wandering which draws from YHWH a mother's compassion and love, the desire to rescue. So, prior to the making of 'my people' (Ammi), and the motivation for their rescue which became the determinative act for the faith of Israel, of Jew and of Christian, was YHWH's compassion for the suffering people. That these feelings are identified with the personification of YHWH as

---

[4]   Genesis 29, Judges 11.

[5]   Mieke Bal, *Lethal Love: Feminist Literary Readings of Biblical Love Stories*, Indiana Studies in Biblical Literature (Indiana, 1987), p. 73.

[6]   Hosea 2.1, 23.

[7]   Phyllis Trible, *God and the Rhetoric of Sexuality* (Philadelphia, 1978) explores this connection, as I discuss on p. 141.

[8]   For example Psalm 139.13, Isaiah 49.5, Isaiah 49.15. Additionally, in the Genesis narratives, we read that 'When the Lord saw that Leah was unloved, he opened her womb', Genesis 29.31.

female is significant in the prophetic literature from the exile. I suggest, therefore, that Lo-ruhamah's gender is significant to the prophetic message, that there is a holistic balance between the two acts of having compassion and people-making, first rejected then re-established. Thus, the naming of a girl here, in contrast to her sisters' anonymity elsewhere in biblical literature, becomes in feminist reading culturally symbolic, redeeming girls from oblivion to a central place within God's saving purpose for humankind.

There is a further feature of interest in this story. When she is named by her father, her mother is sidelined. That a father could imagine such unnatural rejection of his own child is truly appalling. However, Gomer silently rejects the name and its signification. As Sherwood shows, by breastfeeding her daughter for three years, the norm in those days, she 'subverts the master-text'. 'Not loved' *is* loved; by showing that the 'negatively depicted harlot is also a nurturing mother' the father's action is seen to be deviant. This has been commonly overlooked because 'critics usually focus on *what* rather than *how* the text means'.[9] This story, and Gomer's part in it, often disregarded as a mere tool of patriarchy, offers evidence of a resistance to male domination similar to that which in Exodus chapters 1 and 2 has become highly celebrated by feminist scholars.

A Personal Journey

My 'discovery' of Lo-ruhamah comes at a stage in my own journey where I have become aware of the neglect of girls in studies of childhood, and it is this which has motivated my research, the fruits of which are found in this book. For many years, as a teacher, mother, ordained minister and college tutor, I have worked at local, national and international level studying children and their faith, promoting good practice in their care and nurture, and resisting their marginalisation in the church. In the course of my ministry I have experienced gender discrimination to a degree I had not encountered in the teaching profession of my earlier years. In response, my intellectual journey has taken me into feminist theology and hermeneutics in order both to take a stand in dialogue with men on a sound biblical and theological basis against values I consider to be inimical to the gospel of Jesus Christ, and to become more confident in my own identity as a woman made in the image of God.

Along the way, I have become aware not only of discrimination but also of avoidance of discussion of gender on the part of many well-meaning people in the church, both men and women, as if the goal of Galatians 3.28 was to discount gender differentiation in favour of some form of androgyny. This naïve approach refuses to acknowledge the power structures operative in any society, which, as clinical psychologist Robert Kegan holds, translate 'we are really all the same' as

---

[9]   Sherwood, 'The Prostitute and the Prophet', pp. 147–8.

'you are really all like me'.[10] The theology and biblical understanding we live by is primarily constructed by men (overwhelmingly white, western and middle class), and we do not immediately perceive the bias built into our dominant worldview. There is still work to be done to analyse the context and standpoint of those who construct our theologies and ecclesiologies, and open our eyes, and theirs, to the partiality of their vision and to the consideration of other viewpoints. In his first book, *The Evolving Self*, Kegan somewhat idealistically proposes that we seek a 'universal language'[11] that transcends gender and cultural differences. In his later work, in which he addresses his earlier lack of clarity on the importance of gender styles, taking more serious account of the research findings of Jean Baker Miller and Carol Gilligan,[12] he recognises the power games people play, and proposes a way forward in which people would learn self-awareness which would respect all diversity.[13] He still, however, seems to believe it possible to achieve this kind of mutuality by cognitive endeavour alone. He says:

> this kind of learning cannot be accomplished through *in*formational training, the acquisition of skills, but only through *trans*formational education, a leading out from an established habit of mind.[14]

History and faith testify that humans are rarely capable of such transformation by their own efforts. Kegan's vision of crossing a 'consciousness threshold' needs a spiritual foundation, as St Paul recognised.[15]

Even when we have taken into account the cultural differences Kegan identifies, and the divisions in the early church Paul names, there are yet further areas of power differential. One of these is generation. Children are not always treated with the respect they deserve, nor are they accorded the dignity and protection which it is their right to expect and which is enshrined in the United Nations Convention on the Rights of the Child (UNCRC). Girls are particularly vulnerable. My own experiences as a woman in the church, and my work promoting good practice in child protection and supporting survivors of abuse who are mostly female, have fuelled the concern I have for girls within churches. In my own faith story, it was as a girl and early adolescent that I had my most formative spiritual experiences, but growing within a system where faith was defined by men, I moulded these

---

[10]   Robert Kegan, *In Over Our Heads: The Mental Demands of Modern Life* (Cambridge, MA, 1994), p. 207.

[11]   Robert Kegan, *The Evolving Self: Problem and Process in Human Development* (Cambridge, MA, 1982), p. 209.

[12]   Jean Baker Miller, *Toward a New Psychology of Women* (Boston, 1976). Carol Gilligan, *In a Different Voice: Psychological Theory and Women's Development* (Cambridge, MA and London, 1982).

[13]   Kegan, *In Over Our Heads*, p. 204.

[14]   Ibid., p. 232. Author's italics.

[15]   Romans 7.14–25.

experiences to fit existing paradigms, and shaped my life-course within those patterns. I now see that overlooking, or even denying, that my encounters with God were as an embodied woman deprived me at an early stage of owning and therefore integrating an essential part of my identity with my faith journey. Although girls are living now in a time of increased awareness of gender identity, this has not greatly impacted on life and teaching within the church, and the social construction of girlhood still retains vestiges of the patriarchy of my own youth although manifest in different, perhaps more dangerously subtle, ways.

Girls in Theology

Gender is a significant factor in understanding the self during the growth process. Attention to and validation of the different experience of women has been slow to emerge, and the inclusion of girls' experience is still rare. The 30th anniversary in 2009 of the signing of the UNCRC has encouraged more writing on children in the UK. For all their valuable content, however, they noticeably lack any gender differentiation.[16] The church takes little account of gender difference, or knowledge of gendered lives, especially in dealing with children. In biblical hermeneutics and in theology, girls are largely ignored, often assumed to be included in non gender-specific references to 'children', which are not neutral. There are discourses which shape the way churches regard and behave towards girls, of which those who determine policies and attitudes towards girls are largely unaware. From Aquinas' discussion of whether girls and women were 'defective', their birth a result of weak semen or the south wind,[17] through Rousseau's exemption of girls from his 'negative education',[18] girls have been seen as aberrant. Theological reference to and discussion of children, their education and nurture, has been based on boyhood as normative. It has for the most part been ambivalent about children, both recognising their natural innocence and believing their inherent sinfulness,

---

[16]   Examples can be found in: Richard Layard and Judy Dunn and the panel of The Good Children Enquiry, *A Good Childhood, Searching for Values in a Competitive Age* (London, 2009); Anne Richards and Peter Privett (eds), *Through the Eyes of a Child: New Insights in Theology from a Child's Perspective* (London, 2009).

[17]   Although Nolan argues for a more constructive reading of Aquinas here, the 'popular' legacy is a negative one. Michael Nolan, 'The Defective Male: What Aquinas Really Said', *New Blackfriars*, 75.880 (1994): 156–66.

[18]   Rousseau's sexism is explored by John Darling and Maaike Van De Pijpekamp in 'Rousseau on the Education, Domination and Violation of Women', *British Journal of Educational Studies*, 42.2 (June 1994): 115–32. Both Aquinas and Rousseau had unorthodox upbringings in relation to women, which had a bearing on their respective writings.

with greater emphasis on the latter which has led to promotion of abusive child-rearing practices, perpetuated even today among fundamentalist groups.[19]

As 'childhood' emerged in the nineteenth and twentieth centuries as a discrete period of human development, 'a cultural interpretation of physical immaturity',[20] and became an accepted subject of academic enquiry, more theological writing touched on childhood, although almost incidentally until the second half of the twentieth century.[21] Biblical foundations were found in Jesus' actions and teaching: stress was placed on Jesus' blessing of children, his advocacy of them in his ministry, and his emphasis on the child as a model for discipleship. Theologians reclaimed a literal rather than metaphorical understanding of 'unless you become like children', although Jesus' meaning and the qualities signified are debated. Emphasis has also been placed on the positive attitude to children in Israelite, Jewish and Christian culture in contrast to the harsher treatment meted out in the Hellenistic and Roman worlds.[22] Throughout Israel's history, God's choice of children to perpetuate the covenant relationship and to 'rescue' Israel from straying, with its climax in the incarnation, has also been a focus. These children, such as Isaac, Moses, Samuel, David, Jeremiah and Jesus, are all male.

Theologies of childhood and biblically based reflections on children have for the most part been written by men.[23] Significant among these have been Rahner, Moltmann and Jensen.[24] Among women theologians, there has been a reluctance to write about children. Baker notes with some incomprehension how 'white feminists frequently forget to turn an intentional eye toward feminist socialization of younger generations'.[25] Carter concludes that feminist theology's contribution to studies of childhood is indirect, that children are drawn into discussion through

---

[19]   For a brief overview of theological views of children, see Marcia Bunge (ed.), *The Child in Christian Thought* (Grand Rapids, 2001), pp. 3–7.

[20]   Angela Shier-Jones (ed.), *Children of God: Towards a Theology of Childhood* (Peterborough, 2007), p. 188.

[21]   Bunge comments: 'children … do not play a role in the way that systematic theologians think about theological themes', 'Historical Perspectives on Children in the Church: Resources for Spiritual Formation and a Theology of Childhood Today', in Donald Ratcliff (ed.), *Children's Spirituality: Christian Perspectives, Research, and Applications* (Eugene, 2004), p. 43.

[22]   W.A. Strange, *Children in the Early Church: Children in the Ancient World, the New Testament and the Early Church* (Carlisle, 1996), pp. 3–12.

[23]   For example, Hans-Ruedi Weber, *Jesus and the Children* (Geneva, 1979); John Bradford, *Caring for the Whole Child: A Holistic Approach to Spirituality* (London, 1995); W.M.S. West, 'The Child in the Church', in W.M.S. West, *Baptists Together* (Didcot, 2000).

[24]   Karl Rahner, *Theological Investigations*, Vol. VIII (London, 1984); Jürgen Moltmann, *In The End – The Beginning: The Life of Hope* (Minneapolis, 2004); David H. Jensen, *Graced Vulnerability: A Theology of Childhood* (Cleveland, 2005).

[25]   Dori Grinenko Baker, *Doing Girlfriend Theology: God-Talk with Young Women* (Cleveland, 2005), pp. 14–15. She contrasts this with womanist literature where 'young girls are pervasive', i.e. in cultural contexts where girls do not suffer marginalisation.

the writers' experiences of mothering.[26] Even here, gender differentiation is minimal, 'assigned to footnotes'.[27] From a feminist standpoint, Mercer has written on childhood, her aim being to expose the objectification of children in a consumer society, and to address the way in which many churches recreate rather than challenge 'the market's utilitarian self-interested ambivalence' towards children as 'innocents and devils'.[28] Since a significant feature of that consumerism is the inappropriate sexualisation of young girls through beauty competitions and the marketing of suggestive clothing, it would have been appropriate to have discussed the different external pressures to which girls are exposed. Although Jensen's theological reflection around children's vulnerability lends itself to application to girls, Moltmann alone shows awareness of their exclusion and finds a way, on a biblical foundation, to redress this.[29] Pastoral theology has offered a little more to promote understanding of girls, recognising the significance to girls of the menarche.[30]

Rationale and Structure of the Book

There is, then, a discrepancy between the amount of change girls experience in this period of their lives, which is great, and the volume of qualitative research in the field, which is minimal. The transitional stage from childhood to adolescence does not fit neatly with studies of 'children' or 'young people'; change happens at an individual pace, so generalisations are difficult. It is often seen as a stage to be passed through on the way to something else. Both childhood and adolescence are subjected to intense study, but in this interim period, girls in particular suffer notable invisibility.

It was to attempt to speak into this void that I embarked on a study of girls between 11 and 13 who were already on a faith journey, another neglected area of academic study. These girls belonged in different ways to the life of local churches. It was a small-scale piece of qualitative research which makes no universal claims; it is on the basis of my analysis of what these girls shared with me, that I suggest

---

[26]   Marian Carter, 'A Preferential Option for Children: The Creation of a Theology of Childhood within the Christian Tradition' (unpublished PhD thesis, University of Exeter, 2004), pp. 279–80.

[27]   Baker, *Doing Girlfriend Theology*, p. 15.

[28]   Joyce Ann Mercer, *Welcoming Children: A Practical Theology of Childhood* (St Louis, 2005), p. 120.

[29]   Moltmann, *In The End*, chapter 1.

[30]   For example, Mary Lynn Dell discusses pubertal development and body image from the perspective of pastoral and practical theology: 'She Grows in Wisdom, Stature and Favor with God: Female Development from Infancy through Menarche', in Jeanne Stevenson-Moessner (ed.), *In Her Own Time, Women and Developmental Issues in Pastoral Care* (Minneapolis, 2000), pp. 117–43.

ways of understanding their faithing and supporting its further growth that may be valid for others and transferable to other contexts, and propose ideas for a theology which recognises their place as gendered subjects and enables them to find a distinctive place and voice within the Christian community.

In the next chapter, I engage in a thorough review of the literature relevant to the study of girls of this age. This is multi-disciplinary. Despite the paucity of writing on girls in religious and theological literature, much work is being done in other fields. If any further justification were needed for such a broad exploration of childhood, more specifically girlhood, when my goal is theological, one is offered by Shier-Jones, who says the 'exploration must take full account of the interdependency ... between the childhood of the human or natural child, and that of the child of God'.[31]

The methodology needed to carry out qualitative research ethically with children, requires special care so Chapter 3 gives a detailed explanation of the processes. Handling the resulting data also requires attention to particular criteria. The primary data comes from interviews with girls, which I designed around three aims:

1. How do these girls understand themselves as girls and as Christian girls?
2. How do they understand themselves in relationship with God, and 'do' their faithing?
3. What do they need from a church community to make it a healthy environment in which their faithing can flourish?

These three questions give shape to Chapters 4, 6 and 8.

In Chapter 4, I look at girls in the 'transitional space' which is around the age of puberty as they begin to leave childhood behind, with its accompanying sense of loss, and its sometimes fearful anticipation of what lies ahead for them as they emerge into womanhood. Taking my cues from their own words, I explore the growth of identity, and the physical, social, psychological and emotional implications and effects of puberty. I conclude by offering a positive interpretation of living in a liminal place, aligned theologically with the image and experience of being a boundary dweller.

Chapter 6 takes seriously the thoughts and feelings of the girls around their religious experience, which ground my discussion of the meaning faith had for them, and their strategies for living as faithing people. As I identify themes and processes, I create a dialogue with the writings of contemporary theologians to illustrate how, without yet a commensurate vocabulary, the girls are able to wrestle with the same ideas as those of the academy, commanding respect when enough attention is paid to their discourse. The reader will not find in this dialogue a full engagement with all aspects of each theological theme, but a 'taster' from across a spectrum of views, to model a method whereby girls, and all young people, can

---

[31]   Shier-Jones, *Children of God*, p. 183.

be affirmed, and given the tools to continue to mine the depths of spirituality and theology to grow in faith in their peer groups and alongside older pilgrims.

Chapter 8 concludes my analysis as I turn to the 'holding environment' of the church, and suggest a way of thinking about the nurturance of girls from their current gestation to their birth as women. At the opening of each of these chapters, as at the beginning of this introduction, I offer a biblical reflection on pre-pubertal girls and young women whose narrative presence is for reasons other than their role as wives and mothers, thus drawing them out of the shadows of the story of YHWH's people. By this means, I begin to redress the male focus in theologies of childhood, which in its search for biblical authority is rooted in ungendered narrative or foregrounds boys. This breaks new ground, and offers positive images for girls of the part their fore-sisters played in YHWH's story, and may help them identify with people like themselves in the overwhelmingly androcentric narrative.

In between these chapters lie two short 'interludes', or pathways from the subject matter of one chapter to the next. They contain detailed analysis of the 'theologising'[32] of two girls, Lucy and Rosie, whose thinking plumbs depths of a reflective reasoning showing both maturity and originality.

My conclusion imagines a girl-friendly church; besides suggesting other ways girls might be accompanied on their faith journey, I argue for further work to be done to affirm the theological meaning and significance of girlhood.

The purpose of this book, then, is to bring girls out of the shadows, out of anonymity, and offer to those charged with their nurture in churches resources to understand, support and mentor girls, hear them into their own speech instead of 'ventriloquising' others' words and ideas, that they may enjoy abundant living as equal partners with boys and men in the adventure of faith.

Defining Terms: Faith and Spirituality

Both 'faith' and 'spirituality' appear in the title to this book. Some explanation is necessary as to the meanings they hold for me, gained from literature on spirituality which in later chapters I set in dialogue with my analysis of 'girl-talk'. Both 'spirituality' and 'faith' indicate girls' activities and orientation towards life, and the words have specific connotations; I do not use them interchangeably. They signify both the wider and the narrower frames of reference within which girls describe their experiences.

---

[32] Following Gerhard Büttner, I use this term to indicate that as girls 'do theology', their starting points, context and thought forms are different from those of adults but are no less valid: they 'develop their own schemes to structure their theological knowledge', 'How Theologizing with Children can Work', *British Journal of Religious Education*, 29.2 (2007): 138. Although the children who are the focus of Büttner's research are younger, his findings have parallels with my own.

In interviewing girls, I found that some of them were relating personal experiences of transcendence or 'excedence'[33] which did not 'fit' the language of traditional Christian faith as it will have been mediated or overtly taught by church and family. Some also brought into the interview experiences and reflections from outside the church, most notably from school assemblies and Religious Studies lessons. They offered evidence that their spiritual experience was not confined to or solely initiated by the religious tradition in which they were being nurtured, but they were open to 'revelation' which might break in unexpectedly.

Childhood spirituality is an area subjected to much research at the end of the twentieth and increasingly in the twenty-first century, and is yielding rich results in its understanding of a spirituality which is distinctive, and foundational for the transition to adulthood.[34] David Hay's research with Rebecca Nye has contributed significantly to an understanding of children's spirituality. In its 'mapping', they identify three themes which play a part in a spiritual life:[35] these are 'awareness-sensing' (the ability to 'tune in' and 'lose oneself' in an experience), 'value-sensing' (relating to conscience or moral sense), and 'mystery-sensing' (intimations of transcendence inducing wonder and awe). Hay in particular develops the work of Alister Hardy, for whom 'spirituality is not religion (but) prior to religion, a built-in, biologically structured dimension of the lives of all members of the human species'.[36] To Hay, 'spiritual awareness is commonly the context out of which religion grows'. His work with children leads him to respect that spiritual awareness. 'Could it be the case', he asks, 'that children's perceptions of mystery in situations where, from an adult perspective, there is a simple explanation arise from as profound an experience as those of the contemplative philosopher or the theologian?'. Following Popper, he suggests an understanding of science which sees a hypothesis as:

> conjecture which may at any time be refuted, rather than a thesis to be proved. In this way children's perception of mystery develops into a mature insight into the human condition, rather than being dismissed as infantile thinking.[37]

---

[33]   A term used by Terry Veling, *Practical Theology: 'On Earth as it is in Heaven'* (Maryknoll, 2005). Veling means that transcendence is not an '"otherworldly" realm ... rather a desire that stretches our attention to that which exceeds our lives, to a tradition that is larger than (exceeds/transcends) this historical moment, to a wisdom that is older than the nineteenth, twentieth or twenty first centuries', p. 31.

[34]   See pp. 38–9 for further resources on childhood spirituality.

[35]   David Hay with Rebecca Nye, *The Spirit of the Child*, rev. edn (London and Philadelphia, 2006), pp. 65–77.

[36]   David Hay, *Something There: The Biology of the Human Spirit* (London, 2006), pp. 48–9.

[37]   Hay with Nye, *The Spirit of the Child*, p. 72.

Spiritual awareness, however, goes beyond the subjective. Working with Hay, Nye found a 'core category' of children's spirituality which she termed 'relational consciousness', relational indicating 'a child's awareness of being in relationship with something or someone which added value to their ordinary or everyday perspective' and consciousness 'a distinctively reflective awareness of themselves as "subject"'.[38]

Definitions of spirituality from other fields, not specific to children, deepen our understanding.

- Seen through a *philosophical* lens, spirituality could mean: 'our capacity for self-transcendence, a capacity demonstrated in our ability to know the truth, to relate to others lovingly, and to commit ourselves freely to persons and ideals'.[39] This emphasises the outward focus and moral dimension of spirituality.
- *Psychological* definitions focus more on the inner dimension: self-fulfilment through discovery of personal meaning in life, the development of the self–other relationship of object relations theory, or the growth of identity as an individual phenomenon giving personal meaning, for which involvement in organised religion is optional.[40]
- *Sociological* definitions focus on institutional allegiance: 'religiousness is now described narrowly as formally structured and identified with religious institutions and prescribed theology and ritual'.[41]
- Then there are '*popular*' definitions, which can be 'fuzzy' in their subjectivity, emotionalism, mysticism, and connection with new age phenomena, or meditative practices associated with eastern religion.[42]

Each of the above has something to contribute to a Christian understanding. While these definitions are informative, and must be taken note of because, as Schneiders

---

[38]   Ibid., p. 109.

[39]   Joann Wolski Conn (ed.), *Women's Spirituality, Resources for Development* (New York, 1986), p. 3.

[40]   Examples can be found in the works of psychologists on whom I draw in ensuing chapters, such as Erikson and Kegan. A helpful summary can be found in Michael Jacobs, *Living Illusions: A Psychology of Belief* (London, 1993), pp. 23–54.

[41]   B. Zinnbauer and K. Pargament, 'Religion and Spirituality: Unfuzzying the Fuzzy', *Journal for the Scientific Study of Religion*, 36 (1997): 549–64.

[42]   Ibid. In the United States spirituality has a closer popular association with religion than is the case in the UK as a critique of Zinnbauer reveals. Cultural differences between the United States and UK with regard to these issues is important to bear in mind where children's spirituality is concerned as much of the recent research of relevance to children in church communities has been done in the United States where secularism is not as prevalent as in the UK.

comments, 'the subject of Christian spirituality is the human being as a whole',[43] I need to find a satisfactory definition which offers breadth as well as depth within an overtly Christian frame of reference for the study of girls. Schneiders goes on to define spirituality as 'the experience of conscious involvement in the project of life-integration through self transcendence toward the horizon of ultimate value one perceives', a description of a broadly religious understanding of spirituality which, while attending to aspects of spirituality's outer and inner dimensions, importantly locates movement inwards to self-fulfilment and outwards to relationship and moral responsibility in 'ultimate concern' or 'the sacred'. Translating this into the language of Christian faith, Hess defines it as 'a call from the Holy Spirit to the human spirit',[44] and Wolski Conn as involving 'the human capacity of self-transcending knowledge, love, and commitment as it is actualised through the experience of God in Jesus Christ, by the gift of the Spirit'.[45] McIntosh expresses the transformational nature of Christian spirituality which focuses out into the world and prevents self-transcendence from becoming narcissism, or an 'almost imperceptible slide into egoistic self-preoccupation with one's own development'.[46] Such an ethical dimension must surely be a distinguishing mark of Christian spirituality but the definitions above still do not take account of the breadth of spirituality proposed by Hay and Nye as found in children, particularly with regard to relationality. If, however, we locate our spiritual awareness in divine personhood, then perichoresis within the Trinity both draws us in (as visualised in Rublev's icon 'The Visitation of Abraham') and inspires us outwards to a connectedness with the world.[47]

Writers on women's spirituality bring their own subjective experience to bear on their definitions. Slee engaged in empirical research into women's faith, so when among her conclusions we find that connectedness and relationality are features of women's spirituality, this gives us a firmer basis for such an assertion about girls' faith; 'women's identity, development and spirituality are', she writes, 'embedded in a strong sense of connectedness to the other'.[48] Of the authors Slee cites in her extensive review of feminist writings and women's experience, it is

---

[43]   Sandra M. Schneiders, 'Approaches to the Study of Christian Spirituality', in A. Holder (ed.), *The Blackwell Companion to Christian Spirituality* (Oxford, 2005), p. 17.

[44]   Carol Lakey Hess, *Caretakers of our Common House: Women's Development in Communities of Faith* (Nashville, 1997), p. 48.

[45]   Joann Wolski Conn, 'Spirituality and Personal Maturity', in R.J. Wicks, R.D. Parsons and D. Capps (eds), *Clinical Handbook of Pastoral Counselling*, Vol. 1 (New York, 1992), p. 38.

[46]   Mark A. McIntosh, 'Trinitarian Perspectives on Christian Spirituality', in A. Holder (ed.), *The Blackwell Companion to Christian Spirituality* (Oxford, 2005), p. 179.

[47]   See Paul S. Fiddes, *Participating in God: A Pastoral Doctrine of the Trinity* (London, 2000).

[48]   Nicola Slee, *Women's Faith Development, Patterns and Processes* (Abingdon, 2004) p. 159. Although not interviewing girls, Slee suggests this is true for them, too.

Zappone whose definition comes closest to incorporating relational consciousness and the intrinsic interdependence of all reality that describes spirituality, and that distinctive of women. She says: 'In its broadest sense, spirituality centers on our awareness and experience of relationality. It *is* the relational component of lived experience'. Authentic spirituality is then lived 'in ways that nourish relationship between self, others, God and the world *that already exist*'.[49]

In her research into children's spirituality, approached as a psychologist, Nye does not betray significant awareness of feminist literature, so her data analysis is not overtly influenced by feminism. Yet, alerted by her reading of Gilligan, she does acknowledge that her conclusions 'reflect a gendered account of spirituality' and that her 'findings are a perspectival rather than absolute contribution to the body of knowledge'.[50] A glance at the index of recent books on spirituality[51] would suggest that her findings are being regarded as definitive, yet the gender attribution appears only in her unpublished dissertation. This is a matter of regret since the acknowledgement of the clear but spontaneous connection of her findings with the spirituality of women and girls would help in the study of girls' spiritual growth.[52] I wonder whether this is a case of the silencing of a woman's voice in the field of scholarship where normativity is still covertly male. If 'masculinist' perspectives were so declared, 'the world would be a very different place'.[53]

In the light of this discussion, I will use 'spirituality' to indicate imaginative experiments the girls engage in to make meaning of experience, as they strive to explore new dimensions to or ways of expressing their understanding of God. This often breaks new ground for them. As far as possible I will use active verbs for the processes of girls' 'development' since, in interviews with them, I experienced them as active makers of meaning in their lives.[54]

If that is how I understand spirituality, what of the 'faith' of my title? I use it to denote more than the cognitive content of religion, rather a girl's trust in God to give life experience, and life itself, meaning in the context of relationship. Much of what James Fowler understands by faith, following Cantwell Smith, is what I have called spirituality. But Fowler also distinctively uses faith as a verb,

---

[49]   Katherine Zappone, *The Hope for Wholeness: A Spirituality for Feminists* (Mystic, 1991), p. 12. Author's emphasis.

[50]   Rebecca Nye, 'Psychological Perspectives on Children's Spirituality' (unpublished PhD thesis, University of Nottingham, 1998), p. 279.

[51]   For example, Ratcliff, *Children's Spirituality*; Eugene C. Roehlkepartain (ed.), *The Handbook of Spiritual Development in Childhood and Adolescence* (Thousand Oaks, 2006); Hay, *Something There*.

[52]   The majority of ten-year-olds whom she cites in her research are girls.

[53]   Ann Oakley, *Experiments in Knowing: Gender and Method in Social Studies* (Cambridge, 2000), p. 21.

[54]   For faith as an active verb, see James Fowler, *Stages of Faith: The Psychology of Human Development and the Quest for Meaning* (San Francisco, 1981), p. 16.

something done, not a body of doctrine requiring only rational assent.[55] It involves movement – towards it to embrace it, and within it to draw experience into its embrace. Many expressions have been used to describe it. Astley offers several: 'belief-in is belief-that *with attitude*', Wittgenstein's 'passionate seizing', Hick's 'experiencing-as' (that is, our recognition of God's activity in human history).[56] I therefore also use 'faith' as an active verb to denote girls' lively seeking after and trusting, that is, being in relationship with, who they understand God to be for them. In the context in which I am writing, it will also convey the content of Christianity, but as story to engage with both individually and in community rather than a set of fixed doctrines.

From this introduction, we turn now to survey the literature which informs this study.

---

[55]   Fowler, *Stages*, chapter 2.

[56]   Jeff Astley, *Ordinary Theology: Looking, Listening and Learning in Theology* (Abingdon, 2002), pp. 27–33. Author's emphasis.

Chapter 2
Breaking the Silence around
Girls in Transition

Introduction

At this age, girls are becoming adolescent, a word whose Latin roots suggest a process of feeding and growing towards the greater maturity we label 'adult' by a variety of criteria.[1]

The resources I explore in this chapter fall into three groups, shaped by three disciplines. Firstly, I look in some detail at girls through the eyes of social scientists, developmentalists and researchers into the growth of spirituality and faith. Secondly, and briefly, I review the context in which girls are growing, returning to the work of psychologists Robert Kegan and Erik Erikson. Thirdly, I survey literature relevant to a theological understanding of girls and a validation of their theological acuity. Because this is an under-researched field, I shall be reviewing in every section work done on older or younger girls, or girls/boys,[2] and extrapolating findings which I consider significant: we must not forget, though, that by virtue of generation and context girls in this age range may perceive apparently similar experiences differently from those significantly younger or older.

My search was for evidence specifically about girls, texts which faced squarely the different human experiences of girls approaching adolescence through puberty. Beyond the well-known work of Gilligan and her colleagues in psychology, other texts, for example in social sciences, were difficult to unearth, reflecting the marginalisation of girls, their 'erased history', in that field.[3] There is, however, a growing body of cultural studies literature which begins to redress the imbalance,[4] and which I discuss despite its silence on spirituality. It brings helpful insights and

---

[1] G. Stanley Hall, *Adolescence: Its Psychology and its Relation to Physiology, Anthropology, Sociology, Sex, Crime, Religion and Education* (New York, 1904). Hall's contribution to the construction of female adolescence is discussed by C. Driscoll, *Girls: Feminine Adolescence in Popular Culture and Cultural Theory* (New York, 2002), pp. 53–8.

[2] From hereon, except in quotations and unless sense demands otherwise, I adopt the term 'girls/boys' instead of 'children' to highlight the fact that 'childhood' is peopled by both genders.

[3] Driscoll, *Girls*, p. 11.

[4] Anita Harris sees this field as emerging from the 'commonplace disregard for issues of gender within youth studies and age within women's studies' in A. Harris (ed.), *All About the Girl: Culture, Power and Identity* (New York, 2004), p. xviii.

discourses into the debate, and sheds light on the context in which girls construct their identity, or have it constructed, in the early twenty-first century in the western world. In this study of the spirituality and faith of girls who spend most of their time in contexts outside the church, I am seeking an understanding of the interplay between all aspects of their identity and personhood; church offers girls an environment shaped around an integrating set of values and life goals which impinge on all other parts of the lives they bring with them.

Girls in Contemporary Western Society

To understand, then, the wider context in which girls are nurtured we must look beyond the church to writing which emerged since the 1970s and which merits attention. Postmodernism analyses the function and power of discourse.[5] When 'girl' is subjected to discursive scrutiny, it appears as more than a designation of a 'universal, biological condition of female experience':[6] it is seen as a multidimensional social construction whose discourses influence the way in which individual girls live in the present and negotiate the transition to female adulthood. Thus its meaning becomes contested. 'Girl' is caught in the debate between 'sex' and 'gender' as it attempts to analyse and determine the balance between biological and cultural construction.[7] Valerie Walkerdine concludes that in the classroom 'girl' is used to denote someone passive, biddable, relational, even lacking or a failure, whereas 'child' signifies someone engaged in active exploratory learning processes, behaviour discursively associated with male characteristics and promoted as normative.[8] Harrison and Hood-Williams thus recognise the ambiguity of girls' positions, that as girls they are 'rule-following' but as children, active explorers in the search for new knowledge. To counter this, Burman uses the feminine pronoun for 'the child' in her wider deconstruction of developmental psychology to draw attention to individuality, to culture and class difference.[9] Driscoll adds the generational dimension, citing the traditional

---

[5]   I use discourse in the Foucauldian sense of the complex of language, institutions, philosophy, moral proposition, etc., which create and give boundaries to society's accepted thinking about specific subjects and constitute the 'truth' we live by. The knowledge so produced confers power and social control. Michel Foucault, *Discipline and Punish* (London, 1977).

[6]   Sinikka Aapola, Marnina Gonick and Anita Harris, *Young Femininity: Girlhood, Power and Social Change* (Basingstoke, 2005), p. 5.

[7]   A summary of the debate can be found in, for example, Iris Marion Young, *On Female Bodily Experience: 'Throwing Like a Girl' and Other Essays* (New York, 2005).

[8]   This view is proposed by Valerie Walkerdine and the Girls and Mathematics Unit, Institute of Education, *Counting Girls Out* (London, 1989) and discussed by Wendy Cealey Harrison and John Hood-Williams, *Beyond Sex and Gender* (London, 2002), pp. 150ff.

[9]   Erica Burman, *Deconstructing Developmental Psychology* (London, 1994), p. 5.

connection between 'girl' and premarcheal immaturity. She also notes that 'the Subject on which modern popular, public and academic discourses center is never a girl, even for feminism'.[10] She sees no validity in attempting to unify the varied discourse on girls; her own project is to 'analyze how girls are articulated in specific sites',[11] a goal resonating with my own as I investigate how girls see themselves and are seen within a very specific church context.

The corpus of literature on girls and girlhood in social science is growing. Although again much focuses on the 14+ age group, it introduces an important new dimension to any study of younger girls in churches as it reflects and affects the perceptions of the girlhood into which they are growing in popular discourse and in the media. What is revealed here, however, is that contemporary social science ignores the part religion plays in girls' lives: a search among indexes for 'faith', 'religion' and even 'spirituality' has yielded no results.[12] Mercer comments aptly that 'when researchers, fearful or unaware of the multiplicity of religion's presence in women's lives, neglect it in young women's experience, they ignore a vital but complex feature of these girls' lives'.[13] If we accept the results of studies of spirituality such as that of Hay and Nye, the prevalence of spiritual experience indicates a serious omission in psychological and sociological studies of all girls/ boys, but sociologists generally take no account of it despite their emphasis on well-being and fulfilment, although it can also be said of churches that they show little if any engagement with the complex social and political contexts within which girls are attempting to structure their faith life in this first decade of the twenty-first century.

1. Carol Gilligan and the Harvard Project

Carol Gilligan and her colleagues concentrated their attention on what they termed 'loss of voice' among women and girls.[14] Their pioneering work was carried out in the 1980s in the Harvard Project on Women's Psychology and the Development of Girls. The research was grounded in Gilligan's seminal studies on women's 'voice',

---

[10]   Driscoll, *Girls*, p. 9.

[11]   Ibid., p. 5.

[12]   My findings here are endorsed by K. Aune and G. Vincett: 'Gender Matters: Doing Feminist Research on Religion and Youth', in S. Collins-Mayo and P. Dandelion (eds), *Religion and Youth* (Farnham, 2010), p. 218.

[13]   Joyce Ann Mercer, *Girl Talk, God Talk: Why Faith Matters to Teenage Girls – And their Parents* (San Francisco, 2008), p. xxii.

[14]   Gilligan, *In a Different Voice*; Carol Gilligan, Nona Lyons and Trudy Hammer, *Making Connections: The Relational Worlds of Adolescent Girls at Emma Willard School* (Cambridge, 1990); Carol Gilligan, Annie G. Rogers and Deborah Tolman (eds), *Women, Girls and Psychotherapy: Reframing Resistance* (New York, London and Sydney, 1991); Lyn Mikel Brown and Carol Gilligan, *Meeting at the Crossroads: Women's Psychology and Girls' Development* (New York, 1992).

that of Jean Baker Miller on women's psychology, and of Mary Belenky and her colleagues who categorised 'women's ways of knowing'.[15] Their work generated considerable debate. Critics have accused them of, for example: taking insufficient account of how 'the structural forces of gender, race, ethnicity, class and culture constrain and influence the development of one's sense of self'; not taking holistic account of girls' experience especially of their changing bodies which at puberty become sites of new knowledge and self-discovery or construction; and adhering to the dominant psychological autonomy and individualism of western society.[16] Although in her later research Brown identified many examples of resistance, she became aware of the danger of concentrating on the loss of voice, leading her 'to worry that the current rhetoric of low self-esteem and accommodation has become a self-fulfilling prophecy'.[17] This was in large measure due to the publication and popularity of titles which, one-sidedly focusing on that aspect of the Harvard work, pathologised loss of voice, and suggested strategies to combat its destructiveness. Mary Pipher's influential *Reviving Ophelia*, for example, was one of a stream of books responding to this aspect of the work of Gilligan and her colleagues, which have become definitive of female adolescence. They often arose out of the clinical experience of psychologists and psychotherapists: Pipher for example aimed to make some sense of the increased numbers of girls she met in therapy in the 1990s compared with 30 years earlier, and her work helped to normalise the view that girls lose voice in early adolescence.[18] In the educational world, the American Association of University Women sponsored studies to identify and

---

[15]   Gilligan, *In a Different Voice*; Jean Baker Miller, *Toward a New Psychology of Women* (Boston, 1976); Mary Field Belenky, Blythe McVicker Clinchy, Nancy Rule Goldberger and Jill Mattuck Tarule, *Women's Ways of Knowing* (New York, 1986).

[16]   These responses were to an article by Lyn Mikel Brown and Carol Gilligan, 'Meeting at the Crossroads: Women's Psychology and Girls' Development', *Feminism and Psychology*, 3.1 (1993): 11–35. The following year an issue of the journal, Vol. 4.3 (1994), was given over to critical articles. The arguments referred to here are from: M.B. Lykes, 'Whose Meeting at Which Crossroads? A Response to Brown and Gilligan', pp. 345–9; S. Contratto, 'A Too Hasty Marriage: Gilligan's Developmental Theory and its Application to Feminist Clinical Practice', pp. 367–75. For the third, see T. Robinson and J.V. Ward, '"A Belief in Self far Greater than Anyone's Disbelief": Cultivating Resistance Among African American Female Adolescents', in Gilligan et al., *Women, Girls and Psychotherapy*, p. 92.

[17]   Lyn Mikel Brown, *Raising their Voices: The Politics of Girls' Anger* (Cambridge, MA, 1998), p. 201.

[18]   The Shakespearean character Ophelia 'furnishes the name for this discourse' by her self-destruction in the face of competing demands by Hamlet and her father: Aapola et al., *Young Femininity*, pp. 40–41. Some authors describe and analyse the syndrome further, for example A. Garrod, L. Smulyan, S.I. Powers and R. Kilkenny, *Adolescent Portraits: Identity, Relationships, and Challenges* (Needham Heights, 1992); others create opportunities for girls' voices to be heard in resistance to this, for example Sara Shandler, *Ophelia Speaks: Adolescent Girls Write about their Search for Self* (New York, 1999).

help girls overcome pressures of sex, peers and body image which threaten them with 'grow(ing) up too fast'.[19]

2. New Feminisms

By the mid 1990s, second wave feminism was beginning to be replaced by new manifestations of feminism, especially among teenage girls and young women. Girl gangs, girl power, grrrls and zines were among its manifestations.[20] Partly out of resistance to the perceived invisibility and inaudibility of girls, and partly due to political and social changes which encouraged greater individualism and self-realisation, an alternative adolescent subjectivity began to be constructed, invested with power, agency, a strong sense of self and often anger.[21] Girls who spoke their truth assertively at the risk of disconnection were labelled 'mean' or 'brash'.[22] So two discursive strands of response to the inheritance of second wave feminism can now be identified, although they vary according to local context determined by class, race, income and educational expectation: some of the earlier angry response to invisibility was from lower income girls and girls of colour.[23] The danger of polarity between the two, denoted on the one side as power and resilience offering girls opportunity and choice, and on the other as crisis and risk encouraging inequality and victimisation, becomes apparent.[24]

Analysis of these developments in girlhood appears in a wide range of publications. As the work of Miller, Gilligan and others spread more widely across the western world and now globally to urbanised communities, social scientific studies are emerging from many quarters, and 'the category "girl" itself has proved to be slippery and problematic'.[25] Ward and Benjamin plot the shifts in American studies of girlhood, noting particularly the tendency to move away from intergenerational discourse towards an individualism which renders girls

---

[19]   P. Haag, *Voices of a Generation: Teenage Girls on Sex, School, and Self: A Report on Teen Girls from the American Association of University Women's Sister to Sister Summits* (Washington, DC, 1999). Peggy Orenstein, *Schoolgirls: Young Women, Self Esteem and the Confidence Gap* (New York, 1995).

[20]   The story of these and others is found in Brown, *Raising their Voices*, pp. 4–19; Aapola et al., *Young Femininity*, pp. 18–39.

[21]   Brown, *Raising their Voices*, pp. 5–6; Aapola et al., *Young Femininity*, p. 39.

[22]   Brown, *Raising their Voices*, pp. 14–15; Maria Harris, 'Women Teaching Girls: The Power and the Danger', *Religious Education*, 88.1 (1993): 56.

[23]   For example, Valerie Walkerdine, Helen Lucey and June Melody, *Growing Up Girl, Psychosocial Explorations of Gender and Class* (Basingstoke, 2001); Robinson and Ward, '"A Belief in Self"', pp. 87–103.

[24]   Aapola et al., *Young Femininity*, p. 10.

[25]   Harris, *All About the Girl*, p. xx.

responsible for their own futures.[26] This gives rise to particular difficulties for girls from majority world cultures, where the phenomenon associated with western culture is critiqued differently.[27] Aapola, Gonick and Harris draw attention to the danger to girls from adult women, whose girlhood was lived in the very different culture of the 1960s and 1970s, identifying too closely with the Ophelia narrative as a description of *their* story, which they then project onto contemporary girlhood. They agree with Baumgardner and Richards as they question whether many girls in the early twenty-first century do feel vulnerable and at risk.[28]

These early twenty-first-century studies of girlhood respond to the need to 'grapple with theorizing the changing conditions under which young women's diverse self-making occurs'.[29] The struggle for gender equity is reshaped in every generation as legal, political and social changes take place, driven by and driving ideological stances and material factors. It is these 'specificities' which sociological studies seek to analyse, so that girls' studies become more than a lamentation that girls are absent from 'youth studies', a trap I have too easily fallen into myself in the long road to uncover where serious study of girls and girlhood is being undertaken.

There is broad agreement among feminists that second wave feminism from the 1960s onwards enabled girls and young women to achieve increasing levels of equality in social, economic and legal spheres, and if they chose, to create a 'gynocentric alternative lifestyle, glorifying women's ways of doing everything'. However, this was at the expense, Baumgardner and Richards claim, of 'the tabooed symbols of feminine enculturation – Barbie dolls, make-up, fashion magazines, high heels'. Using those things was seen as submission to male gaze.[30] Although women acquired a significant amount of power, contemporary feminist critique acknowledges it was at the expense of 'girliness'. Third wave feminism wants to exert female power and harness the anger, seen for example in the phenomenon of girl gangs, while also being free to adopt a 'feminine' lifestyle. Baumgardner and Richards sum up the distinction:

---

[26]   Janie V. Ward and Beth Cooper Benjamin, 'Women, Girls and the Unfinished Work of Connection: A Critical Review of American Girls' Studies', in Harris, *All About the Girl*, pp. 15–25.

[27]   The voices of girls from the Middle East and Asia but resident in Canada are heard in Yasmin Jiwani, Candis Steenbergen and Claudia Mitchell (eds), *Girlhood: Redefining the Limits* (Montreal, 2006). Adreanne Ormond gives voice to Maori girls in Harris, *All About the Girl*, pp. 243–53.

[28]   Aapola et al., *Young Femininity*, p. 47: Jennifer Baumgardner and Amy Richards, 'Feminism and Femininity: Or How We Learned to Stop Worrying and Love the Thong', in Harris, *All About the Girl*, p. 65.

[29]   Aapola et al., *Young Femininity*, p. 7.

[30]   Baumgardner and Richards, 'Feminism and Femininity', pp. 60ff.

What (feminists) overlooked in this process of ensuring that women were 'taken
seriously' is that some women – and men – are drawn to feminine things (i.e.
'unserious' things). Beyond that, feminine things weren't truly the problem;
being forced to adopt them was. Second wave feminists fought so hard for all
women not to be *reduced* to a 'girl' – they didn't lay claim to the good in being
a girl.[31]

We have already observed that the signification of 'girl' is contested. Brown and
Gilligan use it to indicate the pre-feminist patriarchal diminution of women and
women's issues, but 'girl' or 'girlie' now attempts to reclaim for women and girls
the potentially stereotypical models of being female, as a tool to independent
living.[32] For others, girl power has extended into a 'more expansive form of
femininity', expressed in a wide range of musical, sporting and political activities
not previously thought 'girlie' – and the clothes to match.[33] It is argued that choice
for girls and women is therefore increased, legitimating much that second wave
feminism saw as a betrayal of the cause, for example, marriage and family. A
conflict is thus set up between second and third wave feminists. The danger
that this buys into consumerism and individualism is noted, but legitimated as
the price of a woman's freedom to choose. Much recent work in the UK has
sought to analyse the structuring of girl power and the way girls operate within it,
identifying connections with class and race in its operation.[34] Some writers suggest
that 'niceness' and 'power' are mutually exclusive discourses for girls, but nothing
is ever as simple as that; girls are subject to many influences in their public social
worlds and their subcultures, with which they interact in complex ways. Raby
suggests that hidden resistance underlies much overt conformity or 'niceness'.[35]
'Girlhood' does not represent a coherent and unchanging cultural construction, but
girls construct meaning for themselves in individual and idiosyncratic ways, out of
the mix of personality, context and history.

Among faith groups, two strands have similarly emerged. The first encourages
girls towards empowerment, growing in faith by finding their voice, and thus
resisting the pressure to be 'nice'[36] as the acceptable face of a 'Christian girlhood'.[37]

---

[31]   Ibid., p. 61. Authors' italics.

[32]   Brown and Gilligan, *Meeting at the Crossroads*, chapter 1. Jiwani et al., *Girlhood*,
pp. ix–x.

[33]   Aapola et al., *Young Femininity*, p. 19.

[34]   For example Valerie Hey, *The Company She Keeps: An Ethnography of Girls'
Friendships* (Buckingham, 1997).

[35]   Rebecca Raby, 'Talking (Behind Your) Back: Young Women and Resistance', in
Jiwani et al., *Girlhood*, pp. 153–4.

[36]   Usually meaning quiet and compliant, Brown described it as 'psychological foot-
binding': Brown and Gilligan, *Meeting at the Crossroads*, p. 21.

[37]   For example, Hess, *Caretakers of Our Common House*; Patricia H. Davis,
Beyond Nice: The Spiritual Wisdom of Adolescent Girls (Minneapolis, 2001); Baker,

The second advocates resistance to societal pressures by helping girls 'envision identities that are grounded in Scripture and developed in God's love'.[38] The first, which encourages girls to develop autonomy while remaining connected, is typically to be found in non-evangelical churches, and the latter which promotes connection through compliance with and submission to perceived biblical norms is found in more conservative congregations.

The relational/caring qualities developed from Gilligan's 'ethic of care' by Tina Beattie among others as a female characteristic helped forge an alliance between the socialism of many second wave feminists and Christians who pursued the same agenda in a theological quest for prophetic justice. Beattie critiques the reality behind this new feminism as being no more than pretence; finding support in Gilligan, Elshtain and Irigaray, she exposes it as another form of co-option 'into a society premised entirely upon masculine values and morals'.[39] She argues that this violates a woman's sense of self; the self now is constructed in the interplay between desire and its gratification, which is in reality defined by men or by social forces which keep her captive, for example in marketing conceived and operated on traditional masculine models. Appropriation can become a form of resistance, however, and third wave feminism suggests girls' and women's adoption of multiple identities is intentional and ironic. The rise of 'girl power' offers girls a more assertive way of expressing themselves. However, with the rise in commercial targeting of ever younger girls who lack the experience necessary to be aware of the power of such images to construct identity, the spread of these models of girlhood to 'tweenies' is of concern.[40]

3. Luce Irigaray

Beattie brings into the discussion the writings of French philosopher Luce Irigaray whose reflection on the issue, although sharing some agreement with Gilligan, offers a more radical critique of the patriarchal discourse which shapes female identity. Her work is given little recognition in the United States because, she considers, there is a fundamental misunderstanding of her work based both on its treatment within a literary rather than a philosophical framework, and on

---

Doing Girlfriend Theology; and a series of six manuals from a Roman Catholic project entitled *Voices: Nurturing the Spirituality of Girls*, for example, Marilyn Kielbasa, *Prayer: Celebrating and Reflecting with Girls* (Winona, 2002).

[38]   For example, Whitney Prosperi, *Girls Ministry 101: Ideas for Retreats, Small Groups, and Everyday Life with Teenage Girls* (Grand Rapids, 2006); Ginny Olson, *Teenage Girls: Exploring Issues Adolescent Girls Face and Strategies to Help Them* (Grand Rapids, 2006).

[39]   Tina Beattie, *Woman* (London, 2003), p. 49.

[40]   As expressed, for example, by Christine Griffin, 'Good Girls, Bad Girls: Anglocentrism and Diversity in the Constitution of Contemporary Girlhood', in Harris, *All About the Girl*, p. 35.

poor translation.[41] Irigaray's writing has porous boundaries with psychology and theology; more recently she has written on spirituality, drawing on her Catholic background and integrating it with her early work on gender. Gender difference for Irigaray is primarily ontological, an envisioning of 'a horizontal transcendence' between two mature but irreducibly different subjects, man and woman, in opposition to the equality for which, she argues, feminism strives within the discursive framework constructed by patriarchy. Although accused of espousing 'a form of psychic essentialism'[42] or 'reverting to a biologically deterministic account of femininity',[43] she refutes Lacan and his Freudian analysis of women by which, she says, they are 'reduced to acting a masquerade of femininity'; she argues instead for 'a woman coming to understand herself in her own right, not simply as a vehicle for reproduction'.[44] According to Joy, her feminine imaginary 'encourages women to claim specific engendered or "feminine" characteristics', which she sees as a strategy of refusal to support the symbolic process which determines their silence or 'othering'.[45]

In her attempt to 'redistribute discourse' to create authentic dialogue, Irigaray exposes the way linguistic forms, seemingly neutral, in fact perpetuate sexuate relations, terminology she invented to refer to the biological differences between women and men which are not of a strictly sexual nature.[46] Hirsh and Olson summarise this thesis of Irigaray's:

> in a setting where girls typically use the preposition 'with' in relation to another human subject, boys in the same setting will instead use it in relation to an inanimate object; girls thus construct (and construct themselves within) a subject-subject dialectic where boys construct a dialectic of subject and object.[47]

Irigaray thus strives towards a self-understanding that obviates the need to choose between accommodation and resistance. Although detailed analysis of Irigaray's thinking is beyond the scope of this work, I will at particular points in my

---

[41]   Morny Joy, *Divine Love: Luce Irigaray, Women, Gender and Religion* (Manchester, 2006), p. 2.

[42]   A detailed refutation of the charge of essentialism has been written by Ellen Armour in C.W. Maggie Kim, Susan M. St Ville and Susan Simonaitis (eds), *Transfigurations: Theology and the French Feminists* (Minneapolis, 1993), pp. 164–7.

[43]   Elaine L. Graham, *Making the Difference: Gender, Personhood and Theology* (London, 1995), p. 138.

[44]   Joy, *Divine Love*, p. 11.

[45]   Ibid., pp. 3, 11.

[46]   Luce Irigaray (ed.), *Luce Irigaray: Key Writings* (London and New York, 2004), pp. 10f., 179–80.

[47]   Elizabeth Hirsh and Gary A. Olson, '"Je-Luce Irigaray": A Meeting with Luce Irigaray', *Hypatia*, 10.2 (1995): 93–114.

argument draw attention to aspects of her writing about girls, found principally in
her collection of writings on spirituality and religion.

4. Developmental Theories and Girls

We turn now to developmental theories and the part they have played in the
construction of girls' identity. Kegan describes the theory that human growth
occurs through definable developmental stages as the 'cultural symbolic of our
time'.[48] Developmentalism, interpreting human behaviour 'as directed by a priori
behavioural schemata that precede any and all experience',[49] is still the dominant
paradigm in thinking about childhood and adolescence, and can be traced through
the seminal work in different disciplines from Freud through Piaget, Erikson,
Kohlberg and Fowler. It is criticised in many quarters, and because in a limited
way I draw on developmental schemes in my research analysis, I will discuss these
critiques and justify the qualified use I make of them.

Both feminist psychology and sociological studies of childhood want either to
modify or to deconstruct developmentalism for its tight hierarchical stratification,
its failure to attend to gender and generation as well as race and class, and the
social structuring of childhood.[50] Psychologist Erica Burman asks 'what are
the consequences for developmental psychology of its forgetting of gender as
a structuring dimension of development?'.[51] Developmental schemata claim
universality for structures which privilege values deriving from the western social
and cultural context, and become a tool of social control. They do not allow for
the 'multiple voices' particularly of women across class, race and generation, nor
for the 'complex disorder of individual development'.[52] This applies whether the
paradigms are found in psychology, biology or sociology.

As a psychologist, Sheila Greene agrees with Burman's rejection of prescriptive
and fictionally normative models of development. She advocates a dynamic
developmental theory that includes the whole lifespan, and relates closely to context
and to particular points in time, that is, it takes account of the experience of the
subject in the present.[53] She challenges the presumption that a subject is shaped by,
and is in that sense captive to, past experience, and although she questions scholars
who state this more strongly than she does, she still holds to the power of individual

---

[48]   Kegan, *Evolving Self*, p. 13.

[49]   Wolfhart Pannenberg, *Anthropology in Theological Perspective* (Edinburgh,
1985), p. 33.

[50]   The history is described in A. James and A. Prout (eds), *Constructing and
Reconstructing Childhood: Contemporary Issues in the Sociological Study of Childhood*,
2nd edn (London, 1997), pp. 10–14.

[51]   Burman, *Deconstructing Developmental Psychology*, p. 5.

[52]   Ibid., p. 19.

[53]   Sheila Greene, *The Psychological Development of Women and Girls: Rethinking
Change in Time* (London and New York, 2003).

agency to effect personal transformation, a challenge to developmentalism which has its counterpart in theology: in different ways both Karl Rahner and James Loder argue for the freedom to grow in the interplay between spirit and Spirit.[54]

Several developmental theories derive from the clinical experience of psychologists and there is the further danger that they extrapolate supposedly normative models from the deviations they witness in the consulting room, as already noted in the work of Pipher. Lindner comments:

> Developmental theories and theorists who inform the therapeutic interventions to which non-conforming children will be subjected continually define 'developmental norms' and 'age-appropriate' behaviours too narrowly and, worse, may not describe the trajectories of many children's experiences.[55]

Without rejecting developmentalism but stringently critiquing it, another theological challenge exposes psychologists' focus on pathology, proposing instead an alternative teleology which promotes 'good or optimal development' defined as reciprocal relating. This is created theologically by exploration of trinitarian relationality in reciprocating selves, which enable human–human and divine–human relationship, and is consistent with a feminist perspective in its vision of connectedness over against autonomy.[56]

Within cultural studies, Driscoll implicitly critiques developmentalism by discussing the way the concept of and discourse around adolescence 'functions as an explanation of the indispensable difficulty of becoming a subject, agent, or independent or self-aware person'.[57] Adolescence, she argues, is 'feminised': as the period of instability between two stable stages, childhood and adulthood, it is characterised by immaturity often seen in changeability and malleability out of which the individual, male as well as female, grows to maturity.[58] Postmodernism, however, challenges the idea that any stage has stability, as we change according to our discursive contexts. Lee argues that contemporary society has no certainties even for adults; he discusses the element of provisionality that postmodernism brings, with the result that questions of identity remain open throughout life, so that people of all ages are united as both 'beings and becomings'.[59]

---

[54]   Karl Rahner, *Theological Investigations*; James Loder, *The Logic of the Spirit: Human Development in Theological Perspective* (San Francisco, 1998).

[55]   Eileen W. Lindner, 'Children as Theologians', in Peter B. Pufall and Richard P. Unsworth (eds), *Rethinking Childhood* (New Brunswick, 2004), p. 66.

[56]   Jack O. Balswick, Pamela Ebstyne King and Kevin S. Reimer, *The Reciprocating Self: Human Development in Theological Perspective* (Downers Grove, 2005), p. 28.

[57]   Driscoll, *Girls*, p. 6.

[58]   Ibid., p. 54.

[59]   N. Lee, *Childhood and Society: Growing up in an Age of Uncertainty* (Maidenhead, 2001), chapter 1.

Much developmental theory presumes the fixed goals of modernism. As noted in the discussion of girlhood, feminist critics in many disciplines agree that girls still face the choice in their search for subjectivity between, on the one hand, renouncing 'femininity' to conform to social norms which disconnect self and body and are deemed 'mature' and, on the other, being 'girlie' which connects them with their embodied female identity but which in its changeability and particularity is deemed 'immature'.[60] The pattern of 'development' is from the body/earth nexus to the 'higher' level of mind/spirit, a legacy bequeathed by the Enlightenment, maturity patterned on a male model, commonly characterised as individuated, autonomous, rational and oriented towards rights. Girls, especially at puberty, are very conscious of change both internal (bodily maturing) and external (social and cultural expectations) and receive mixed messages as they learn to adapt to them, whether to embrace or hide them. Driscoll argues that 'girlhood in late modernity is constituted in processes ... The association of girlhood with immaturity has interpreted these processes as uncertain and as opposed to majority, agency, citizenship, and other markers of maturity', and she advocates an 'analysis of girl culture (which) is not a matter of just finding out more about girls, however fascinating and pleasurable those things are, but of considering their interaction with discourses that name and constitute them'.[61] Developmental paradigms contribute to that infantilising in gendered discourse, perpetuating the view that that which is in process is immature, that which is relational is overly dependent, and that which has 'arrived' at a supposed level of stability and autonomy is mature.

Greene, however, still wants to retain a developmental framework as 'enhancing our understanding of the psychology of women and girls' for the common sense reason that 'periodization' characterises everyone's life course;[62] in adopting this approach, it is useful to keep in mind the questions Burman asks about whose interests the developmental schemata serve, whose goal is being pursued and the desire for, or exercise of, power and control it may represent. Greene contributes to the understanding of girls in the church by emphasising the formative influences of social context which change with each generation: she describes this as 'cohort particularity' which 'casts doubt on any over-generalized statement about women's psychology and the course of women's development. As well as knowing about women's socialisation we must locate them in historical time'.[63] The age and context of a girl's identity formation and socialisation are, however, not segregated but intergenerational, so account needs to be taken of context in this sense, as Kegan does in his work on the holding environment. Both Hey and Brown identify the influence of family and society and their covert and manifest values through girls' 'ventriloquism', a term they adopt from Bakhtin to indicate

---

[60]   Raby, 'Talking (Behind Your) Back', p. 140.

[61]   Driscoll, *Girls*, p. 304.

[62]   Greene, *Psychological Development*, pp. 15, 37.

[63]   Ibid., p. 120.

girls' articulation of values particularly of parents in which they 'recirculate(ed) and inflect(ed) cultural appropriations from their own ... communities'.[64]

The girls whom I studied are legally children, dependent (not having any legal independence), and immature (below the age of criminal responsibility). However, since by 13 most will have completed the major physical pubertal changes, I maintain that they should not be classed as children when the word is used discursively to diminish them and suggest they and their voice are of less worth than those of older people, as Driscoll and others highlight. Much contemporary social theory emphasises the importance of agency, implying its incompatibility with dependence. The construction of self, including the spiritual, takes place within a formative environment; girls are still subject to and strongly influenced by not only parents and teachers, but peers who take a leadership role in their wider life; in the cases I am studying, this is the church. If we follow the often normatively accepted stages of structuralists, girls at 11–13 are likely to have the capacity for formal operational thinking (Piaget), and be negotiating identity formation versus role confusion (Erikson).[65] As I have indicated above, 'development' is rightly contested as a value-ridden term when, from its dictionary definition of 'unfolding', it is understood to mean a movement towards something 'more', perpetual improvement on the way to an ideal or goal. The way I shall use it will be free of any suggestion of such 'progression', but reflect an understanding that change takes place in all people's lives, hence the importance of theories such as Erikson's which encompass the whole lifespan, and 'may at times be directional and linked to innate capacities and maturation particularly in childhood'.[66] I introduce later a theological perspective which carries with it its own teleology.

5. Transitional 'Stages': Kegan's Evolution of Selfhood

Retaining a healthy suspicion of developmentalism as outlined above, I now discuss in more detail the frameworks of development which I have found helpful in studying girls, principally Kegan and Erikson. The relevant stage of Erikson's lifespan theory concerns the 'crisis of wholeness', the achievement of which he calls 'a sense of inner identity'[67] on which I concentrate here, but because of the wide range of his writing, I shall return to him in a number of places. Although both start out from an exclusively male perspective, they move away from male normativity as they adjust their theories to female difference, Kegan more successfully.[68] Erikson and Kegan, although not overtly addressing faith, are open

---

[64]   Hey, *The Company She Keeps*, p. 84; Brown, *Raising their Voices*, chapter 5.

[65]   Kegan charts Piaget's stages, *Evolving Self*, p. 34; Erik Erikson, *Identity: Youth and Crisis* (New York, 1968), pp. 128–35; both Kegan and Gilligan consider Erikson's stages inapplicable to girls.

[66]   Greene, *Psychological Development*, p. 19.

[67]   Erikson, *Identity: Youth and Crisis*, p. 87.

[68]   Kegan, *In Over Our Heads*, chapter 6.

to exploring the spiritual or religious side of human experience, and acknowledge that the physical changes (development) for a girl at puberty are accompanied by her internal re-organisation in her view of herself, her identity, the balance between 'self and other'.

Kegan, a clinical psychologist, studies the way we make meaning for ourselves at different stages of life, through our relating to others. The question he is asking and answering is: how do we achieve autonomy/individuality healthily while remaining in connection with others? He does not endorse theories which promote independence and autonomy as the goal of human maturity, recognising the need for balance between autonomy and the interdependence found in relationship. Thus he creates a bridge between traditionally male and female understandings and experiences of maturity. Although in his theory of 'constructive developmentalism' he is suggesting a developmental phenomenology (styles or stages of being), he is also seeking 'liberation from a static view of phenomena'[69] through identification of a dynamic process between forms, thus focusing more on transition than on the forms themselves.

In *The Evolving Self*, Kegan offers a way of understanding the development of personality which allows for both the affective and cognitive to be held together, finding an underlying organic system by which theories of development can be unified to overcome the tension between, for example, emotion and thought, which is reflected in the perceived dichotomy between psychoanalytic and cognitive theory.

For Kegan, to be a person is inseparable from the activity of making meaning as we organise experience, and 'organic systems evolve through eras according to regular principles of stability and change'.[70] He argues that, unlike in structural theories, these evolutionary eras are not developmental stages, but processes which create the conditions in which cognitive, moral and psychosocial development takes place. His book is therefore 'an organized way of wondering what happens if the evolution of the activity of meaning is taken as a fundamental motion in personality'.[71] Here, he is exploring ideas consistent with those of Hay, Nye and Murphy who in their research highlight the 'roles played by emotion and forms of experience not confined to rational cognitive capacities' which are essential ingredients of spiritual and religious experience.[72]

Kegan notes the linguistic connection between motion and e-motion, and introduces a further dimension to the process of making sense of experience, validating for meaning-making our 'knowing', the emotional response to experience, a felt or intuitive rather than a rational interpretation. His usage of

---

[69]   Kegan, *Evolving Self*, p. 13.

[70]   Ibid., p. 13.

[71]   Ibid., p. 15.

[72]   David Hay, Rebecca Nye and Roger Murphy, 'Thinking about Childhood Spirituality: Review of Research and Current Directions', in Leslie J. Francis, William K. Kay and William S. Campbell (eds), *Research in Religious Education* (Leominster, 1996), p. 48.

the word is far from any contemporary sentimental connotations it may have, but the felt experience of a motion; he is thus 'putting forth a candidate for a ground of consideration prior to, and generative of, cognition *and* affect'.[73] It is here that James Fowler, whose work on faith development I discuss later, typifies the difference between his faith stage structure and Kegan's work where he describes the 'self in motion' as Kegan's 'dance' whereas his is the '*self-Other-ultimate environment trialectic*'.[74]

'Development' for Kegan is a process, and is evolutionary. In this there is some sense of hierarchy, but he does give an intrinsic value to each 'evolutionary truce'. He himself uses stages as diagnostic tools in therapy on which most of his empirical evidence is based, but he describes their existence as a natural and healthy dimension of human living and being.

He models his theory as a helix, suggesting that each evolutionary balance represents a psychologic which alternately favours independence and inclusion; he thus takes account of the tension between the two in all forms of development theory, but deliberately tries to assimilate within his system the criticism levelled at theorists from Freud to Piaget, Kohlberg and Fowler that their constructs are derived predominantly from observation of male subjects, which do not take account of or give value to the different female characteristics evident from empirical research such as that of Gilligan, Slee and others. In his later work, having taken more account of feminist criticism, he accepts that the 'inclusion' side with its emphasis on relating, favours and is inhabited more readily by women, while the 'independent' side more often describes men. Rejecting any suggestion of hierarchy between the two, neither of which is normative but instead reflects a difference of orientation or style, he introduces flexibility into his theory to allow for each gender to operate both autonomously *and* relationally in each balance.[75] The advantage of the helical model to the understanding of the growth of faith, in contrast to the linear model of Fowler, is that it is not closed; the spiral movement allows each stage to build on and relate in some ways to earlier stages while still being discrete.

Although Kegan only suggests broad guidelines of age for his six 'evolutionary truces', it is evident from his descriptions that the 'Imperial' and 'Interpersonal' stages or selves and the transition from the one to the other are those that relate to pre- and early adolescent girls.[76]

The Imperial stage or balance describes girls/boys who have moved away from infant dependency, who know themselves to have a 'child' role and possess a private world. Now having control of their earlier impulses, they are agents in their own world. They are embedded in their own needs, interests and wishes. School

---

[73]   Kegan, *Evolving Self*, p. 81. Author's italics.

[74]   James W. Fowler, 'Faith Development Theory and Postmodern Challenges', *International Journal for the Psychology of Religion*, 11.3, (2001): 164. Author's italics.

[75]   Kegan, *In Over Our Heads*, p. 217.

[76]   For full discussion of these 'stages', see Kegan, *Evolving Self*, pp. 161–220.

and family are recognised as institutions of authority. In role, the girl or boy is confident, self-sufficient and creative, providing that the context offers stable routine and personal affirmation.

The Interpersonal balance can, he says, be reached at any time from early teens onwards. Kegan suggests the interpersonal self has moved from self-sufficiency (evident in the strength and courage which Brown and Gilligan hear in younger girls' voices)[77] to be embedded in mutuality and interpersonal co-operation. Other people's feelings and opinions feature in a girl's decision-making, reliability grows as she takes more account of the needs of the other: she no longer *is* her needs, but *has* needs, Kegan's version of subject–object shift which occurs in each balance.

For Kegan, adolescence begins when the evolution of meaning becomes interpersonal; the physical and psychological ages for this may therefore be different. 'A girl's body can begin to take the shape and features of a woman. She can speak with the sophistication associated with adolescence or adulthood … (b)ut until the evolution of meaning becomes interpersonal, there is a very real sense in which the person is not yet adolescent'.[78] According to this structure, girls from around 12–16 are likely to be in the transitional stage between the Imperial and Interpersonal stages so adolescence becomes a late teen destination rather than a transitional process. This does not cohere with more holistic views of adolescence, which recognise the interweaving of the many facets of change, all of which affect and are affected by a sense of self. Driscoll draws attention to a widely applied social distinction between physiological and psychological maturity, and concludes feminine adolescence to be 'an assemblage of transitions'.[79] It is more appropriate, then, across a range of disciplines including the psychological to regard adolescence as a process, testing out a new way of being and relating rather than an achieved balance. The peer group has a particularly significant role to play in the transition period, and research into friendships indicates an experimentation with peer relationships which oscillate between domination and mutuality, without having yet reached the 'mutuality of reciprocal one-to-one relationships',[80] which for Kegan is a mark of the new balance. Interpersonal relating is being learnt during this period of shifting identities so it may be that by definition, the Interpersonal can only be in process.

Hess adopts Kegan's developmental theory as an aid to understanding and exposing the dualism inherent in the identity choices facing girls at puberty, whether to maintain connection and lose self (the nice girl) or retain self and lose connection for independence (the mean/brash girl). For her, the interpersonal stage highlights the danger of 'relationship addictions'[81] and gives a theoretical

---

[77] Brown and Gilligan, *Meeting at the Crossroads*, p. 3.

[78] Kegan, *Evolving Self*, p. 178.

[79] Driscoll, *Girls*, pp. 48, 58.

[80] Kegan, *Evolving Self*, p. 190. Hey's research endorses this, *The Company She Keeps*, pp. 57–8.

[81] Hess, *Caretakers of our Common House*, p. 65, quoting Anne Wilson Shaef.

framework for devising strategies for awakening girls to the reality of social and cultural pressures and achieving both relationships and autonomy. In her own experience as a mother and teacher, Hess resonates with the relational crisis identified by Gilligan. She approaches this from a Christian standpoint, so interprets women's oppression in theological terms, drawing attention to those traditions and writers (for example, Niebuhr on the sin of pride) which result in 'prophetic torpor', meaning self-abnegation and a diminished capacity to care for others.[82]

Relationships with others are therefore important to girls at puberty as they explore new identities, so the reality is not, then, as clear-cut as the structural developmental theories suggest. In these relationships, intimacy particularly within the peer group is imperative to most girls. Social science studies suggest these relationships act as sites of resistance to the hiding or repression of a 'strong sense of self' associated with 'niceness': beneath overt compliance lie strategies of self-assertion in peer group relationships. The successful achievement of intimacy with another is one of Erikson's developmental stages, but in his sequential scheme it follows identity formation for which Gilligan is critical of Erikson; for her, it is in intimate knowing that identity is formed.[83] Although Kegan sees a correlation between Erikson's identity formation stage and his own 'Institutional' balance, there is some correspondence with the 'mutually reciprocal one-to-one relationships' of his 'Interpersonal Self' through which identity also grows.[84] Kegan is realistic about the danger that 'the self confuses the other with itself'; he advocates the 'nurturance of a cooperative community' to support the movement, but as he draws his conclusions from dysfunctional subjects met in therapy, he does not pay sufficient attention to the development of identity in 'normal' family or peer relationships. Erikson does allow for some flexibility in his stage sequence, as 'each item exists in some form before its critical time normally arrives' and once a crisis has been resolved, the 'achievement' feeds subsequent stages; the process is therefore cumulative.[85]

6. Transition in Identity: Redeeming Erikson

It is not, however, Erikson's 'stages' on which I wish to draw further, but his writing on the growth of girls through puberty and its contribution to the construction of their identity, itself a contested area. My discussion of identity will, however, be limited, in recognition of its relative position in my overall argument. My approach to it, initially from a psychological perspective, leads into contemporary research on childhood faith and spirituality, although James Loder's work forms

---

[82]   Ibid., pp. 42–7.
[83]   Gilligan, *In a Different Voice*, p. 12.
[84]   Kegan, *Evolving Self*, p. 190.
[85]   Erik Erikson, *Childhood and Society* (Middlesex, 1965), p. 262.

a bridge into engagement with theology, for example through Pannenberg and German scholarship; some resources such as Erikson are common to both strands.

Among questions of concern for girls entering the transitional stage of puberty are: 'who am I?' and 'who will I become?'. They seek to answer these questions as they interact with the environments of home, school and church within which they move, still dependent yet moving towards an increasing independence, acquiring agency while remaining connected with family and friends. So identity and individuality are formed in growing awareness of the gifts, skills and interests of self and others.

'Identity' is fundamental to Erikson's developmental schema for adolescence, yet he recognises its complexity and refuses a clear definition. Being 'for the most part unconscious except where inner conditions and outer circumstances combine to aggravate a painful, or elated, "identity-consciousness"', the nearest he comes to a definition locates it in a reciprocal harmony between one's own and others' perception of self. It is therefore, importantly, located both *in the core of the individual* yet also *in the core of his* [*sic*] *communal culture*, a process which establishes ... the identity of those two identities'.[86] Loder attempts an explanation of his meaning for adolescence as 'a consistent sense of oneself', as one learns to steer a course between unthinking conformity to adult expectation and 'subjective self-absorption'. In relation to others, it means that 'the inner sameness and continuity sensed in oneself is matched by one's meaning for others'.[87] Despite its flaws, Erikson's theory offers a helpful guide to the understanding of the development of identity, and along with Kegan shows how the individual makes meaning for herself in the environments in which she is embedded. Erikson knew that identity was not monolithic: he stood by the necessity of 'the many faces of identity he created ... in order to understand how individuals maintained and retained a sense of continuity and wholeness in a world of contending forces'.[88]

Others have worked with Erikson's ideas and attempted to systematise them. One such was Marcia, who acknowledged his negative attitude towards testing his concept of identity empirically, fearing its trivialisation.[89] The value of Marcia's work for my research is his classification, suggested by Erikson's writings, of four identity statuses which can be applied to the progress of identity development. These lay stress on the effect of the context on identity formation and so, when used in conjunction with Kegan's work on holding environments, offer a critique on the way these operate in relation to the individual. Erikson saw the need for a 'sequence of expectable environments to resolve each developmental crisis',[90] which Kegan translates into the ideal functions of the holding environment as

---

[86]   Erikson, *Identity*, pp. 22–3. Author's italics.

[87]   Loder, *Logic*, p. 207.

[88]   Jane Kroger, 'Identity in Formation', in Kenneth Hoover (ed.), *The Future of Identity: Centennial Reflections on the Legacy of Erik Erikson* (Maryland, 2004), p. 65.

[89]   James Marcia, 'Why Erikson?', in Hoover, *The Future of Identity*, p. 43.

[90]   Erikson, *Identity*, p. 222.

being 'holding on', 'letting go' and 'staying put'. A less than ideal environment holds either too loosely or too tightly. In between outright success and failure, which Erikson terms achievement and diffusion, Marcia names two further identity statuses: moratorium and foreclosure. The responsibility laid on the holding environments which nurture girls between 11 and 13, in a crucially formative stage of identity formation because of the losses of the past and uncertainties about the future, is to hold them in moratorium, and avoid foreclosure. In moratorium, girls would be 'exploring alternatives and their commitments are usually vague, although they can be very passionate about certain social issues. They give the impression of struggling to find life direction and consequently appear as anxious … Their reasoning about moral issues, whether in terms of justice or care is especially acute'. In foreclosure, they would be 'committed in important life areas, but these commitments are those which they have adopted from childhood authority figures. One might say that their identities are conferred upon them and willingly received, rather than being self-constructed'.[91] Marcia overstates the level of independent agency in identity formation, but his description resonates with the part authority plays in the faith development of Fowler, and the style of the affiliative and searching stages of John Westerhoff.[92]

7. Faith 'Development'

Thus far, faith has not featured in the discussion, although Kegan and Erikson acknowledge a spiritual dimension inherent in human experience. In *Women's Faith Development*, Nicola Slee offers an overview of faith development theories; although she concentrates more on the adult stages (I use 'stages' loosely here, and not in a structural sense), she does have an eye to the placing of girls within that, and like Greene and Burman exposes its male orientation. Her focus on Fowler acknowledges the importance of his seminal work in understanding faith, although he 'offers only a partial account of women's faith and its development'[93] and on this ground she accounts for much opposition, including her own, among feminists. She recognises Fowler's partial revision of his theory to include women, but also the absence of any radical reworking.[94] Unlike other feminists, however, Slee does not reject his faith development theory fully. Indeed, as she analyses her data, she finds the processes she observes in women's faith cohere with the transitions between Fowler's stages, and some faith content matches Fowler's descriptions.

On Fowler's analysis, I would expect the girls in my study, at this time of transition in many areas of their lives, to show characteristics of both his second

---

[91]   Marcia, 'Why Erikson?', p. 45.

[92]   J.H. Westerhoff, III, *Will Our Children Have Faith?* rev, edn (Harrisburg, 2000), pp. 91–5.

[93]   Slee, *Women's Faith Development*, p. 32.

[94]   Fowler takes note of it, as Slee points out, in a German edition of *Stages of Faith*.

and third stages, mythic-literal,[95] and synthetic-conventional faith.[96] I note, however, two difficulties with his stages. The first is the inconsistency in his criteria for defining stages: Stage Two appears to be determined primarily by the content revealing the 'level' of cognition (Piaget's concrete operational thinking), but Stage Three primarily by the relational needs at the adolescent stage of ego development (Kohlberg's mutual interpersonal perspective taking).[97]

The second difficulty is with his methodology which, when evaluated according to best practice identified by researchers into girls/boys, is seriously flawed;[98] this casts doubt on the reliability of his stage definitions. Fowler constructs his interviews in line with his Piagetian assumptions about levels of cognitive skill. Despite detailing his methodology and interview process with adults, he summarises the variations needed for interviewing girls/boys in four lines, omitting any discussion of methodological principles that might legitimate alteration to questions in the interview while maintaining significant parity. Issues of power, for example, need careful consideration when interviewing girls/boys. If questions are altered on the basis of the expected 'level' of response, then those expectations are likely to be realised, that is, the interviewer gets out what they put in. So, for example, when the interviewer conducting Fowler's research asks what God looks like, a question not put to adults, the literal answer is classified as anthropomorphic, when it may demonstrate a struggle to formulate an answer on the interviewer's terms, as may be the case with ten-year-old Millie.[99] Fowler describes these anthropomorphisms as 'pre-personal, lacking the kind of nuanced personality in relation to which one could know oneself as being known deeply'.[100] This contrasts with the findings of Rebecca Nye in whose data ten-year-old Maggie revealed a close sense of relationship with God.[101] In Fowler's research, questions about religious experience, a significant category for adults,[102] formed no part of the interview process for children. Nye notes the 'several different

---

[95]   Mythic-literal faith: 'mythic' denoting a 'more linear, narrative construction of coherence and meaning' and 'literal' denoting reliance of the surface 'truth' of a story whose actors are viewed as anthropomorphic. Fowler, *Stages*, p. 149.

[96]   Synthetic conventional faith: 'synthetic' denoting a convergence of values and information as the young person's world expands, and 'conventional' denoting its conformity to the expectations of significant others while the young person still lacks a sufficiently autonomous sense of personal identity to 'construct and maintain an independent perspective'. Ibid., pp. 172–3.

[97]   Fowler, *Stages*, pp. 63–5, 72–5.

[98]   See Chapter 3 for my discussion of appropriate methodologies for research with girls/boys.

[99]   Ibid., pp. 138–9.

[100]   Ibid., p. 153.

[101]   Hay with Nye, *The Spirit of the Child*, p. 101.

[102]   Fowler, *Stages*, p. 311.

languages' children use to voice their spirituality.[103] In exploring answers to other questions, Fowler discerns something of this in Millie's ability to handle paradox, to construct another's (God's) perspective, and her individual processing of parental beliefs.[104] Nye recognises that children's ability to communicate the unknowable is limited by the language at their disposal, determined by context, and the range of experience which is age, gender and class dependent; but in her analysis she also becomes aware of the children's 'resourcefulness' in speaking of their spiritual lives, finding each child had an individual 'signature'.[105]

Content versus form remains a particular controversy in the debate over Fowler's theory, and although he maintains that 'movement in stage development, properly understood, is a *byproduct* of teaching the substance and practices of faith',[106] his work is primarily associated with a pedagogical approach to faith formation. Despite his individualism, he recognises, along with feminists and Kegan, our reliance on a relational environment for nurture, but envisages spiritual awareness as primarily resulting from 'narratives and the practices that provide experiences of God's love, and that convey – as we guide, teach and discipline the child – that he or she is a gift of God, loved by God, and loved and honored by us as Children of God'.[107] In subsequent writing, Fowler has argued more clearly for a less rigid approach, stating that 'the formal structuring of stages is at best only half the story as regards the shaping and maintaining of a person's or group's worldview'.[108]

A significant view contrary to Fowler's is offered from a Reformed tradition by Loder, who criticised him for his emphasis on rationality and his failure to account adequately for the spiritual nature of human beings. Fowler himself was critical of Loder's early writings on the grounds of their lack of empirical research.[109] Both studied as practical theologians and practised as educators coming under the same wide-ranging influences in theology, psychology and sociology from the 1950s to the 1980s, yet both were formed by their particular life experience and contexts, which included their church traditions.

Loder's faith was transformed by a near-death experience, which initiated for him a move towards a reversal of accepted developmental theories originating in

---

[103]   Hay with Nye, *The Spirit of the Child*, p. 122.

[104]   Fowler, *Stages*, p. 140.

[105]   Hay with Nye, *The Spirit of the Child*, p. 98.

[106]   Fowler, 'Faith Development at 30: Naming the Challenges of Faith in a New Millennium', *Religious Education*, 99.4 (2004): 417. Author's emphasis.

[107]   Ibid., p. 413.

[108]   Fowler, 'Faith Development Theory and the Postmodern Challenges', p. 169.

[109]   The relationship between Fowler and Loder, and story of the origin and development of Loder's work is explored in D.R. Wright and J.D. Kuentzel, *Redemptive Transformation in Practical Theology: Essays in Honor of James E. Loder Jr* (Grand Rapids, 2004). Loder developed his 'alternative understanding of human development' in *The Logic of the Spirit*.

the human sciences.[110] Where Fowler attempts to map a structural theory of growth in faith as universal as the capacity for faith itself, Loder's starting point is located firmly in Christian faith, which leads him to ask 'What is theological about human development?' and to transpose the Chalcedonian view of Christ onto the same resources on which Fowler drew. He premises his work on his conviction of the primacy of the human spirit,[111] 'which both transcends and implements the life of the psyche', and that 'theological categories have ontological priority over those in human sciences'.[112] His theological thinking draws on the work of, among others, Kierkegaard, Barth, Luther and Pannenberg. He finds evidence of that primacy within psychological theory itself by the 'pervasive concern that each foundational theorist had for religion, particularly the religious life of the individual'.[113] He strikes a careful balance between the understanding of and co-operation between the human spirit and the Holy Spirit, holding a highly creative view of both in their interaction to bring about transformation. In the face of the fundamental choice humanity makes between meaning and meaninglessness, the human and divine spirit are relationally interacting, being 'designed to replicate the relationality of the divine and human in Jesus Christ'.[114] While the human spirit remains rooted in the human psyche and the Holy Spirit in God, there is an analogous relationship between them. Understanding the human spirit to be 'exocentric', a term he adopts from Pannenberg signifying 'human openness to the world and self-transcendence',[115] Loder invests Pannenberg's term with a more 'expansive self-transcending power of the human spirit (driving) toward a transformation of every obstacle in its path',[116] that is, a transformational pattern in which the Holy Spirit calls the human spirit out of futility, negation and death towards its origin and goal in the *imago dei*, to become the new creation in Christ. Only there, Loder claims, 'can (it) be true to itself without losing its distinctive nature as *human* spirit and human *spirit*'.[117] Thus he develops a spiritual as distinct from a psychological axis of development, which releases us from entrapment within a deterministic view of destiny against which we have seen Greene and Burman also argue. It also introduces the teleological dimension to development after which Balswick et al. are striving when, developing Loder's work, they criticise psychological and sociological developmental models for their 'empty teleology', proposing

---

[110]   Loder tells his story in *The Transforming Moment*, 2nd edn (Colorado Springs, 1989), pp. 9–13.

[111]   He defines the human spirit as 'the dynamism that drives human development forward'; it is 'inherently relational, transformational, self-transcending and the dynamic basis of choice', *Logic*, p. xiii.

[112]   Ibid., p. 41.

[113]   Ibid., p. 20.

[114]   Ibid., p. 17.

[115]   Ibid., p. 5.

[116]   Ibid., p. 33.

[117]   Ibid., p. 36.

instead a developmental goal which is relational, as modelled in divine reciprocity. Human selfhood is only fulfilled in its orientation outwards.[118]

Loder does not, however, dismiss the psychological, stressing the need to understand human development as a reminder that, although the spiritual is both prior and ultimate, spiritual experience has a psycho-neurological foundation. Indeed, he attempts a synthesis, or reconfiguration, between his own theory and both the linear approach of Fowler and the overlapping and mutually interacting epigenetic stages of Erikson, recognising that reality defies schematisation. Thus he describes his configuration as picturing human development as a 'circumambulation of the human spirit around the center, who is the one Triune God'.[119] Loder's hypothesis is thus allied to work on spirituality approached from other perspectives, for example David Hay whose research on the human spirit is located in biology,[120] and theologian Sarah Coakley who among many others connects the three stages of ascent in mystical theology (purgative, illuminative and unitive) with spiritual development cautioning, as we have seen others do, against the danger of 'elitist progressivism'.[121]

Where do girls fit into this writing? Loder recognises that gender differentiation plays an important part in psychological development in puberty. Like Fowler, he was the father of two daughters: as with Erikson, it is interesting to speculate on how far their experiences of their own daughters' negotiation of puberty influenced their theories. Stressing the relational nature of adolescent development, he acknowledges the milestone for girls represented by the menarche, and the societal influences which may lead to repression or diffusion of identity. He decisively counters Erikson's assumption of the anatomical determination of destiny for a girl: of her potentiality for motherhood, he says 'it is important … that this aspect of sexual formation be recognized and affirmed but not become a declaration of one's destiny'.[122] However, he fails to take account of the influence of gender on bodily perception and ideology, but fixates on girls' sexuality at the expense of wider issues. Practical theologians Wright and Dean, while not foregrounding female experience, integrate Loder's themes and apply them specifically to youth ministry in a way which, I suggest, draws on their experience and reflection as women. Without denying that their arguments apply, perhaps in varying degrees and modes of expression, to both genders and are supported by the writing of malestream as well as feminist theologians, their focus on relationality and affectivity in structuring their theological approach to and understanding of adolescence illustrates the findings of other writers that these

---

[118]   Balswick et al., *The Reciprocating Self*, pp. 18–22.

[119]   Loder, *Logic*, pp. 72–7.

[120]   Hay with Nye, *The Spirit of the Child*, chapter 1.

[121]   Sarah Coakley, 'Deepening Practices: Perspectives from Ascetical and Mystical Theology', in Miroslav Volf and Dorothy C. Bass (eds), *Practicing Theology: Beliefs and Practices in Christian Life* (Grand Rapids, 2002), p. 93.

[122]   Loder, *Logic*, p. 221.

are distinctive of the spirituality of women and girls.[123] Slee, for example, records the passionate engagement of women in the stages of their faith journey,[124] and as we have already seen, Nye attributes to her gender her identification of relational consciousness as a feature of children's spirituality.

Stage theories are still accepted in some recent works on girls'/boys' spirituality, but only as forming one strand in a growing understanding which now takes full account of other factors, including gender, context and environment. As a Christian researching from a biological perspective, Hay is dismissive of the work of developmental theorists, arguing that 'their stress on the development of intellectual and moral reasoning in children means that they downplay the spiritual dimension', which he summarises as self-transcending awareness.[125] Others see spiritual development as a dimension of human life and experience which not only relates to cognitive, emotional and social development, but serves as a core process which integrates these different aspects of development.[126] In their summary of the contemporary scene, Roehlkepartain, Benson, King and Wagener conclude that spiritual development is more appropriately seen as a continuous process which must remain in dialogue with stage theories despite the latter being based on discontinuity and implying inevitability. Their conclusions have other antecedents besides Fowler, as others in the United States have researched the content of girls'/boys' spiritual and faith lives. Mostly from a psychological and sociological background, such scholars include Coles (who like Fowler was influenced by Erikson), Heller, Hart, and Benson and Roehlkepartain at the Search Institute's Center for Spiritual Development in childhood and adolescence.[127] While they understand spirituality as a universal human phenomenon, the Search Institute joins with other North American and British researchers and practitioners in the triennial Children's Spirituality Conference to locate it within a more overtly Christian framework.[128] In the UK, a similar diversity is in evidence. The most substantial work on childhood spirituality has been undertaken within the context of the public education system, in the Warwick Religions and Education Research

---

[123]   Dana R. Wright with Kenda Creasey Dean, 'Youth, Passion and Intimacy in the Context of *Koinonia*: James E. Loder's Contribution to a Practical Theology of *Imitatio Christi* for Youth Ministry', in Wright and Kuentzel, *Redemptive Transformation*.

[124]   Slee identifies the stages as: alienation, awakening, relationality in *Women's Faith Development*, pp. 107, 113, 149ff.

[125]   Hay with Nye, *The Spirit of the Child*, pp. 50, 21–2.

[126]   Roehlkepartain, *Handbook of Spiritual Development*, p. 9.

[127]   Robert Coles, *The Spiritual Life of Children* (London, 1990); David Heller, *The Children's God* (Chicago and London, 1986); Tobin Hart, *The Secret Spiritual World of Children* (Makawao, 2003); articles, books and research papers from the Search Institute can be accessed through the Center's website: www.spiritualdevelopmentcenter.org.

[128]   Papers from the first two conferences are published in Donald Ratcliff (ed.), *Children's Spirituality*, and Holly Catterton Allen (ed.), *Nurturing Children's Spirituality: Christian Perspectives and Best Practices* (Eugene, 2008).

Unit[129] and in the Children and Worldviews Project and the related Association for Children's Spirituality.[130] The work of Hay and Nye makes a substantial contribution to a generic understanding of girls'/boys' spirituality which, although stemming from research carried out in state schools, can more readily than the others be applied to the life of faith in a church community.

8. Research on Girls and their Faith

Around 12–13 years old, quantitative research reveals that the religious affiliation of all girls/boys declines. Hay suggests its cause is socially constructed (or rather destructed) and, he argues, a European phenomenon. His contention is that *spiritual experience* does not decline, only *religious observance*.[131] In one study, Kay and Francis found that up to age 15–16, girls were more positive than boys in their attitude to Christianity,[132] and in another, using a 'scale of attitude towards Christianity', Francis and Wilcox, using gender orientation theory,[133] found that among 13–15-year-olds, 'sex continues to be a significant predictor of attitude towards Christianity'; their research differentiated between biological sex and gender orientation. They concluded that younger girls appear to have more positive religious attitudes because it is less socially acceptable for boys to appear religious, i.e. they are more likely to deny their gender orientation at the same age.[134] Francis and Wilcox theorise only in the psychological and social domains but signs of differentiation are found in others too, for example increased understanding of brain structure brings neurology into the picture, and the relatively new study of spiritual intelligence.[135]

---

[129]   See Eleanor Nesbitt, 'Researching 8 to 13-Year-Olds' Perspectives on their Experience of Religion', in Ann Lewis and Geoff Lindsay (eds), *Researching Children's Perspectives* (Buckingham and Philadelphia, 2000).

[130]   Associated with the work of Clive Erricker, Jane Erricker and Cathy Ota: see www.childrenspirituality.org.

[131]   Hay with Nye, *The Spirit of the Child*, pp. 57ff.

[132]   William Kay and Leslie Francis, *Drift from the Churches: Attitude Toward Christianity During Childhood and Adolescence* (Cardiff, 1996), p. 218.

[133]   They used the Bem Sex Role inventory, one of several psychological theories they cite which traditionally account for difference in attitude to religion between men and women. Bem herself believes the link between sex and psychology is overstated in the West: her position is critiqued by Greene, *Psychological Development*, p. 14.

[134]   Leslie Francis and Carolyn Wilcox, 'Religiosity and Femininity: Do Women Really Hold a More Positive Attitude Toward Christianity?', *Journal for the Scientific Study of Religion*, 37.3 (1998): 462–9.

[135]   An overview of recent developments in this field is found in Kate Adams, Brendan Hyde and Richard Woolley, *The Spiritual Dimension of Childhood* (London, 2008), pp. 15–18, 88–102; Danah Zohar and Ian Marshall, *SQ: Connecting with our Spiritual Intelligence* (New York, 2000). SQ is 'the intelligence by which we address and solve problems of meaning and value … our ultimate intelligence', pp. 3–4. The authors make minimal links

Together, these studies support the need for research focusing on girls' faith especially at puberty, offering a significant corrective to studies of children in the church which avoid gender differentiation. With the decline in church attendance and consequent exposure of young people to religious knowledge and influence, Heynes cites the argument that Religious Education (RE) in schools is becoming increasingly important 'as a means of understanding one's self and society', and on that basis conducts research in schools with 14–18-year-old girls. Her findings reveal the masculinist nature of the content of RE, which serves as a significant deterrent to teenage girls' engagement with religion.[136]

There is therefore strong motivation for giving attention to girls in this younger age group to prepare them for and accompany them in the exposure to wider ranging influences which will impact the internal processing of their maturing faith as they attempt to mould their lives holistically towards adulthood, offering support and nurture which will help them enrich their relationship with God, and flourish as women. Increased understanding of girls' growth and its impact on how they 'do' faith will therefore help the community of which they are a part to offer more informed support.

When we look for research into the content of girls'/boys' faith, we find some qualitative studies carried out among pre-adolescents. Most UK based work has been multi-faith and, as above, conducted in secular, commonly educational, contexts. Gender has not been used as a criterion of analysis. Elsewhere, David Heller in the United States investigated children up to 12 in faith communities in the 1980s, and in Finland, Kalevi Tamminen undertook a longitudinal study of children and young people between seven and 20 in Finnish schools in the 1970s and 1980s; both used gender as one criterion for analysis of their data.[137] A major piece of sociological research has been carried out more recently in the United States among teenagers between 13 and 17,[138] and in the UK, Christian Research carried out a survey in churches and schools in 2001 into attitudes of children between ten and 14 to 'God, the Church and themselves' in response to falling numbers of that age group in churches.[139] Both also, in a limited way, assessed results by gender.

---

with research into children's spirituality, but connections can be made by those working in that broader field.

[136]   Jeannine Heynes, 'Engaging with Teenage Girls' Understandings of Religion and Gender', in Collins-Mayo and Dandelion (eds), *Religion and Youth*, pp. 123–30.

[137]   Both do, I believe, produce results which, despite their different cultural contexts, offer relevant comparative data. Heller, *The Children's God*; Kalevi Tamminen, *Religious Development in Childhood and Youth* (Helsinki, 1991).

[138]   Christian Smith with Melinda Lundquist Denton, *Soul Searching: The Religious and Spiritual Lives of American Teenagers* (New York, 2005).

[139]   Peter Brierley, *Reaching and Keeping Tweenagers* (London, 2002).

Some more recent qualitative research in the United States has focused solely on girls, but from 16 to 18.[140] While acknowledging that younger girls need the encouragement of such attention in their faith journey, both Baker and Mercer worked with the older age group on the grounds that they would bring more life experience to the task. Although their work brings insights for comparison, the difference in age and context limits its usefulness to my study.

Turning now to survey the processes of these research projects, and broadly summarise their findings, I begin with research across both genders.[141] Tamminen, Heller and Brierley, and the 2005 National Study of Youth and Religion (NSYR) survey of teenagers in the United States all found it to be consistently true across a wide variety of religiosity variables that, corroborating Francis and Wilcox's findings, girls practise religion more than boys. However, it is important to note the degree of difference: in Smith and Denton's research, 'on each of the six religiosity variables examined, girls scored higher than boys. The differences are not enormous but … they are statistically significant'.[142] These variables are: religious attendance, importance of faith in daily life, personal commitment to God, involvement in a youth group, frequency of prayer alone and closeness to God. Tamminen's results are similar, applying not only to 'the religiousness of boys and girls as such but also in the line of development': he finds that girls' earlier development, particularly in abstract thinking, correlates with the normal age they reach puberty.[143]

Where research has investigated girls' beliefs and religious practice more closely, there is marked similarity across western cultures. Heller's was conducted entirely through semi-structured interviews; the others gathered statistics though questionnaires, selecting smaller samples for one-to-one or small group interviews. None was undertaken solely in church communities. Heller's 40 4–12-year-olds were recruited from local schools and places of worship, the interviews taking place on a university campus. Tamminen's three stage study over a 12-year period, questioning well over 2,000 7–20-year-olds with roughly equal numbers of girls and boys, took place in schools in Finland where membership of the Lutheran church was high and religious education compulsory for the majority. Brierley's research among 10–14-year-olds from churches, schools and unspecified Christian parachurch organisations, drew 2,172 responses to a questionnaire, and was followed up by two Focus Groups attended by 17 young people divided by whether they were church or non-church attenders. The NSYR study with 13–17-year-olds was conducted with unstated numbers by telephone, and followed by 267 interviews with subjects selected to gather a broad range of difference across a range of demographic variables including gender. The authors' comment is valid that 'any book aspiring to present general overview of the results of such an inclusive study of national teen religiosity,

---

[140]   Baker, *Doing Girlfriend Theology*; Mercer, *Girl Talk, God Talk*.
[141]   I discuss the detail alongside my own data analysis in Chapter 6.
[142]   Smith with Denton, *Soul Searching*, p. 277.
[143]   Tamminen, *Religious Development*, p. 308.

yet lacking an analysis using these kinds of demographic variables, would be incomplete'.

Brierley's research is the only one which broadly coincides with my targeted age group, so in each of the others, I am searching out the age-appropriate data. Despite similarities, context does affect some outcomes. While Tamminen wrote up his findings for an international readership, drawing on current European and American literature in his analysis, Heller, the NSYR and Brierley are speaking into their own national contexts, and are therefore culture specific. The purpose of each study was different. Heller undertook wide-ranging research into 'deity representation and their personalized meanings' and aimed to write a 'descriptive essay and analysis of what I observed'; his research followed Robert Coles' phenomenological model and included Jewish and Hindu children alongside Christian. Tamminen wanted to 'clarify as extensively and comprehensively as possible the religious development of children and young people in its different dimensions'. The NSYR aimed to 'help develop a better scholarly and public understanding of the religious and spiritual lives of American adolescents'.

The publication of Brierley's research findings was of an intentionally popular nature, and lacks the rigour of a truly academic study. Nevertheless because it was supported and welcomed by a number of Protestant denominations and parachurch organisations in the UK, it has been formative of attitudes to girls/boys of this age, and for this reason its data gathering process and analysis must be challenged. It was planned with a Steering Committee comprising representatives of denominational and evangelical parachurch organisations, and its initial report was reviewed by a wider specialist group. However, female representation in the design of and reflection on the process and its findings was minimal: only one woman was on the Steering Committee of eight (with staff changes, nine men participated overall), and only four of the 12 to whom the draft manuscript was distributed for comment were women. This is in marked contrast to the other studies cited; where authored solely by men, they include in their consultative processes and bibliographies feminist research or research by women. Among the respondents to Brierley's questionnaire, 53 per cent were girls, but the Focus (discussion) Groups consisted of seven girls and ten boys, whereas Heller's gender mix was equal, in all but one of Tamminen's samples girls slightly outnumbered boys, and although the NSYR survey does not record gender proportions, it aimed 'to capture a broad range of difference'. Brierley's research aimed to study the reasons for the substantial numerical decline in under 15-year-olds attending church in the UK over the previous decade, its purpose intentionally missional, to offer churches resources to 'stop the haemorrhage'.[144] The research covered a range of issues and attitudes beyond the religious, most data being gathered by questionnaire, presenting limited response options which reflect the stance of the researcher. The limitations of such questionnaires in

---

[144]   Brierley, *Reaching and Keeping Tweenagers*, pp. 3–4. The report has an accompanying *Workbook*. For Brierley's conclusions about the role of girls, see p. 191.

discovering much of value about faith is expressed by Dykstra: of answers to similar research questions in the United States, he says: '(it) does not tell us much about what "God" means for those young people or whether these affirmations arc in any way significant for their lives, much less what that does to their ways of thinking and speaking and what they perceive the nature of reality ultimately to be'. It only tells us, he says, that they have come across faith claims, and 'for some reason or another' they agree (or disagree) with the statements.[145]

Brierley appends a brief description of his methodology for the quantitative study, but not that for the Focus Groups; the information gleaned from these is used sporadically in the report. He admits to extensive 'desk research' and to incorporating 'extracts from the findings of others who have undertaken research among this age group', although many studies cited were for different purposes and with no overlap with this age group. There is clear gender bias in his use of such material, especially with regard to girls. Sexual activity was deliberately excluded from the questionnaire, and he admits that there have been relatively few studies of sexual behaviour of young people in churches. Yet he makes girls' sexual activity a feature of his report, by drawing on studies of older subjects. This is translated into a conclusion which suggests their promiscuity, and places the onus on girls both to exercise restraint for themselves and to direct their relational skills to influencing boys to do the same. This is founded on his suggestion that boys may be 'feeling intimidated by high performing girls'; a feature of the research is the link it makes between religiosity and academic achievement. Girls are also to be diverted from sexual activity by encouraging their involvement in church projects 'so that their Christianity has a practical and social dimension'. This is despite evidence gleaned directly from the research that girls experience lower self-esteem, and that in addition to being statistically more friendly and caring, which he concludes renders them more confident, they were also more scared, something he does not elaborate. Brierley's conclusions ignore the complexity of living in the contemporary context for a girl, and the struggles of girls in the church to be affirmed in their bodily as well as their spiritual growth when such matters are not openly discussed and role models are rarely presented to them. The sexuality of boys, and the social construction of a sexualised identity for girls, is not considered.

Some of Brierley's research conclusions may be harmful for girls in the largely evangelical circles in which it is read and so, despite not having academic credibility, I will make occasional reference in later chapters to its findings where my own corroborate, qualify or challenge his.

---

[145]   Craig Dykstra, 'Youth and the Language of Faith', *Religious Education*, 81.2 (1986): 177–8.

The Church as Holding Environment

It is the contexts in which girls are growing in faith to which I now turn. The individualism of much faith development theory does not give sufficient weight to the environments of home, church, school and peer group which bear much of the responsibility for facilitating its growth. Westerhoff recognises this inadequacy, and uses as a theological model for the nurture of all in interdependence the 'image of communal life' in the persons of the Trinity.[146] This dynamic image is employed increasingly to explore and explain the nurturance of girls/boys in faith, signifying as it does a mutuality between people of all ages but different experiences within the community.

To help give substance to the role of the community, I draw again on the work of Kegan, since he paid attention not only to the evolutionary truces in human growth but to the transitional stages. Westerhoff and Fowler both understood that movement from one stage or style to another usually occurred through an external event which triggered new thinking and opportunities for reflection on faith, but paid little or no attention to puberty, the threshold girls cross in perhaps the most significant life-change, a bodily experience with potential to birth deeper faithing.

Kegan sees the role of the holding environment not only as offering support but as contributing actively to the change process, recognising also the danger of the opposite, that it might stifle growth: he thereby encourages reflection by the community on its identity as a holding environment and the part it plays in the nurturance of its members. Winnicott developed the terminology out of his clinical observation of the conditions by which infants were able to separate successfully from their mothers. The holding environment denotes the psychic space between mother and child within which the child begins the process of self-identification and separation, the transition to becoming differentiated while remaining within relationship. In this space, the mother mirrors the infant's self when responding to her needs rather than projecting the mother's own self onto the child. Thus, the image has its origins in the birthing of identity. Its appeal to Kegan lies in its dual properties of containment and intermediate space; for him it symbolises the conditions which facilitate growth and development which are not achieved by the individual alone, but only with caretakers in a social structure – parents in the home, teachers in the school, friends in peer group(s) and, for the purposes of my research, leaders and members within a church. Kegan's development of the concept of the holding environment is therefore useful for exploring how girls can flourish in a church context; this is explored further by Carol Lakey Hess.

The holding environment is fundamental to 'a life history of cultures of embeddedness'. By culture, Kegan means both the 'accumulated history and mythology' of the community, and the medium of growth as in a Petri dish, a mixture of inherited tradition and an ethos and structure generated within its influence by its current members. He thus affirms that differentiation is only

---

[146]   Westerhoff, *Will Our Children Have Faith?*, p. 75.

one half of a life story, that 'a person is an "individual" *and* an "embeddual"'. The evolution of the self takes place as a person is sequentially held and let go by the holding environment into the next balance. If growth is not apparent, the healthy holding environment will offer the challenge to move on. An unhealthy environment will hold on too tightly and not release the subject: Kegan describes this as 'developmental detention', which has parallels with Erikson's 'foreclosure'. The healthy holding environment remains in place when the person grows and the relationship changes, so that it continues to include even as distinctness is emerging. Through resistance to the 'culture of embeddedness', the child re-negotiates her relationship to her environment; it holds the story of her transformation, a narrative which she must translate in the process of creating or finding her new self. Kegan comments that 'the normal experiences of evolution involve *recoverable* loss; what we separate from we find anew' (author's italics). Although taking account of the psychological theories of Freud and Jung, Kegan aligns himself more with the psychosocial approach of Erikson, who sees personality development as occurring 'in the context of interaction between the organism and the environment, rather than through the internal processes of maturation alone'. What Kegan does not do, however, is to allow for the complexity of the dialectic set up between the agent (the girl) doing the interacting, and the context within which the process occurs.

Hess develops out of Kegan's writing her theoretical base on which she builds her practical theology of girls' growth to maturity incorporating and subverting the social forces which repress girls' voices. As an educationalist and theologian, she proposes a method whereby the church can become 'the kind of holding environment where men and women can speak their voices and stay connected to one another', characterised by 'hard dialogue and deep conversation' with one another, with scripture and tradition and with God. Thus we come at last to the third category of literature.

Girls in Theology

In the absence of theologies dedicated to reflection on girlhood, I must tease out of theologies of childhood, and of such feminist theology as attends to them, material helpful in locating girls in God's purposes, and affirming them in their gendered bodies.

Although there are strong female role models in scripture, there is a fundamental problem that at the heart of the Christian faith lies God's male incarnation. Moltmann, criticised for failing 'to break the rigid hold and privileged status of masculine imagery for God' when he coined the phrase 'motherly father',[147] has more recently addressed the issue of the maleness of Jesus in his essay on the theology of childhood. He does this by focusing first on the hope

---

[147]   Mary Grey, *Introducing Feminist Images of God* (Sheffield, 2001), p. 28 referring to Jürgen Moltmann, 'The Motherly Father: Is Trinitarian Patripassianism Replacing

of a messianic child in prophecy, which he argues is only one of two traditions by which Jesus is identified. The child of habitual expectation was to be a *son* of David (e.g. 2 Samuel 7.12f., Isaiah 9.6). Insofar as Israelite tradition looked to children as the guarantee of God's faithfulness, the harbinger of the new as well as preserver of the old dispensation, the inheritance only came through a male heir. Although Israel did not adopt the custom of exposing girl children, Moltmann claims 'daughters must be avoided' (he doesn't suggest how!). Trible likewise notes that the girl child was 'less desirable in the eyes of her parents than a male child'.[148] Questioning the gender exclusive understanding of the promise, Moltmann looks to the Wisdom tradition for identification of the daughter: unlike Fiorenza, Ruether and Day,[149] however, who only see in the *hokma* figure an adult 'daughter of God', he interprets the Wisdom figure of Proverbs 8 as the wise *child* which the playfulness of one reading of the disputed text of verse 30 might suggest. He argues that 'later Israelite traditions fused the two figures of hope' into an explicit Wisdom Messiah. If wisdom is a presence of God in creation, she is more than a human virtue, he suggests: Jesus is 'presented in the New Testament both as Israel's Messiah and as the wisdom of creation, so that not only is the Christ mystery both male and female' but the infant Christ is daughter as well as son.[150] In the theological reflection on childhood he constructs on this foundation, Moltmann affirms the new values Jesus teaches when he welcomes children and holds them up as models of discipleship, as for example in Mark 10.14, concluding that Jesus as the messianic child of promise fulfils all messianic expectations so that male privilege is at an end and 'daughters and sons are the bearers of hope for humanity'. Sadly, like many who construct theologies of childhood, Moltmann seems to leave it in a 'bubble', unconnected with his work on, for example, power and patriarchy. Ruether argues a similar transcendence of the Christ of theology over the human maleness of Jesus,[151] but despite evidence of dependence on the Wisdom tradition through the use of the feminine *sophia* in christological texts such as 1 Corinthians 1.23–4, the Jesus of history and the Christ of faith are distanced from the 'female side of God' by, for example, the choice of the masculine Logos in John's Prologue. Regardless of such discussions, the question of how a girl can relate to Jesus born a boy presents

---

Theological Patriarchalism', in Schillebeeckz and Metz (eds), *Concilium* (Edinburgh, 1981), pp. 51–6.

[148]   Phyllis Trible, 'Feminist Hermeneutics and Biblical Studies', in A. Loades (ed.), *Feminist Theology: A Reader* (London, 1990), pp. 23–9.

[149]   Elisabeth Schüssler Fiorenza, *Wisdom Ways: Introducing Feminist Biblical Interpretation* (Maryknoll, 2001); Rosemary Radford Ruether, *Sexism and God-talk* (London, 1983); Linda Day, 'Wisdom and the Feminine in the Hebrew Bible', in Linda Day and Carolyn Pressler (eds), *Engaging the Bible in a Gendered World: An Introduction to Feminist Biblical Interpretation in Honor of Katharine Doob Sakenfeld* (Louisville, 2006).

[150]   Moltmann, *In the End*, pp. 11–12.

[151]   Ruether, *Sexism and God-talk*.

as an issue for girls as for women.[152] Divine Wisdom, which Fiorenza describes as a 'submerged tradition', offers such a resource for use with girls.[153]

Of other theologians who have written on girls/boys, Rahner offers the richest resource, in an essay which has stimulated two recent practical theologies of childhood. In 'Ideas for a Theology of Childhood', Rahner reaffirms the mystery and value of childhood by rejecting the developmental paradigm with its implied subordination of childhood, reclaiming human subject status, self-possession and therefore self-worth throughout the lifespan. Therefore,

> We do not lose childhood as that which recedes ever further into our past, that which remains behind as we advance forward in time, but rather we go towards it as that which has been achieved in time and redeemed forever in time.[154]

Childhood for Rahner 'must take the form of trust, of openness, of expectation'. Counting himself a pastoral or practical theologian, Rahner saw his wider theological quest as leading people 'into the presence of the one, same, and all-embracing mystery of God', so in relation to childhood he 'is concerned not only with what a child *is* in the sight of God, but how God as mystery is revealed in the experience of childhood'.[155] Rahner inspires Hay and Nye in their rejection of developmentalism, and promotion of attention to 'signals of transcendence', a term they borrow from Peter Berger.[156] Nye in particular seeks such signals in girls'/boys' total communication: a category of data in her research was the children's 'casual chatter', studying what they revealed aside from intentionally religious talk.[157]

Jensen is the first theologian I will cite to be influenced by Rahner. In *Graced Vulnerability*, he develops Rahner's assertion of the intrinsic value of a child who needs no becoming and to whom are already attached 'the values of imperishability and eternity', who is 'related with absolute immediacy to God himself [*sic*]'.[158] Relationality becomes a key theme for Jensen, who identifies in human vulnerability the *imago dei*, arguing that relationality, in the Triune as in human life, risks vulnerability. This is the outcome of his search for a

---

[152] The issue is regularly revisited, as in Julia Baudzej, 'Re-telling the Story of Jesus: The Concept of Embodiment and Recent Feminist Reflections on the Maleness of Christ', *Feminist Theology*, 17.1 (2008): 72–91.

[153] For example, J. Claussen with J.A. Keller, *Seeking: Doing Theology with Girls* (Winona, 2003), pp. 68–76.

[154] Rahner, *Theological Investigations*, p. 37.

[155] Mary Ann Hinsdale, '"Infinite Openness to the Infinite": Karl Rahner's Contribution to Modern Catholic Thought on the Child', in Bunge, *The Child in Christian Thought*, pp. 417–18.

[156] Hay with Nye, *The Spirit of the Child*, p. 60.

[157] Nye, 'Psychological Perspectives', p. 229.

[158] Jensen, *Graced Vulnerability*, chapter 6; Rahner, *Theological Investigations*, p. 37.

theology inclusive of all humankind including people with the most profound learning disabilities, which leads him to reject any association between human capability and the divine image; thus he moves away from a gendered (or any other) dialectic. Despite that, the two themes of vulnerability and relationality are ones which touch but do not prescribe girls' lives. His work thus contributes to a theological understanding of girlhood. A psychological counterpart to Jensen's theology can be found in Kegan's search for an integrating ground for mutual understanding and relating prior to what he regards as culturally originating and defined differentiations. One of his goals in studying the evolution of meaning is to enable people to see the 'other' better through seeing ourselves more clearly and this 'increases our vulnerability to being recruited to the welfare of another': such recruitability, or relationality, is necessary not just for our survival but for our flourishing. Kegan aligns his ideas theologically with Tillich's 'centered unity' which in order to be enlarged and strengthened must 'give up something of what I now am', indicative of the 'sacrificial character of all life',[159] language which feminist theology and psychology would align with the lived experience of women and girls acting and being acted upon. So these ideas can lead us inductively from female experience to the being of God taken up, for example, by Paul Fiddes when he explores ideas of God's power and self-chosen vulnerability in the perichoresis of Trinitarian and human relating, by which he includes so-called gender-difference within divine life.[160]

Implicit in Rahner's writing are three attributes of girls/boys which are marks of spiritual pilgrimage: imagination, play and paying attention. Jensen identifies these, as does Mercer, the second theologian whose work owes much to Rahner's influence.

As a feminist theologian Mercer surprises herself by her attraction to the work of a Catholic priest, whose experience is far removed from hers as a woman and a mother, but she approves his affirmation of the value of childhood for itself and in its role in 'our eschatological future'. Indeed, the focus in the theologies of Moltmann and Rahner is refreshingly different from many other theologians whose major discussion of childhood is on sin, election or sacraments. Although Rahner offers no practical application of his ideas for the nurture of children, Mercer uses his insights to challenge educational practices within her own and other Protestant churches, concentrating on the context in which children are being nurtured and the positive formational potential of an affirming theology. In her experience, Christian education has become 'instructional downloading of moralistic sound bites delivered to children through entertainment-oriented styles of teaching in a context sequestered from the practices of the wider

---

[159]   Kegan, 'Where the Dance is: Religious Dimensions of a Developmental Framework', in C. Brusselmanns, J.A. O'Donooe, J. Fowler and A. Vergote (eds), *Toward Moral and Religious Maturity* (Morristown, 1980), p. 42, in which he quotes from Paul Tillich, *Systematic Theology*, Vol. 3 (Chicago, 1967).

[160]   Fiddes, *Participating in God*, pp. 89–96.

community of faith'.[161] Likening this to Freire's banking model of education, she advocates instead a 'community of practice' within which girls/boys can develop their Christian identity as they make meaning out of the faith stories in the context of their daily lives.[162] Mercer recognises, as Kegan in discussing holding environments does not, that this also involves openness on the community's part to transformational self-reflection. This model of growth is relational, and open to the encouragement of the co-operative work between human and divine (s)Spirit of which we have seen Loder speak. Mercer emphasises the relational contexts which offer girls/boys support in the process of identity and discipleship formation in the face of material consumerism, places where they are valued as full members of the community of faith, and which take seriously the theological dimension of Jesus' welcome of children.

It is primarily Carol Lakey Hess in *Caretakers of Our Common House* who, starting from the standpoint of feminist rather than childhood theology, focuses on a similar issue, how the church can become a community which both holds and nurtures into wholeness its more vulnerable members, who for her are women and girls. She transfers Brown and Gilligan's findings on girls' loss of voice in the school environment to the church where she finds a parallel situation. She argues on biblical and theological grounds for a Christian education which is conversational, building on women's strengths of caring and connection as well as promoting voice. Her intentional learning process of 'hard dialogue and deep connection' has three conversation partners – peers and adults, scripture and tradition, and God – enabling voices to be heard from the 'underside' of suppressed or silenced female lives and voices. Her work is grounded in exegesis of biblical stories: female resistance to patriarchy by Rachel and Leah, Vashti and Esther, and the leadership of God's people by Deborah, to the end that, by 'tak(ing) control of the household gods as did Rachel ... they learn to use the master's tools and establish themselves in the household'.[163]

'Household' is only one of Lakey Hess' images for communities of faith, but it is a favoured one, emphasising the intergenerational nature of the community, but one whose purpose goes beyond preservation of the status quo to empowerment of girls in 'creative defiance' to 'wrestle together to prevail against those things that deprive women of their well-being'.[164] It represents a safe house in which girls can be coached and mentored, learning to resist compliance but be critically inquiring, and challenge interpretation of texts and discriminatory practices which dehumanise, inhibit or deny their flourishing. Hess recognises that the church can be restrictive, even abusive, as does Kegan when he describes a holding environment which holds on too tightly. Nevertheless the image of a safe space

---

[161] Mercer, *Welcoming Children*, p. 163.

[162] Ibid., pp. 168–172. Paulo Freire, *Pedagogy of the Oppressed*, rev. edn (London, 1996).

[163] Hess, *Caretakers of our Common House*, p. 166.

[164] Ibid., p. 181.

ideally offered in household or home is a strong one, to which I shall return in my analysis. In anticipation, it is interesting to return briefly to Moltmann who makes a theological link between the safe nurturing space for a child in the covenant community and the mutual indwelling between God and humankind, which are both part of everyday experience and our eschatological hope.[165]

Nye rightly warns of the danger that over-attention to gender may lead to stereotyping of girls on the part of adults who 'may miss valuable diversity and individuality'. Contrary to the body of research cited above, she asserts that 'the research evidence … has not provided much to support th(e) idea' that 'gender issues affect spirituality in childhood'. She proceeds, however, to offer contradictory evidence from her own experience of working with boys as well as girls which lead her to concludes that the desire to please others at the expense of acting and thinking independently is 'alarmingly engrained' in girls, and she, like Hess, recommends positive action to support them in their growing spirituality.[166]

Hess is aware in her own culture that the message girls receive about their role and identity encourages them into 'giving themselves away': in response, her 'conversational education' is a strategy to help them to 'take themselves back', finding 'voice' or 'meaning' or succeeding in Loder's 'transformative reconstruction'. She sees the intergenerational holding environment of a church ideally offering girls what culture denies, a place where they can learn resistance and be supported as they develop their identity through strong relationships with others and God. In Slee's analysis, she finds similar tensions are experienced by women in churches in Britain. Church communities will not always be safe places for girls: the experience among Southern Baptists in the United States of which Sue Monk Kidd writes was extreme,[167] but girls in the UK, like their adult counterparts, still find restricted views of their place and role, and expectations of behavioural 'niceness'.

A more systematic attempt to create a method of 'finding voice' with girls and young women as advocated by Hess has been undertaken by Baker. Again taking 'loss of voice' as axiomatic, 'shorthand for a series of transitions that seem to occur as girls begin to belie their inner sense of knowing',[168] she explicitly names spirituality as already an intrinsic component of girls' resistance. To establish that this is so, she wants to encourage girls to tell their own stories, 'to tease out of (them) the embodied strategies they use to confront oppressive forces that seek to diminish their humanness' by developing a 'process of bringing to voice the "God-talk" that emerges when adolescent girls and adult women "meet at the crossroads" to share everyday experiences'.[169] She gathered together small

[165] Moltmann, *In The End*, p. 16.
[166] Rebecca Nye, *Children's Spirituality: What it is and Why it Matters* (London, 2009), pp. 88–9.
[167] Sue Monk Kidd, *Dance of the Dissident Daughter* (New York, 1996).
[168] Baker, *Doing Girlfriend Theology*, p. 13.
[169] Ibid., p. 19, quoting the title of Gilligan and Brown's book.

groups of teenage girls and adult women aged from 14 to 40 to 'do theology'. Despite having accepted that the transitional process which she is trying to forestall begins at the younger age, she chose an older age group (the youngest girl whose voice we hear is 16) to bring greater life experience to the research conversations 'although a younger population might have allowed me to test this method as an intervention'. So her claim to create an 'intervention tool helping girls find and maintain voice',[170] cannot be fully justified although she claims this does not invalidate her research as the phenomenon of silencing beginning in early adolescence continues into adulthood. By her own admission, though, her connection with the work of Brown and Gilligan, whose research finds that the 'hinge' age is around 12–13, is loosened.

Baker's method is narrative, her participants a mixed-age, faith-based but not singularly Christian nor necessarily practising group, her process adopted and adapted to follow an action/reflection model for 'doing theology'. This involves four discrete stages: story-telling, reflection first as 'experience near' (based on personal association) then as 'experience distant' (bringing identified themes into dialogue with theology and scripture), and concluding with 'going forth' to act on insights gained. There are strong links here with a traditional 'pastoral cycle' model.[171] In each two-hour session, up to four teenagers would be led through the conversational process by one or two adults. Baker found her research confirmed the value for girls of the companionship and mentoring by women at 'the crossroads of souls', and initiated 'not so much a finished product as … an ongoing process' in which shared story as 'sacred text where God continue to reveal Godself' continued in memory to inform and illuminate the faith journey.[172] Three of the four stories quoted were introduced by the girls who therefore set the theological agenda. The chosen themes were: the complexity of relationship, issues of life and death, and experiences of epiphany.

What is evident from the interaction recorded is the safety felt by the girls to speak with authority of their experiences, thoughts and feelings, to disagree with adults and resist the power of their superior status and knowledge. In describing her methodology, Baker does not address the issue of power differentials; she is promoting a method yet does not analyse the interaction between woman and girl, the quality and influence of input, and the way the girls themselves structured their theological reflection. She does, however, identify theological statements made by the girls which stress their own stories and the world as places of encounter with an omnipresent God, at work with healing potential in church and world, a God, she reflects, 'in many ways … different from the God most of the girls inherited from the faith tradition'.[173] Further research will evaluate her strategy, which combines

---

[170]   Ibid., p. 38.

[171]   For example, Laurie Green, *Let's Do Theology: Resources for Contextual Theology* (London, 2009).

[172]   Baker, *Doing Girlfriend Theology*, p. 171.

[173]   Ibid., p. 173.

existing models of theological reflection with feminist methodology, and assess its longer-term results in the lives of girls. Nevertheless, Baker's work comes closest to my own and offers some useful material for comparison with my findings.

Chapter 3
Methods for Learning from Girls

Introduction

Throughout this chapter, I recount a personal research journey. The very nature of my subject, subjects and context demanded a distinctive investigative pathway.

Research with girls/boys is not easy, hedged about as it necessarily is with ethical guidelines, and the need for special attention in its execution and analysis to many specifics – of context, of personhood and personality, of life experience, and above all of power. To explore my three research questions, I needed to construct an empirical process, locating and talking with particular girls in my chosen age group. Empirical research draws its data from the experience of particular people both from the researcher's observation of them in their own context and from intentional conversations designed to explore aspects of their thinking and experience which will then be subjected to analysis. Fundamental to my research process was the valuing of girls' experience of the world, and the conviction that their responses would give rise to genuinely new knowledge, able to stand its ground when tested in the ecclesial as well as the academic world. Gender awareness was intrinsic to my research with girls, so a feminist methodology was appropriate, drawing on the model developed by Slee in her study of women's faith: much qualitative research with girls/boys is in any case now conducted along lines which have become associated with feminist research methodology, so there were other resources upon which to draw.

Recognising the difficulty of establishing 'truth' between different and often conflicting experiences, Fraser offers three qualities which should mark it out and assist in its validation in academia: it should be demonstrably systematic, sceptical about existing truth claims, and ethical in its responsibility towards participants. It will provide a full account of its design and process, expecting its methods and findings to be open to scrutiny. Such systematic investigation, he argues, does not presume a quantitative methodology, but that with qualitative methods we can also systematically understand 'perceptions directly through what children and young people say, draw, sing, wear etc.'.[1] All this provided me with a useful framework within which to construct a methodology. So, in this chapter, I demonstrate the systematic nature of my research design and process of analysis, and the attention I gave to ethical considerations informed both by good safeguarding practice and

---

[1]   Sandy Fraser, 'Situating Empirical Research', in S. Fraser, V. Lewis, S. Ding, M. Kellett and C. Robinson (eds), *Doing Research with Children and Young People* (London, 2004), p. 19.

by the understanding of relevant 'developmental' issues which drove responsible interview procedures. I drew on resources and models of good practice from sociology, anthropology and psychology, since most research on children and young people, whether quantitative or qualitative, is carried out in 'secular' institutions, state or voluntary, which deliver services in education, health, social care or leisure activity. However, I never lost sight of variations appropriate for church and faith contexts, where 'profundities of human existence – matters of the greatest personal importance to people'[2] require sensitive handling.

Narrative of Research Design

Undertaking research alongside my work as both minister and teacher, I was not able to follow a tidy process. This is itself, I believe, a dimension of feminist research, which many women undertake full- or part-time alongside commitments to work, family and wider society which enriches the outcomes but makes the research process itself a struggle, especially if, as for many women and researchers in contextual or practical theology in general, and with girls/boys in particular, the project does not excite interest in, or is regarded as inferior by, the academic world. Many engaged in feminist research are dependent for informed support and interaction on small groups of scholars engaged in similarly complex juggling.

I wanted to interview girls who came from across a wide range of churches in terms of size, and social context with a mix of racial identity, also from at least one church with a woman minister in sole pastoral charge. For ease and speed of contact and establishment of my ethical credentials, I sought out churches and ministers from my existing networks, established over many years working with churches on educational projects and children's issues. Therefore they were all from within Free Church traditions; this serves as an important counter to much current published work in the UK on girls'/boys' spirituality which emanates from the Anglican church.[3] I interviewed 17 girls in five churches, mostly in the Midlands and North West of England, with one in London. They were selected to present a range of social context and demographic and theological profile. Two were inner city churches, both in areas of significant deprivation; one was experiencing infrastructure regeneration in the locality, while the other was facing the challenge of a decaying building alongside pressing social need among an extensively multi-ethnic population. Three churches were in different small urban settings, two of which had high unemployment through the loss of traditional manufacturing industries. One was a large church (around 100 members), two were medium sized (around 50 members), one was small (12 members). They represented a variety of theological position from broadly 'liberal' to evangelical/

---

[2]   Hay, *Something There*, p. 181.

[3]   For example Nye, *Children's Spirituality*, and Richards and Privett, *Through the Eyes of a Child*.

charismatic. All were served by ordained ministers, of whom three were men, one a woman, and in the fifth church a woman and a man shared pastoral charge. One had a tradition of strong female lay leadership, in another women did not hold key leadership positions. Fifteen of the girls were white, two were black African. Although I did not enquire into social background, I believe the girls to be broadly middle class determined not by income but by education and career aspiration. None were physically disabled or had learning difficulties. While visiting the churches I also interviewed all the ministers and some of the youth leaders.[4]

In accordance with best ethical practice, I had access to the girls only through the minister or youth leader, acting as gatekeeper. I discussed my project with them at an early stage, and when ready to begin interviewing, made another approach to check that the girls identified still met my age criterion. Preparing for the interviews over a two-year period, by the time our meetings took place two girls had just passed their 14th birthday, but I proceeded on the grounds that the difference a week or two made was minimal. I decided on a size limit of four to each group, small enough for me to get to know each girl, build a trusting relationship and ensure that every girl's voice could be heard, large enough to give the girls confidence through peer support. There was no opportunity in every case for the girls to evaluate the interview process, but my impression is that relationship building was successful: their openness and fluency, especially among those accustomed to conversing regularly with non-parental adults in the church, as distinct from encounters of a more didactic nature, suggests positive outcomes.

The amount of time I spent with the girls in each church context varied. I visited three of the churches on several occasions; in the other two, I spent a large part of a day with the two girls in each, and interviewed them together. In the same three churches, the group of girls was larger, so I met with them in a whole group, and then either in pairs or individually as they chose. I recorded each 15–20 minute interview with the girls' consent.

The context of each visit to four of the churches was Sunday worship; in the other, I attended their normal weeknight meeting which incorporated worship. The interviews in three churches took place in the girls' own space in the building; for the others, we were invited to a home where we shared a meal together. In each, therefore, I was a guest in their space, which helped to reduce the power imbalance and enabled them to relax quickly. Nesbitt sees strong advantages in interviewing girls/boys on their home ground: 'children know that in-group language and many community activities and details of ritual practice are unfamiliar to outsiders. The fieldworker's attendance, repeatedly where possible, encourages children's confidence in speaking about these areas of experience'.[5] In three cases, I interviewed the complete group who normally met on a Sunday; in the other two, I asked the gatekeepers to select girls from a larger group. The mix overall not only

---

[4]   See Table 3.1 for interviewees and churches.

[5]   Nesbitt, 'Researching', p. 143.

of age, but of personality and background gave me a sufficient range of difference within the whole sample.

Once the girls had been identified, the gatekeepers secured the agreement of the girls and permission of their parents, and I provided them with a summary of my aims to share with church leaders as appropriate. Safety was of paramount concern: all were given access to my CV, and informed of my Enhanced Criminal Records Bureau Disclosure.[6] Where I could organise it, I took great care in setting out the interview space so that our conversations were observable, and the girls could leave the room unhindered if they chose. I talked with the girls at the outset about their control of the process, which entitled them to end the interview at any time; they also had the choice whether or not to answer any question.

In designing the interviews to provide sufficient material for analysis, I established clear criteria, drawing on the experience of those who have engaged in research interviews with girls/boys. The questions were open-ended, to allow them to 'structure the nature and extent of their responses';[7] I aimed only to prompt if they did not understand the question, but quickly discovered the need to differentiate between my role as researcher and my 'day job' as teacher which I had to set aside along with any comment and information I was tempted to input. Nesbitt advises that 'teachers have to learn to speak less than they would as teachers' and notes Piaget's recognition of this tension in his instruction 'to let the child talk freely, without ever checking or side tracking his [*sic*] utterance'.[8] Heller believes his data on girls'/boys' views of God were enriched by following tangents in the conversation,[9] although with a two-hour time slot for each, he had more flexibility than I had. In group work, I found some of these tangents were attempts by one or more girls to dominate, so on occasion I did direct a return to the original, or a move to the next, subject. This is not to deny the importance of 'chatter' for building a fuller picture of the girls, as Rebecca Nye observed.

I allowed the girls time to think around the questions, often needed in the one-to-one conversations, and exerted judgement over a girl's silence or hesitation as to whether it indicated serious reflection or lack of anything to say; the latter was rare. Although I aimed for parity between each conversation to enhance validity of analysis, there were minor variations between each setting as each developed its own character according to the girls and the context, particularly as they taught me the depth with which they were able to handle complex theological issues.

The starting point to each conversation was crucial, as I was deliberately seeking their perspectives on faith as *girls*. The objective of my first question was

---

[6]   A statutory requirement in the UK for anyone working with children or vulnerable adults.

[7]   Julie Dockrell, Ann Lewis and Geoff Lindsay, 'Researching Children's Perspectives: A Psychological Dimension', in Lewis and Lindsay, *Researching Children's Perspectives*, p. 55.

[8]   Nesbitt, 'Researching', p. 141.

[9]   Heller, *The Children's God*, p. 17.

both to break the ice in a 'fun' way and more seriously to encourage awareness of themselves as gendered, and to think 'girl'. I had a hunch, correctly as I later learnt, that discussion of their own gendered identity, of God's view of them as girls, and of women and girls in the bible, opened up new perspectives for self-discovery. Although subsequent questions were 'gender neutral', the girls knew the purpose of the interview, and I hoped that this introduction would keep gender awareness in their minds and give them a different frame of reference in which to construct their thoughts.

The extent to which the views they expressed were their own or derived from adults or the church environment is difficult to assess. Nesbitt questions 'the extent to which and the age at which children can articulate a perspective on religion, and to what degree they are able to articulate a perspective other than that learned from parents and influential elders'.[10] In Scott's experience, 'most children of 11 and older are fully able to articulate their perceptions, opinions, and beliefs'.[11] Kegan's theory and Gilligan's research illustrate the tendency of girls at this 'stage' to over-dependency on significant others, but to seek for totally independent thinking is to adopt a traditional 'malestream' agenda, emphasising the autonomous individual at the expense of connection which feminism espouses. So I would expect to find reiteration in traditional language of faith and doctrine by which the girls can identify with and be attached to their environment, whether they understand the full meaning of words and concepts or not. Tamminen comments that understanding religious language is not a problem only for children.[12] What I looked for was the ability to 'say what I think rather than what I ought to think'.[13] Through comparison of vocabulary used in interviews with ministers and youth leaders and from observation of teaching methods, I was able to determine instances of dependence and derivation, and by the same criterion to uncover questions, concerns or beliefs which reflected attempts to critique the biblical interpretation and theology passed on to them. In my analysis it was this skill I was trying to discern, regardless of my own view of the theological perspective being presented. Although this learned language, and the theology and power structures which shape it, may in Marge Piercy's poetic rendering 'bind you like a halter/you have learned to pull inside',[14] it is not the task of the researcher to raise questions which might lead to the 'unbinding' of the girls, but where appropriate to suggest critical resources which leaders might use within the holding environment to 'let go'. The researcher, given permission

---

[10]   Nesbitt, 'Researching', pp. 141–2.

[11]   Jacqueline Scott, 'Children as Respondents', in Pia Christensen and Allison James (eds), *Research with Children* (London and New York, 2000), p. 102.

[12]   Tamminen, *Religious Development*, p. 23.

[13]   The words of Karen, one of my interviewees.

[14]   From Marge Piercy, 'Maggid', quoted by Hess, *Caretakers of our Common House*, p. 55.

to work with young people, must be conscious of ethical consequences of their position of trust by not destabilising the girls' faith.

I did not rely solely on a question and answer format, but employed other activities to add variety, and to test for myself methods other researchers into girls'/ boys' faith have found to be effective in creating data. Firstly, in his investigation into girls'/boys' views of God, David Heller used drawing, story-telling, play and writing in addition to direct questioning, to guard against loss of attention or interest, allow for different age-related skills and abilities and to draw out different perspectives of the girl's/boy's inner life. Secondly, an element of writing featured among Tamminen's methods, as well as response to photographs, his projective-photograph instrument used with girls/boys aged between nine and 16. Here participants were given pictures of individual children, matched according to gender, in poses showing a range of emotions (smiling, fearful, contemplative) and states both neutral and overtly religious (gazing out of a window, reading the bible, chatting with a parent). Beneath a description of the situation, sentence openings were printed inviting completion. In their research with primary school girls/boys, Hay and Nye adapted Tamminen's method using, to stimulate conversation, pictures with no explicit religious connotation, but which suggested the themes of awareness-, mystery- and value-sensing.[15] Pearmain developed Hay and Nye's method with older girls/boys because by the very nature of spirituality, 'the researcher needs to find the means to open deeper levels of communication', and she considered images an appropriate medium. She reflects on the exercise as creating something 'shared between researcher and participant as a relational and embodied experience, as something known because it is felt'.[16] With a younger age group Scott, too, advocates visual stimulus as being a more inclusive method.[17]

Building on these models, I gave the girls the opportunity to respond in whatever way they chose to pictorial images and I experimented with both written (simple sentence completion) and oral formats. My resources were predominantly photographic, some deliberately chosen for their artistic merit to encourage the girls, as Pearmain suggests, to 'feel' a response and by that means to 'tell it slant', a phrase originating with the poet Emily Dickinson, drawing out connections not dependent on cognition alone. Where possible, this was to be an individual exercise, hence the attraction of writing, so that the quieter girls could 'speak' unhindered and uninfluenced by their peers. In the end, context dictated format: where we were meeting in homes, neither the atmosphere nor the furniture facilitated writing. An oral format enabled some discussion where girls' interpretations differed and I found little evidence of dependence. The resources I selected were all commercially available in stores and in teenage girls' magazines, therefore intentionally consonant with the girls' surrounding culture.

---

[15]   Hay with Nye, *The Spirit of the Child*, p. 89

[16]   Rosalind Pearmain, 'Evocative Cues and Presence: Relational Consciousness within Qualitative Research', *International Journal of Children's Spirituality*, 12.1 (2007): 80.

[17]   Scott, 'Children as Respondents', pp. 101–6.

My research was conducted on the basis of seeing the girls primarily as subjects, setting aside judgements based on social maturity and cognitive ability, so giving full value and respect to their experience. They are of equal value to adults in the present time, persons in their own right, 'beings' *and* 'becomings', a position argued strongly by contemporary sociologists engaged in 'reconstructing childhood'.[18] They are 'social actors whose actions can both shape and change social life'.[19] The 'actor' image implies that the interaction is not individual but in relation to others within the environments in which they participate. It is this communal context which, according to the theory of socialisation, shapes growth: 'individual development ... becomes embedded in children's collective weaving of their places in the webs of significance that constitute their culture'.[20] Translating the social actor concept into theological terms, Miller-McLemore prefers to regard them as human actors, agents in a developing personal relationship with God. Although she writes from the perspective of Christian parenthood, her argument is a helpful corrective to the institutional focus of sociology.[21]

Ethnography

As I prepared for the interviews, I was modelling my approach on particular ethnographic strategies. In their study of 'other' cultures, ethnographers involve themselves in the field, observing, interviewing and participating where appropriate. It is a method particularly suitable for use with marginalised groups and therefore with girls/boys. Ethnography is a broad field: levels of participation vary greatly, from the anthropologist living with a community for an extended period of time, to more limited observation coupled with subject interviews, through all of which the researchers 'set out to be "taught" the ways, language and expectations of the social group they seek to study'.[22] It recognises the role of the researcher as a player in the process. That it has become widely used with girls/boys in sociological research is indicative of two key changes in attitude to them. Firstly, 'childhood is socially, culturally and temporally specific'[23] and therefore commands respect as a distinct social world. Secondly, adults must first set aside

---

[18]   Allison James, Chris Jenks and Alan Prout, *Theorizing Childhood* (Cambridge, 1998), pp. 206–7.

[19]   Pia Christensen and Alan Prout, 'Anthropological and Sociological Perspectives on the Study of Children', in Sheila Greene and Diane Hogan (eds), *Researching Children's Experience: Approaches and Methods* (London, 2005), p. 50.

[20]   Ibid., p. 50.

[21]   Bonnie J. Miller-McLemore, *Let the Children Come: Reimagining Childhood from a Christian Perspective* (San Francisco, 2003), pp. 158–9.

[22]   Ruth Emond, 'Ethnographic Research Methods with Children and Young People', in Greene and Hogan, *Researching Children's Experience*, p. 124.

[23]   Ibid., p. 124.

what they think they know from their own memories: 'the filtering of information through our own experience of childhood and its associated meanings can distort what children are telling us', being careful not to 'dislocate children from all other aspects of social life' but to find similarities.[24] Baker treads a different path. Her own story openly influences her conduct and interpretation of conversations with girls; she names her method 'autoethnography', arguing that to weave 'autobiographical fragments from my own adolescence into my discussion of the theory and practice of girlfriend theology' is 'in keeping with feminist objectivity' understood as acknowledging the researcher's partial perspective as an imperative precursor to interpreting another.[25] The danger of her method is the presumption already identified, that one context and generation can interpret that of another through her own story. I may share gender and faith with the girls, but I needed to retain awareness that there was gulf of experience and context lying between us.

Ethnographic methods are also consistent with feminist research in setting aside traditional views that the researcher retains a critical distance to maximise objectivity, which Warren argues embraces 'an objective/subjective dualism that gives much research a masculinist imperative'.[26] It recognises that the quality of data is strengthened if relationships are developed with subjects, consistent with the desire for connection. My position varied with each encounter, from substitute 'leader' to guest in a home. The girls' responses, at least at first, mirrored those expected in their 'normal' group activity: in some, the discussion-starter triggered free and lively debate, in another where the girls were more accustomed to a prescribed format, I quickly realised my discussion starter was being taken as a question demanding a 'right' or 'wrong' answer, and there was a protocol of putting up their hands to be given permission to speak, which I quickly stopped although remained alert to the fact that quieter girls might need to be invited to speak. In homes, the dynamic was different again. I experienced the ease of relationship between interviewer and interviewee resulting from meeting girls on their home ground, which Nesbitt recommends particularly for research into religion. In my case, this applied to both home and church but particularly the former where I was a guest and the power dynamics were more equal. This echoes Corsaro's experience with pre-school girls/boys in Italy where he developed 'a participant status as an atypical less powerful adult' by not speaking the language fluently nor knowing the school's routines.[27] Corsaro's method of role-reversal

---

[24]   Ibid., p. 136.

[25]   Dori Grinenko Baker, 'Future Homemakers and Feminist Awakenings: Autoethnography as a Method in Theological Reflection and Research', *Religious Education*, 96.3 (2001): 400.

[26]   Simon Warren, 'Let's do it Properly: Inviting Children to be Researchers', in Lewis and Lindsay, *Researching Children's Perspectives*, p. 130.

[27]   William A. Corsaro and Luisa Molinari, 'Entering and Observing in Children's Worlds: A Reflection on Longitudinal Ethnography of Early Education in Italy', in Christensen and James, *Research with Children*, p. 180.

is attested in ethnographic research, enabling the girls/boys to be valued as the experts they are, and becoming the teachers without the researcher patronising them, presuming or pretending to be like them. Emond adapted the method for an older age group when she went to live with them in a 'children's home'. Although the teenagers saw her adult status as representing authority, she adopted the principle of being 'taught the ways, language and expectation of the social group', recognising there could never be full acceptance because she was never one of them: 'participant observation by its very nature allows children to control the level of acceptance and involvement. The role of the researcher is therefore negotiated rather than imposed'.[28]

In summary, then, as a feminist researcher, I wanted to build a relationship with each group which 'values openness to intimacy and striving for empathy (but) should not be confused with superficial friendliness'.[29]

Empathy

Empathy with the girls was another feature of the feminist model I was working with. Generically, empathy means 'the power of understanding things outside ourselves', but in relation to human interaction, 'the power of entering into another's personality and imaginatively experiencing his [*sic*] experiences'.[30] Although it presupposes identification with another's experience, it is an exercise in imagination which must remain rooted in awareness of one's own self. It retains a sense of distance and limitation. Miller-McLemore describes it as 'the capacity to think and feel oneself into the inner life of the child'.[31] The danger here is of over-identification, of losing sight of the subjectivity of the other, of failing to recognise the *imaginative* nature of the exercise, and the need constantly to be listening to the voice of the girl as other in order to keep a check on adult over-interpretation. Bryan balances closeness with an awareness of the bigger picture when she says of empathy that it 'serves to reduce the psychological distance between individuals and enlarges the context in which the relationship is present'.[32] Empathy is more than coming alongside and being at one with subjective feelings; in an enlarged relational context, it stands apart in its own wider experience and has a role in setting boundaries and identifying latent desires. Hess uses Noddings' term, 'engrossment', meaning to focus attention fully on the other. Slee records with honesty the time and effort needed

---

[28]   Emond, 'Ethnographic Research Methods', pp. 124, 136.

[29]   Shulamit Reinharz, *Feminist Methods in Social Research* (New York and Oxford, 1992), p. 68.

[30]   *Chambers English Dictionary* (Cambridge, 1988).

[31]   Miller-McLemore, *Let the Children Come*, p. 48.

[32]   Jocelyn Bryan, 'Being and Becoming: Adolescence', in Shier-Jones, *Children of God*, p. 153.

to understand another, especially when their position and context are so different from one's own. The greater the difference the harder the task, but hearing and honouring those differences and representing them with integrity where they conflict with one's own views is a tension with which one lives as researcher. Hess, possibly with intentional theological undertones, describes it thus:

> Empathy involves a degree of emptying oneself and opening oneself to vulnerability and change. Rather than telling another who they should be, the empathic person listens to who the other says she is; rather than judging another for not matching previously determined norms, the empathic person grants integrity to the differences of another; rather than seeking to convert another to one's viewpoint, the empathic person seeks to learn and is willing herself to be changed by the encounter.[33]

I have discussed empathy here in relation to the methodology of data collection and interpretation, but it enhanced the quality of the interview experience. As I listened to the girls, especially one-to-one, I was impressed by the level of trust placed in me; they were ready to share intimate details of their family lives, inner journeys and faith stories, confident that I would take them seriously and trusting my confidentiality. In most instances I wondered how often they had been given the opportunity to speak so freely about some of the deepest concerns of their lives. Westcott and Littleton point out 'it is easy to forget that children may rarely be spoken to, or seriously listened to, unless they have done something "wrong"'.[34] The researchers responsible for the NSYR study also had the sense that 'for many of the teens we interviewed, *our interview was the first time that any adult had ever asked them what they believed and how it mattered in their life*'.[35] It was clear that, for many teens contacted for their research, very little in their lives had prepared them to be able to explain, even in basic terms, what they believed and how that fitted into their lives. This was in contrast to the level of discussion about other areas of life. In the interviews, I was asking questions which encouraged new areas of self-awareness, and the girls were processing fresh ideas and integrating different parts of their experience, which I received through empathic listening.

Feminist Perspectives

Feminist research has influenced the gathering of empirical data from girls'/boys' lives, and its interpretation. Robinson and Kellett name the centrality of gender in 'the construction and framing of knowledge' as a key theme among variants

---

[33]   Hess, *Caretakers of our Common House*, p. 97.

[34]   Helen L. Westcott and Karen S. Littleton, 'Exploring Meaning in Interviews with Children', in Green and Hogan, *Researching Children's Experience*, p. 141.

[35]   Smith with Denton, *Soul Searching*, p. 133. Authors' italics.

of feminism; aware that women and children often inhabit private space and their lives and concerns are deemed invalid for research in the public forum, they note the role played by feminists in bringing into view these so-called private worlds in order that they take their place in knowledge construction. By these means, they say, discrimination and abuse have been brought into the open.[36] Feminist research has highlighted the importance of the standpoint of the researcher, that there is no neutrality or 'pure' objectivity in design or in analysis; therefore the person of the researcher and her influence on the gathering of data must be foregrounded.[37] Slee narrates the development of feminist research methodology, and identifies five epistemological principles informing the research design and which she employed in researching women's faith:[38] these also connect closely with the advocacy of a feminist methodology as an appropriate tool for working with children. These are: the grounding in the subject's experience, listening and looking for difference, advocacy, a non-oppressive methodology, and reflexivity in analysis. These and other characteristics regarded as distinctive of feminist research, such as participation, interaction and relationality, are all incorporated in my research design and criteria for analysis.

The Difference Age Makes

In developing a research methodology with young girls, the question of difference in chronological age needs to be addressed. Research directly involving girls/boys, rather than with adults observing them or recalling their own childhood, is now more widely practised and has given rise to the literature in the fields of sociology and psychology already drawn upon in this chapter, where their epistemologies and methodologies are relevant to my task. Researchers with girls/boys must decide how far to adapt methods devised for adults or create child-led methodologies. This involves making a decision on girls'/boys' competence as research subjects and whether what developmentalists such as Fowler might demean as immaturity is in fact inexperience. So to what level can girls/boys be active participants in the research process?

Although dependent and under the control and care of adults in all societal structures, they also have an increasingly independent sense of self, and the right according to age and maturity to have their views respected. In the contemporary context of the UK, girls'/boys' right to be heard, in accordance with the UNCRC, is incorporated into law and social work practice.[39] In popular perception, however, the

---

[36]   Chris Robinson and Mary Kellett, 'Power', in Fraser et al., *Doing Research with Children*, pp. 82–3.

[37]   Emond, 'Ethnographic Research Methods', p. 126.

[38]   Slee, *Women's Faith Development*, pp. 46–52.

[39]   The UN Convention on the Rights of the Child (1989), Article 12, states: 'States Parties shall assure to the child who is capable of forming his or her own views the right

value attached to girls'/boys' voices is determined by the dominant developmental paradigms, which, based on structuralist understandings of the life course, claim they are not yet fully formed; their thoughts and opinions are 'lacking' in a variety of ways. The temptation to view children in this way is stronger in churches than in wider society where children are more readily accepted as in some sense social actors and agents. Within Protestantism, faith often has a significant cognitive and therefore age-related dimension, and 'following Christ' is often more about correct articulation of doctrine than relationship with a person, so there is

> a widespread assumption that children are largely unaware of, or at least incapable of, articulating their own spiritual and religious longings. Indeed, many would question whether children have the requisite cognitive capacity to formulate conceptual understandings of existential realities, their own or those of others.[40]

The expectation in churches is that in teen years, girls/boys will undergo a rite of passage signifying personal ownership of faith, through confirmation or believer's baptism; how far 'readiness' for this is based on repetition of credal formulae, conformity to normative ecclesial language or genuine spiritual experience will vary. There exists a temptation in many Protestant churches to diminish the credibility of girls'/boys' voices in matters of faith prior to that 'stage' being reached.

Nelle Morton's famous words, 'you heard me to my own speech',[41] expressed one purpose of my interviews. The needs of girls between the ages of 11 and 13 do not generally feature in textbooks or age-related church programmes. By 13, not only are many fully mature physically, but according to some of the structural developmental schemes already discussed, have also reached a 'level' beyond which many adults do not 'progress'. Although I have called developmental schemata into question, they do serve here to illustrate the point that girls can function in much the same way as adults but are not credited with the value and respect they deserve. So hearing them into speech is not just about bringing their thinking to a hearing public, but advocacy[42] (with its deliberate philological connection) to promote serious attention being paid to them. Where girls are concerned, it has more to do with redressing girls' silence and invisibility in ecclesial settings, as argued by Jensen, than its more common usage in feminist theology to oppose oppression.

---

to express those views freely in all matters affecting the child, the views of the child being given due weight in accordance with the age and maturity of the child'. www2.ohchr.org/english/law/crc.htm. Incorporated in The Children Act 1989, and Children Act 2004. www.opsi.gov.uk/acts/acts1989/Ukpga_19890041_en_1.htm.

[40]   Lindner, 'Children as Theologians', p. 60.
[41]   Nelle Morton, *The Journey is Home* (Boston, 1985).
[42]   Jensen, *Graced Vulnerability*, p. xiii.

If I then ask, as above, what 'allowances' I need to make in my method for girls' age and 'immaturity', I am already situating myself in a particular structural paradigm which I want to challenge. Even though I approach my research from a theological and epistemological standpoint which respects the faith of girls who have a meaningful relationship with the living God, I still have to allow for the fact that the 'level' at which they engage with the issues in the interviews will depend on their range of experience, acquired vocabulary, and practice at dialogical self-expression, on which they are context- and time-dependent, that is, on the opportunities offered during their shorter lifetime in school, home and church to construct and reflect on narrative, their own and others', to sort and critique arguments, to learn and employ a wide range of vocabulary, and so on.

Regarding language, Scott in a review of both quantitative and qualitative research with girls/boys, concludes that, although 'questions have to be pertinent and relevant to the children's own experience or knowledge', little adaptation is needed of questions designed for adults;[43] this supports my critique of Fowler's methodology. Fraser agrees that questions must make sense for each age group: lack of vocabulary does not imply a lack of reasoning powers. Any adaptation in method must therefore take account of the world of the subject. Westcott and Littleton argue that 'we need to guard against theorizing children's immaturity, when their responses in interview contexts reflect inexperience rather than immaturity'.[44]

My aim, then, was to use research instruments similar to those which I would use with adult women, but make a deliberate attempt at culturally appropriate rather than age-related language and format, and be constantly attentive to learn of the culture the girls were revealing and sharing with me, making adjustments as I proceeded. There is a fine distinction here, for 'if children are competent social actors, why are special "child-friendly" methods needed to communicate with them?',[45] to which Fraser's response is that 'participant-friendly' is a more appropriate terminology than 'child-friendly' since methods will be culturally contextual, 'contingent on the frames of cultural reference of researcher and participants'.[46] In facing this issue, Miller-McLemore describes it as a 'temporary inequity between persons', which does not diminish recognition but requires the community (family or church) constantly to make adjustments – of care, language, level of participation and so on – in accordance with the girl's needs, one of which is to *be* a girl and depend on the adult's greater '(hopefully) life-earned wisdom and maturity'.[47] The temporal nature of dependence is a helpful way of looking at this. The result will be negotiated compromises.

---

[43]   Scott, 'Children as Respondents', pp. 99–101.

[44]   Westcott and Littleton, 'Exploring Meaning in Interviews with Children', p. 146.

[45]   S. Punch, 'Research with Children: The Same or Different from Research with Adults?', *Childhood*, 9.3 (2002): 321–41.

[46]   Fraser, 'Situating Empirical Research', pp. 24–5.

[47]   Miller-McLemore, *Let the Children Come*, pp. 130–31.

Woodhead and Faulkner, reflecting on this newer methodological approach
with girls/boys, share the view expressed by Miller-McLemore that cautions
against overlooking the differences between younger and older human beings;
rather than 'throw out the baby with the developmental bathwater', they name the
new responsibility of the adult community to structure girls'/boys' environments
appropriately to facilitate their communication over issues that affect them 'in
ways consistent with their understanding'.[48]

Generation and Power

Attention to the inequities above requires constant vigilance for power imbalances,
identified by many researchers as one of the greatest challenges in working with
girls/boys. Although there was commonality between us, I represented the power
of adulthood. However, as a stranger in the girls' world, in each session I was
learner as well as researcher, modelling the mutuality of feminist methodology
and Freirean pedagogy. Although conducting an interview and not a lesson, I
was using a methodology informed by Freire's conviction that participants are
'active, creative subjects with the capacity to examine critically, interact with and
transform their world ... which encourages freedom for students in cooperative
dialogue'.[49] Thus I employed tasks consistent with a problem-posing methodology.
Such a choice is a necessarily conscious one caused by the generational difference
between subjects and interviewer, in order to guard against the interview process,
especially where biblical texts and Christian tradition are being discussed, slipping
into a banking model whereby knowledge is being transferred.

However, the question remains: was I hearing authentic voices or were they
distorted by power differentials? Some researchers in schools note how girls/
boys subvert or mock adult enquiry into their lives, dissemble or offer bland or
expurgated versions of events as a strategy of resistance to adult intrusion into
their private lives and thoughts.[50] While I found no evidence of similar responses,
some answers to questions may have been 'scripted' to seek approval, but as the
interviews proceeded, most girls gained more confidence in my separation from
church 'authority', and the respect with which I treated them and their views.
Nevertheless, Westcott and Littleton's warning is relevant, that 'the fact that
all situations are constructed – no matter how naturalistic they are', as is their

---

[48]   Martin Woodhead and Dorothy Faulkner, 'Subjects, Objects or Participants?
Dilemmas of Psychological Research with Children', in Christensen and James, *Research
with Children*, p. 31.

[49]   R.W. Pazmiño, *Foundational Issues in Christian Education: An Introduction
in Evangelical Perspective*, 2nd edn (Grand Rapids, 1997), p. 76, summarising Freire,
Pedagogy of the Oppressed.

[50]   Sheila Greene and Malcolm Hill, 'Researching Children's Experience', in Greene
and Hogan, *Researching Children's Experience*, pp. 10f.

exposure of the hidden agendas of interviews, that they are designed to reveal rather than to create understanding because 'the experimental paradigm ignores gaps between reality, experience and expression'. The 'life as told' can never, they suggest, reveal life as lived by the girl/boy as it fails to take account of the motivational and contextual factors with which they co-construct the process.[51]

Active participation in the research process is one means by which power imbalance can be countered. It has a dual meaning in qualitative research. The minimalist definition applies where the interviewee, who is the subject of a predetermined process, participates by responding to the interview questions. A variety of levels operate from here to a maximum possible level of participation when subjects contribute to the research aims, design, fieldwork, analysis and dissemination. Examples of higher levels of involvement are rare, but such participation has been undertaken in the fields of health, social science and education. Although time did not allow me actively to engage my subjects in the design of the research process, their participation enabled me to adjust it in order to redress any avoidable power imbalances. Some girls to whom I was a stranger were shy when being interviewed alone: I therefore introduced the small group interview which gave them more confidence to give voice.

Generation, Power and Discourse

This introduces a further dimension of the issues connected with generation and power, the way in which experience is articulated through the language and meaning situated in and structured by the culture of the groups to which we relate, that is, their discourse. Adults in leadership positions in a church have an authority theologically and institutionally sanctioned, for example by the ordination of a minister, which gives them the power and control to create and perpetuate the discourse by which faith and Christian discipleship are constructed. They bring to that discourse knowledge constructed in other areas of their lives, which will rarely be explicit. Feminist theory, in the view of Alldred, exposes 'how knowledge claims entail plays of power',[52] and in the work she has done with Burman, she asserts the validity of analysis which highlights the cultural specificity of data. 'Children's voices', they say, 'cannot be heard outside of, or free from, cultural understandings of childhood and the cultural meanings assigned to their communication', or following Foucault, 'what it was possible for them to say'. Data collected and analysed on this understanding is not seeking to establish paradigms or universal truths but recognises the local construction of knowledge, and without diminishing their credibility allows girls to express views which may

---

[51]   Westcott and Littleton, 'Exploring Meaning in Interviews with Children', p. 143.

[52]   Pam Alldred, 'Ethnography and Discourse Analysis: Dilemmas in Representing the Voices of Children', in Jane Ribbens and Rosalind Edwards (eds), *Feminist Dilemmas in Qualitative Research, Public Knowledge and Private Lives* (London, 1998), p. 156.

appear contradictory: 'at another time and in a different context, we may occupy quite different subject positions', a factor not indicative of limited cognitive ability but of 'the multiplicity of discourse in circulation'.[53]

Greene and Hill challenge the monopolistic stance of discourse theorists in that, while acknowledging its importance, 'to conclude that experience is entirely constituted by discourse is going a step too far since it negates the material and sensational foundation of some forms of experience',[54] a qualification which opens the way for some originality in creating meaning out of spiritual experience. This conflicts with the position of Alldred and Burman who situate both data collection and analysis within a discursive framework, denying there can be any neutral process of data collection or any interpretation 'unmediated by our perceptions and unchanged by our practices of description and representation'.[55] Hendrik is an ally here, arguing strongly against the view that girls/boys have no alternative but to speak with the voice of the dominant discourse; he regards such a view as 'locking children into *our* experience'; accepting that girls/boys are intimidated by a 'dominant discourse', he claims that though 'they may speak through the discourse, thereby altering it in subtle ways, all dominant discourses contain within them resistant themes. To suggest otherwise is to deny children any potential for their own voices. It refuses the oppressed the agency to impact upon "power" and, consequently, to make a difference'.[56] The task of the researcher, to Jackson, is to grasp 'the grammar of someone else's discourse' to guard against the projection of one's own feelings or attitudes into the situation.[57]

Although not denying the influence of my own perspective, the advocacy dimension of my analysis will attempt to identify and represent both their inherited and their alternative discourse. By 'giving voice' to girls, I am situating myself within a epistemological and methodological framework which offers 'a way of constructing (them) as active subjects not objects and of recognizing that they may have distinct perspectives on the world', by implication questioning/undermining the wide acceptance within churches of the developmental paradigm by which 'they are more easily disqualified as participants of research'.[58] In my biblical reflections, I give examples of how such resistance can be found in scripture as a resource for the empowerment of girls in the church context. Amongst the girls interviewed, Karen stressed her desire to think for herself, and with others in her group wanted to speak to 'power' in her church about community living and about mission. Yet respect for authority was also strong: Amber spoke of the influence

---

[53]   Pam Alldred and Erica Burman, 'Analysing Children's Accounts', in Greene and Hogan, *Researching Children's Experience*, pp. 179–80.

[54]   Greene and Hill, 'Researching Children's Experience', p. 5.

[55]   Alldred and Burman, 'Analysing Children's Accounts', p. 175.

[56]   Harry Hendrik, 'The Child as Social Actor in Historical Sources', in Christensen and James, *Research with Children*, p. 52. Author's italics.

[57]   Quoted by Nesbitt, 'Researching', p. 138.

[58]   Alldred, 'Ethnography and Discourse Analysis', pp. 148–50.

on her spiritual understanding of 'one of the more senior members of the church', Rosie of the informal structure of a church service where the minister's guiding hand is still valued.

Data Analysis

The above discussion reveals that generational difference and imbalance of power relates not only to the interview design but also to the interpretation of data. The challenge in any ethnographic research is to interpret a world to which neither readers nor hearers belong, so while on the one hand I am developing empathy with my research subjects, I am also translating their thoughts and feelings into a language which will have meaning for and build respect in an adult audience. For Alldred, the role of the researcher is of re/presentation, suggesting an inherent ambivalence between re-presenting the original data and an account which 'is actively produced by me and embodies my perspective'.[59] I am aware of the danger of imposing personal agendas on the girls' responses, but also fearful that faithful representation of the girls' meaning may inhibit creative interpretation of underlying nuances and connections. Situated as I am within a discourse conditioned by the paradigmatic developmental understanding of children which minimises girls' capability of 'mature' conceptual thought, I may unwittingly allow myself to be conditioned by it. For example, when Lucy, one of my interviewees, designates God as 'shapeshifter', I have to judge whether she was beginning to stretch beyond a hitherto anthropomorphic view of God, transferring a fictional image[60] onto a deity who is equally a figment of human imagination, or demonstrating a skill at theological reflection by which she found and transformed a resource in contemporary culture to express a spiritual truth that YHWH transcends human imagining and meets us in different ways at different times. In its context I deduce she intended the latter, choosing a metaphor from within her recent experience to explain what she could express in no other way, and as such I represent the words of this 11-year-old.

So what of reflexivity? It signifies the researcher's self-awareness at every stage of the process, awareness of her standpoint and particularly the way in which it affects the construction of new knowledge from the data. Originating in ethnography and taken up substantially by feminist writers, it acknowledges research to be subjective, that the person of the researcher is permitted to 'intrude' into the analysis, and that 'the lens of the observer or researcher inevitably distorts'.[61] This leads to what Slee describes as 'transparency', an honest first person narrative of the research trail, the pursuit of hunches, the changes to or

---

[59] Ibid., p. 149.

[60] The image may be derived from the *Harry Potter* books by J.K. Rowling and the films they inspired.

[61] Greene and Hill, 'Researching Children's Experience', p. 8.

confirmations of her own assumptions, all to promote a method of knowledge construction which seeks 'integrity within the research enterprise and work(s) to establish a new set of conventions in the world of scholarship which will demand, and not merely allow, the statement of the conditions of production under which knowledge is pursued'.[62] It bares all, therefore exposes itself to a more detailed critique, but its conclusions convey the integrity of the researcher. It alerts to instances where predetermined agendas affect outcomes. Yet the adult analyst must exercise critical skills based on a broader understanding of the way girls are viewed and treated in the culture being studied or the result will be no more than a collection of girls' voices. Driscoll speaks instead of 'min(ing) for a revelation they cannot themselves make and may be utilized in prescriptive analysis of their situation from positions that are not theirs'.[63] To draw themes out of the texts which are faithful to the meaning of these often naïve thoughts and experiences of girls is part of the researcher's task of advocacy.

Handling the Data

My data consisted of 14 sets of interviews with girls, group and individual, and six with adults. I also compiled research logs, narrating and reflecting on the experience after each event, and my feelings about each interview, noting my impression of each girl as an individual, features of their interaction with one another and with me. Strauss and Corbin validate such subjective reflection, not as data but as material to 'be drawn on for the purposes of sensitizing the researcher to the properties and dimensions in data, always with considerable self awareness of what the researcher is doing'.[64]

I transcribed each interview, keeping as close as possible to the words spoken, noting pauses, changes in tone or emotional intensity of speech, group reaction and interaction, and interruptions. Para-linguistic features or contemporary idiom were included in the transcription (for example, 'really really' for 'very', and 'like' when not signalling use of metaphor, although occasionally I had to make a judgement on this). Where girls had soft voices or a strong local accent, it was not always possible to reproduce every word exactly, so I summarised the sense of her speech unit; aware of this danger during the interview, I reflected back to the girl what she had said, and by so mirroring encouraged her to confirm her meaning, or to amend or amplify her statement. Thus I believe my record of words and meanings is as accurate as it can be. I was aware that the power differential might be operative here, as she might agree with my interpretation even if it did not reproduce what she meant. Sharp listening, for inflection and nuance, were

---

[62]   Slee, *Women's Faith Development*, p. 52.

[63]   Driscoll, *Girls*, p. 169.

[64]   Anselm Strauss and Juliet Corbin, *Basics of Qualitative Research: Techniques and Procedures for Developing Grounded Theory*, 2nd edn (Thousand Oaks, 1998), p. 58.

important skills to employ, and constant reflexivity. Each interview was physically and emotionally draining.

After my initial transcription, I adopted Slee's method whereby 'each line of text represented one unit of speech',[65] each line marking progression in the girl's argument or narrative. Then I divided each according to the subject areas to view contributions horizontally and analyse data initially across each location to draw out similarities and differences. I read and re-read transcripts to immerse myself in the data, followed textbook protocols for analysis to develop grounded theory which emerges out of the data instead of being imposed upon it, seeking categories through sequential coding.[66] I used both inductive and deductive strategies, and engaged in something akin to the 'free-flowing dialogue' Slee describes to draw out themes and categories against the background of my reading of social and psychological theory of girls, of physical change, and growth of faith. I also followed hunches, to wander in fields of 'interpretative creativity'[67] about what was going on for the girls at this time of transition, both from informal interaction and from other texts, both adult reminiscence and fiction, and why it remains in memory to be reproduced in autobiography and literature.[68] My analysis was not a neat process.

Reliability of the results of qualitative research can be enhanced by the use of triangulation 'which increases scope, depth and consistency in methodological proceedings'.[69] The triangulation I employ is internal and methodological, achieved by constructing different exercises for the girls, such as using pictorial media to draw often indirect or latent connections between visual stimuli, prior experience and thought, and emotion. The results added new dimensions to the interview data, often drawing out underlying feelings which shed fresh light on responses to questions. When my results are set alongside existing theories within the study of girls, of gender, of faith growth and of theology, a degree of consistency serves as another form of validation while not stifling originality.

My research goal was to create situated knowledge. Early feminist research struggled to free itself from notions of 'scientific objectivity', exposing the fact that all research is conditioned by the partiality and bias of the researcher, and is never value-neutral.[70] But if its opposite is subjectivity, it can tend towards relativism,

---

[65]   I found this helped me follow and appreciate the construction of sometimes convoluted argument. Slee, *Women's Faith Development*, p. 57.

[66]   Strauss and Corbin, *Basics of Qualitative Research*, p. 12.

[67]   Slee, *Women's Faith Development*, p. 57.

[68]   I note with interest the abundance of fictional writing in which girls around this age are the subjects, for example, George Eliot, *Mill on the Floss* (Harmondsworth, 1979); Sue Monk Kidd, *The Secret Life of Bees* (Harmondsworth, 2003); Margaret Atwood, *Cat's Eye* (London, 1990).

[69]   Uwe Flick, *An Introduction to Qualitative Research* (London, 2002), p. 227.

[70]   Ibid., p. 23.

by which feminism is 'politically dismembered'.[71] Feminism's emphasis on experience as the primary resource for the creation of knowledge does raise questions about the kind of truth claims that can be made. To be true to feminism's valuing of varieties of experiences dependent on person and context, the idea of unified or privileged knowledge is inconsistent. Smith holds that the 'authority of experience is foundational to the women's movement' while not foundational to knowledge. Haraway favours partial visions and socially-situated knowledge yet recognises that all are not equally valued, but in the judgement of Ramazanoglu and Holland she fails to establish criteria for 'what constitutes "truer" or "better", indicat(ing) a continuing tension over validity'.[72] As girls are speaking from a subjugated position, this could question the validity of their 'voice' as heard and represented in the research process. Although not claiming universality, I expect my findings to be regarded as having a measure of 'authority' by the integrity of its methodology and data gathering, and transparency of analysis; that these girls in these situations thought and felt in this way adds to the knowledge of what it is like to be girls of faith in these contexts.

Table 3.1　　　Churches and interviewees

Church context	Assumed name	Age
Urban, medium sized, theologically mainstream	Karen	13
	Sarah	13
	Lucy	11
	Hannah	11
	Georgia	13
Urban large, evangelical/charismatic	Amber	13
	Ruth	12
	Bethan	11/12*
	Bryony	12
Inner city, medium sized, theologically mainstream	Martha	13
	Julie	11
Inner city, small, liberal	Rosie	13
	Suzanne	13
Urban, medium sized broadly evangelical	Michelle	13/14*
	Mary	13/14*
	Holly	12
	Victoria	12

* These girls had birthdays around the time of the interviews.

---

[71]　Caroline Ramazanoglu with Janet Holland, *Feminist Methodology, Challenges and Choices* (London, 2002), p. 57.
[72]　Examples from Smith and Haraway in ibid., p. 76.

Chapter 4
Girls in Transitional Space

Introduction

This chapter marks the beginning of the analysis of the data generated in the interviews, and reflections on my findings. This is also the place where I return to biblical girls, to develop links between experiences recounted in scripture and the issues both practical and theological girls face today, to offer resources for women and girls to earth themselves more fully in their identity as daughters of God.

Girls of this age are in transition; on the cusp of adolescence they face two ways, back to childhood which they are ambivalent about leaving, and forward to womanhood which holds both fears and excitements. I begin with a biblical girl living through such a time, then hear from the girls I interviewed about their own experiences of being at this transitional stage. As I begin to draw on my empirical data, I will attempt, in presenting the results of my analysis, to honour what Burman reminds us are the personal costs in growing up; her warning applies to ecclesial as well as other communities that to turn 'the complex disorder of individual development into orderly steps to maturity reflects explicit social interests in maintaining social control with and between social groups'.[1] Driscoll also notes that the transitions of feminine adolescence are 'culturally specific, subject to interpretation and regimes of power'.[2] I turn, then, to interpretation of some of the girls' experiences, in the specific cultures they inhabit.

Jairus' Daughter[3]

At 12 years old, Jairus' nameless daughter was in transition, from girlhood to womanhood, from life to death – to life again. Her story, paired with that of the haemorrhaging woman, is habitually understood by commentators to have been included in the synoptic gospels to illustrate faith, Jesus' power of healing, and his transgression of Jewish purity laws to include marginalised people, here unclean through death and supposed uterine or vaginal bleeding. The intertwined stories form part of the corpus of material featuring women, which affirmed their central place in the new community as witnesses to Jesus' life, death and resurrection. Some contemporary exegesis has, however, reinterpreted the story on the basis

---

[1]   Burman, *Deconstructing Developmental Psychology*, p. 19.

[2]   Driscoll, *Girls*, p. 58.

[3]   Mark 5.21–43, Matthew 9.18–26, Luke 8.40–56.

that the impurity theme is not necessarily inferred. In Levine's understanding
of the Matthean version, for example, the point of the story is that Jesus returns
the sick and the dead to health, and that women's bodies, suffering and healing
are models for the body, suffering and resurrection of Christ.[4] Horsley takes this
further by detecting in Mark's gospel a women subplot: he traces through the
narrative how women represent those who faithfully follow and witness to Jesus,
paradigms of faith contrasted with 'the twelve' who are unable to understand the
nature of discipleship. The raising of Jairus' daughter, who in her passivity cannot
actively participate in the construction of this paradigm, evokes the parallel stories
of the restoration of boys by Elijah and Elisha, representing in Israel's narrative
history God's rescue of the people when in desperate straits.[5]

In spite of the radical reinterpretation suggested here, there is still no recognition
among scholars of the enormity of the recipient of the healing being a girl. If girl
children were of little value in Israelite society, then Jesus' recapitulation of the
Elijah/Elisha stories by raising a girl as a precursor to his own resurrection becomes
paradigmatic of the centrality of girl- as well as boy-children in the kingdom. The
enormity of Jesus' action is heightened when we consider that 'the halakhah places
women in the same legal category as children and Canaanite slaves ... (and) a
woman by virtue of her sex can never leave this category' whereas 'male children
and slaves are at least full Jews *in potentio*'.[6] Luke's addition of the detail that she
was Jairus' only child, and his paralleling of the story with that of the raising of
the widow's son at Nain, Luke 7.11–17, reinforces this interpretation. Moloney,
while accepting the im/purity interpretation, suggests another dimension to Jesus'
daring. The girl being of marriageable age, it would be taboo for a man outside the
immediate family who was not her future husband to touch her; in so doing, Jesus
raises her not just to life but to womanhood, facilitating her transition to a new
status in which she too can give life, the intertwining of the two stories making
manifest that the flow of blood marking the generativity of her womanhood is not
bad or impure but the way women are intended to 'live in the well-being of God's
reigning presence'.[7]

[4]   Amy-Jill Levine, 'Discharging Responsibility: Matthean Jesus, Biblical Law, and
Haemorrhaging Woman', in A.-J. Levine with M. Blickenstaff (eds), *A Feminist Companion
to Matthew* (Sheffield, 2001), pp. 77, 87. Levine's interpretation, although based on the
Matthean version, applies equally to Mark.
[5]   R.A. Horsley, *Hearing the Whole Story: The Politics of Plot in Mark's Gospel*
(Louisville, 2001), p. 212.
[6]   Melissa Raphael, *The Female Face of God in Auschwitz: A Jewish Feminist
Theology of the Holocaust* (London, 2003), p. 25. Author's italics.
[7]   F.J. Moloney, *The Gospel of Mark: A Commentary* (Peabody, 2002), p. 111. Similar
arguments are developed by Frances Taylor Gench, *Back to the Well: Women's Encounters
with Jesus in the Gospels* (Louisville, 2004), chapter 2.

Girls in Transition: In Their Own Words

When asked what they liked about being a girl, my interview subjects initially defined themselves in contrast and opposition to boys. They saw their own qualities (for Karen peace-loving, for Bethan emotional, for Martha relational, for Rosie obedient and attentive) and the wider range of choices (for Julie in sports, for Victoria and Michelle as consumers, for Martha in bodily self-expression) as marks of possessing a greater freedom than boys. Although there was some sense of superiority over boys on the grounds that their own behaviour was more mature (Rosie: 'girls have got their heads screwed on'), Karen and Holly showed concern at the pressure boys are under to behave in ways that conform to stereotypes, such as being competitive and fighting; this included not being 'girlie' by showing emotion or enjoying shopping. Limited male consumer choice was for Mary an injustice. 'Maturity' was defined both as behaviour which earned adult approval (Rosie), and having the inner confidence that didn't need to compete (Sarah). Some were aware of game playing with adults for their own ends, displaying the irony with which they deal with gender stereotyping. There was a strong sense of agency here, particularly among the older girls in my sample.

As the girls became more reflective of their experience, and I encouraged them to talk about the negative side of being female, they reported more examples of ways in which as they grow older their freedom is circumscribed. The restrictions outweighed the freedom they first expressed, so that ironic behaviour such as Rosie admitted to became a mechanism to exercise an inner freedom where they could express themselves fully. In the privacy of Mary's bedroom, she and Michelle could put aside the vulnerability they felt at school and 'feel quite peaceful'. They were clear that these restrictions were the result of newly evident gender construction in family, school and society, although Hannah and Lucy reported discrimination by teachers in primary school over who did the more physical jobs, boys being selected for these regardless of size and strength. With puberty, however, girls regretted the lost opportunity to participate in traditionally male sports: mixed teams are no longer permitted, and 'female' school sports like netball and hockey were not mentioned, so seemed to exert no draw. The message came not only from adults, but also from boys who expected them to conform to gendered norms: again, football was an example cited.

It was in self-care and personal relationships, however, that they recorded the greatest change. Most enjoyed paying more attention to looks:

> When I was younger
> I didn't really bother about what I looked like …
> but I'm like sort of bothered about it more
> since I've been a teenager. (Holly)

There was an underlying sense, however, that how a teenager should look was constructed to encourage conformity. They showed clear signs of resistance to such stereotypes, and a desire for freedom to be girls in the way that best suited them. This was consistent with the findings of Walkerdine that girls do not passively adopt a stereotypically feminine role but struggle through conflicts and contradictions 'to accept the position to which she is classically fitted'.[8] Lucy thought there was 'too much pressure about fashion', and Karen was incensed by a magazine illustration of a girl,

> drawn in a typical way of drawing teenagers;
> a teenage girl would be drawn
> with either a miniskirt or flared jeans
> and you will always find a teenager in a picture,
> she will always be wearing much the same things
> and always looking much the same
> and … everybody is different.

Resistance showed, too, in circumscription of friendships. Unlike at a younger age, homosocial friendships were expected to be the norm, heterosocial relationships becoming overlaid with sexuality. Lucy reflected:

> you think of boys differently;
> cos you don't think of it as friends any more
> and I think that's actually a shame
> because there's quite a few boys in my class
> who I get on really really well with,
> but if you're seen with boys
> it's considered straightaway that it's girlfriend/boyfriend
> and it's not!

Mary valued a gender balance:

> it's nice to have both aspects
> like if you're thinking about something
> and you've just got the girls' side of it,
> and to have the lads' view.

Telling it Slant: Awareness of Loss

These insights were offered in open conversation, but in other forms of interaction I heard a deeper response to the transition, which opens up a window onto their spirituality which I address more explicitly in the next chapter. The stimulus was

---

[8]   V. Walkerdine, *Schoolgirl Fictions* (London, 1990), p. 88.

the set of pictures I prepared for them.[9] These were of two kinds: the first showed people from baby to adult, mostly girls and women, in their own context, either alone or in relation to one another; the second was of aspects of the natural world but devoid of people.

By identifying the picture to which the greatest number of girls gave the highest priority, as well as their choices overall, and by analysing the comments and narrative they were engaging in when looking at the pictures, I detected a deep sadness and feeling of loss. This sense of loss, consistent with what they had already revealed, was for their childhood's carefree enjoyment of life and friendships. As they looked at particular images, some expressed nostalgia for the days when they could rock with uninhibited laughter, show their knickers, walk arm-in-arm with boys, without any other preoccupation, self-consciousness or sexual innuendo. True happiness was characterised by a freedom they found echoed in nature when, for example, animals behave entirely consistently with their environment; dolphins leap gladly from the water and even sharks, though predators and hostile to human kind, are following their own nature in their destructiveness. Some drew a comparison with humans and their capacity for oppression and destruction of their own kind causing division and disharmony, an unnatural way of living which, as girls move out of the protected state of childhood, will increasingly impinge on their lives. This is a spiritual condition. They have learnt about the equality of all people God has built into creation:

> everyone talks about God
> being like he created everything
> and he loves everyone
> and everyone's equal. (Rosie)

Yet they are already beginning to experience division and discrimination; as girls are increasingly stereotyped, the extent and quality of relationship with older generations will be more limited, sexuality informs people's judgements and expectations of them, and they expect to be misunderstood by adults who will not listen to them or take them seriously. Amber saw, in a picture of water drops descending into a pool, a sea of tears always being added to mostly through sadness, fear and loneliness, and only occasionally from happiness. I have already noted girls' awareness of marginalisation by adults, of gender not ability determining role (girls don't carry heavy boxes), of sexual innuendo about friendships with boys, of pressures on appearance. Some were beginning to play gender games in response to adult expectations, which may result in 'loss of voice', perceived or actual. They were also grieving for the way changes of school and in personality and interests altered friendships. Sarah said of a loss of a friendship at the move to secondary school:

---

[9] See p. 58.

we used to be really really good friends
and when we went into year 7
she started being horrible to me
saying I was bullying her and everything,
so we're not that good friends any more,
and I found that really hard.[10]

They were conscious of the effects of living in an imperfect world, showing their awareness of the dis-ease of the world which rendered them, and other small and weak people, vulnerable. They were able to interpret their sadness in spiritual and religious language. Several pictures evoked an unexpectedly sad response, such as one of an adult holding a baby's hand, which to Julie spoke of finitude because someone had died and was being 'replaced', a manifestation of the 'cycle of life'. The same picture made others reflect on their own vulnerability and the need for support in the face of the struggles, often unspecified, to come. Bryony wrote:

when I look at this,
I feel like it's me reaching out to God for help
+ even when I'm just so upset
im [*sic*] still holding on.

Responding to a picture of large and small feet, Bethan and Martha separately introduced sadness although it does not appear to be an obvious interpretation; it reminded Bethan of happy family times but 'it's not always like that and the children grow up', and for Martha it could be mother and son or daughter but she envisaged separation, for

if the mother is not there,
they'll still be with their child in their heart,
they can still carry on finding people to be with.

A picture of footprints in the sand triggered memories of the footprints 'poem' which for three girls spoke of being carried through difficult times; one who was not familiar with it, connected the picture with human despoliation of creation, reflecting again the sadness of fracture. Julie alone selected a picture of two girls on swings talking to one another, an image with no obvious hint of sadness; although seeing its representation of girls' friendship as positive and a gift from God, her thoughts immediately moved on to the function of friends to be there for one another in sad or lonely times.

---

[10]   With regard to friendships many of their experiences here and elsewhere corroborate the research of Valerie Besag, in *Understanding Girls' Friendships, Fights and Feuds: A Practical Approach to Girls' Bullying* (Maidenhead, 2006).

The interest in pictures with an intergenerational theme was consistent with their inclusion, in talk of their own families, of photos of grandparents, or in church of an older church member who had died: a recognition of mortality and its attendant sadness was now entering their experience, but treasured gifts or rituals still had the power to make the presence of the lost one tangible, as Hannah and Rosie both described, of a grandmother and an elderly church member respectively.

Empathy with those who suffer was freely offered. Karen spoke of her negative reaction to the trivialising of suffering on the part of some of her peers at school in response to photographic images of suffering, for example of children in extreme poverty, used in lessons. Relationships of all kinds were vital for surviving suffering: of a picture of grieving women in the aftermath of the 2004 massacre at Beslan, Russia, Martha said:

> it's good that they've got people to comfort
> because they'd be really sad if it was just them by themselves ...
> it's like people give,
> it's good to have friends to give you a cry.

The girls' own sense of loss felt in the transition from girlhood to womanhood gave them a new lens through which to view the world, recognising other losses, and feeling an existential sadness. They were passing through a grief process.

Gilligan and Rogers acknowledge that girls suffer this sadness at the onset of adolescence with its changing relationships with self, others and the world. Their research suggests to them that while the Oedipal relational crisis of Freudian psychoanalytic thought takes place for boys in early childhood, it is delayed for girls until early adolescence, but the time delay means girls are entering this transformational stage with a far wider experience of relationships and at a later stage in their development. Relationships have come to mean more to them. Most of the girls in my interviews talked in some detail about their friendships, what they valued about them, and with sorrow about how some have become changed or broken by internal (disparate development) or external (change of school, societal evaluation) factors. Gilligan argues that girls have a far greater awareness of the cost of becoming adult with its expected disconnection from things which build psychological health, 'from the body, from feelings, from relationships, from reality'; they resist such disconnection, although society presses them 'to take on images of perfection as the model of the pure or perfectly good woman: the woman whom everyone will promote and value and want to be with',[11] or as Hess describes it, to be 'sweet, well-mannered and compliant'.[12]

The struggle to negotiate the balance between self, others and society's models for womanhood can result in disturbance leading to psychological problems which

---

[11] Gilligan, 'Women's Psychological Development: Implications of Psychotherapy', in Gilligan et al., *Women, Girls and Psychotherapy*, p. 24.

[12] Hess, *Caretakers of Our Common House*, p. 126.

often manifest themselves in some form of self-harm. For Hess and others, this is linked with the overlay in Christian communities of niceness with a theology or spiritual virtue of 'self-sacrifice', which leads girls to give themselves away and not learn to say 'no'. Hess uses the tale of *The Giving Tree* by Shel Silverstein as 'an allegory of the beauty of (women's) self-sacrifice', to highlight the way in which such ideas feature in fiction girls are encouraged to read, especially in Christian contexts.[13] One consequence of this, she says, can be in eating disorders, and case numbers are rising among younger teenagers. Gilligan suggests that girls are being forced into disconnection from the 'rich relational tapestry of their childhood'.[14] Alone among my interviewees, Michelle admitted to having had an eating disorder. This seemed to be overcome with support from her church which helped her to increase her self-esteem: she attributed the anorexia partly to her parents' divorce and her mother's subsequent depression, causing her to feel deprived of love.

From a philosophical perspective, Irigaray puts forward a similar argument to Hess, that 'holiness is often presented to women as being a relation to the other gender through self-abnegation'. She agrees that girls are in danger of losing their identity at puberty, but for her it is from the male construction of the surrounding culture. Like Gilligan, she rejects Freud's Oedipal theory in relation to girls, but sees a girl as privileged by sharing gender with her mother, through and with whom 'from birth (she is) in a familiar *I-you* dialogue', being and forming herself in 'subjectivity and intersubjectivity', where nature and language are not in opposition as in masculine culture, but 'in harmony to communicate, to hold dialogues, to love'. In Irigaray's thinking this does not blur the boundaries between mother and daughter and therefore lead to identity confusion or failure to separate: she describes the role of the placenta as mediating the autonomy of the child, so that 'holding real dialogues with the child keep(s) the *I* and the *you* distinct'. Thus, she reconfigures the mother/daughter relationship as a process of separation by which the daughter does not 'have to unconsciously "reproduce" motherhood' and the mother has to cultivate 'a dialogical relationship with the daughter, preventing reducing her to the same as oneself, the one who will do later what I do now'.[15] Irigaray's view of transition to adolescence is closer to the experiences expressed by several of the girls, particularly in their relationships with their mothers.

Here I make a tentative exploration of the untranslatable term 'jouissance' of French philosophy, which may paradoxically connect with the sadness I was hearing from the girls and which the paradigm set up by Gilligan and adopted by Hess does not fully address. For girls it might indicate uninhibited pleasure or joy, although not yet fully in the orgasmic sense Irigaray's use signifies for adult

---

[13]   Hess, *Caretakers of Our Common House*, pp. 32–6.

[14]   Gilligan, 'Women's Psychological Development', p. 24.

[15]   Irigaray, *Luce Irigaray: Key Writings*, pp. 154–60. Author's italics

women;[16] being both corporeal and spiritual it carries with it a spectre of loss[17] or incompleteness, 'a dimension which is never complete and never reversible'; they may experience its 'perpetual deferment' or its production 'more in their interior, in their innermost heart'[18] when externally masculine culture dominates and silences women. For these girls, then, jouissance might connote the girlish bodily abandon whose loss they mourn, in which case the journey through puberty is into a refiguring of that delight in the sexuate body which in the context of Christian faith may find its fulfilment in communion with God, a journey the girls are only just beginning.

Menarche

Normally between 11 and 13, but nowadays often earlier, a girl's body changes, and she takes on her mature adult shape, features and capacities. The physical changes (breast and hip growth through increase in fatty tissue, maturing of ovaries and uterus leading to the menarche) are gender specific and add up to a dramatic change in bodily and therefore self-image: 'puberty represents a period of dramatic physiological change that is unparalleled in development. Not surprisingly, this maturational process has a profound impact on the psychological functioning of youth'.[19] Brown discusses these far-reaching changes which, in addition to the physical and cognitive, involve re-examination of beliefs now coming under new scrutiny, and clearer self-definition in terms of gender, bringing alteration to earlier mixed sex relationships.[20] As the girls have testified, it can appear as a narrowing of their world, which brings anger as well as sadness, and often a desire to resist even while they experiment with identities. Lucy faced the choice between resistance (heterosociality) and living with sexual innuendo, and compliance (homosociality) to be seen as 'nice'.

Developmental schemata largely ignore the effect of physical change, particularly the menarche, perhaps because many are constructed by men, but also,

---

[16] Tina Beattie, *God's Mother, Eve's Advocate: A Marian Narrative of Women's Salvation* (London, 2002), p. 27. This is not to say that puberty does not bring with it intimations of orgasmic pleasure, but thankfully, for the majority, it is disconnected from sexual experience.

[17] Beattie quotes Kristeva's description of the experience: 'In sensual rapture I am distraught'. *God's Mother*, p. 103. John Keats captured the transitory nature of beauty and joy which intensifies its pain, when he wrote in his *Ode on Melancholy* of 'Joy, whose hand is ever at his lips/Bidding adieu'.

[18] Luce Irigaray, 'Women-Amongst-Themselves: Creating a Woman-to-Woman Sociality', in Margaret Whitford (ed.), *The Irigaray Reader* (Oxford, 1991), pp. 190–91.

[19] Eric Stice, 'Puberty and Body Image', in Chris Hayward (ed.), *Gender Differences at Puberty* (Cambridge, 2003), p. 61.

[20] Brown, *Raising their Voices*, pp. 7–8.

suggests Greene, because 'many feminist writers have promoted a minimalist view of the impact of menstruation on a woman's life' in a society where many women still experience negative discrimination during menstruation, where these 'inner periodicities'[21] are believed to affect rational judgement, or to render a woman unclean.[22] Brown does girls a disservice by alluding to but not naming menstruation when she discusses girls' 'shock, sadness, and anger and a sense of betrayal' at their adolescent 'awakening'.[23] Frost notes the pathologisation of a girl's gendered subjectivity at this time, and the effect of her socialisation into 'an inferiorised, physically imprisoned being in need of medical attention'.[24] Negativity around menstruation, with the result that their first menstrual bleeding often makes them feel dirty and unclean, requires girls to 'negotiate an experience of disgust and dislike of their own bodies'; that it 'may produce some sense of disjuncture and discomfort would seem probable'.[25] Young writes of girls' alienation from their bodies, and describes its cultural construction as placing women in a 'menstrual closet'.[26] Of the girls whom I interviewed, Georgia alone referred to menstruation, and even then by euphemism, reflecting that its discussion is taboo outside close female relationships. The desire for invisibility is evidenced through media representation of menstruation, which promotes its concealment, and denial of its messiness: for example, TV advertisements in 2007 for sanitary protection stressed product invisibility, and blood flow is coloured blue. This may be a socially constructed response, but one that is reinforced by religious discourse which connects menstrual bleeding with impurity and inadequacy, as the popular interpretation of the story of Jairus' daughter indicates.

Hormones

Myths around hormones may be another linguistic means of hiding pubertal changes and societal failure fully to understand girls. For Amber, they defined adolescence. Since, however, most girls negotiate adolescence without serious behavioural difficulties and 'empirical findings have not demonstrated such resounding effects of puberty on behaviour', Graber concurs with the mythical nature of the claim. She continues:

---

[21] Erikson, 'Womanhood and Inner Space', in *Identity*, p. 284.

[22] Greene, *Psychological Development*, p. 84.

[23] Brown, *Raising their Voices*, pp. 15–16.

[24] Liz Frost, *Young Women and the Body: A Feminist Sociology* (Basingstoke, 2001), p. 74.

[25] Ibid., p. 73.

[26] Young, *On Female Bodily Experience*, pp. 100–4, 111.

even if specific hormonal changes unique to girls were associated with onset or increased rates of a particular disorder, models would still have to explain why all girls do not develop the disorder.

She argues instead for a multidimensional approach which studies 'how pathways from childhood to adolescence may differ depending on the broader context of an individual's development' because 'it was not puberty per se but the context in which it occurred that was salient to understanding subsequent adjustment in … girls'.[27] Greene sees 'hormones' as 'the modern version of floating wombs or cold, moist complexions', a view of women from Aristotle onwards, that is, a male construct to reinforce the belief that women are subject to their biology, while men transcend their physicality to espouse rationality.[28] Moodiness may in part be the result of frustration when community or family do not hear, see or understand a girl's perplexity over bodily and emotional changes, and the grief which I have identified as a feature of their journey through transition.[29] Bohler is positive about the effects of a healthy environment on girls' negotiation of puberty and their coping with grief: reflecting on images from the popular literature, she likens most girls to Alice (in Wonderland) who 'learn(t) to swim in her tears' rather than to Ophelia who drowned herself, which contrasts with Pipher's thesis in which Ophelia's suicide is held up as the tragic outcome to which all her girls' stories may tend, literally or symbolically.[30] Georgia knows menstruation results in her 'being moody' and she adds 'I get tired, I sleep most of the time, especially at school'. Far from being disaffected as it may have appeared to her teachers, Georgia showed strong commitment to learning, finding the discipline and structured activities offered by the Army Cadets a positive environment within which to develop leadership skills (she was proud of her recent promotion to Lance Corporal) and nurture ambition for herself:

> I want to go in the army,
> then go in for an officer
> cos you go to college then or university.

Amber attributed to hormones the changes which made her, for example, reluctant any longer to hug and kiss her father, but this could stem from the conditioning of

---

[27]   Julia Graber, 'Puberty in Context', in Hayward, *Gender Differences*, pp. 308–9.

[28]   Greene, *Psychological Development*, p. 76.

[29]   For example, Katherine Sanborn and Chris Hayward, 'Hormonal Changes at Puberty and the Emergence of Gender Differences in Internalizing Disorders', and other chapters in Hayward, *Gender Differences*.

[30]   Carolyn Bohler, 'Attending to Alice: The Subjective Aims of Adolescent Girls', in J. Stevenson-Moessner (ed.), *In Her Own Time: Women and Developmental Issues in Pastoral Care* (Minneapolis, 2000), p. 146. See also M. Pipher, *Reviving Ophelia: Saving the Selves of Adolescent Girls* (New York, 1994), p. 4.

her church environment: her minister cited 'raging hormones' as the cause of erratic teenage behaviour. Other possible causes might be her awareness of her growing sexuality, and the openness of discussion about child protection in churches. The myth does, however, need to be challenged, and the environment itself subjected to critique to assess its contribution to girls' tears as well as their laughter.

On the Verge of Womanhood

Through external pubertal changes, girls become consciously sexual; through the internal pubertal change, girls enter womanhood with its cyclical rhythm and attendant capacity for reproduction and consequent necessity to take responsibility for others. Much feminist writing discusses the tension between sexual/maternal desire and identity, the girl as actor and acted upon, power differentials in the cultural perceptions of sexual maturity, and 'the apparently contradictory imperative to distinguish between the physical and the psychological'.[31] In her analysis of puberty, Driscoll draws on many sources in psychology and philosophy including Freud, de Beauvoir, Kristeva, Butler and Grosz. Dell sets the menarche in the context of biblical, physiological and psychological issues for a girl, commenting that it 'has not received the attention in pastoral theology circles to the same extent as childbirth, general sexuality or menopause'. Blaming the neglect on what Ruether describes as the 'social and cultural appropriation of biological differences in a male-dominated society', evident in biblical and theological writing, Dell wants to reclaim for girls a spiritual relationship to bodily function from a feminist perspective.[32] Wright importantly asserts that the site of female difference is menstruality not maternity,[33] yet little further work has been done on this in theology or spirituality where the dominant interest in bleeding is as it connects with birth and mothering.

   To inform this relatively empty space, I return here perhaps unexpectedly to the work of Erikson, and begin with some biography. His early career was as an artist. Moving in his twenties to study psychoanalysis under Freud, he retained a creative rather than a systematic approach to his writing. His books are collections of essays around themes connected with his personal search for identity: as he journeyed from Europe to America, from his Freudian training to his theory of ego development across the lifespan, from a Jewish origin to a fascination with the Jesus of John's gospel and Christian theology, Erikson engaged in wide-ranging academic pursuits. Although confessing no religious faith himself, Erikson supported his theory of stage development of the ego by studying Luther as a

---

[31]   Driscoll, *Girls*, p. 85.
[32]   Dell, 'She Grows in Wisdom', p. 140.
[33]   Verena Wright, *Maid in God's Image: In Search of Unruly Women* (London, 2008), p. 11.

young man: he enjoyed theological dialogue with Paul Tillich and among his last writings was 'The Galilean Sayings and the sense of "I"'.

His writing cannot be divorced from his life story. As he himself gained in life experience, so he adapted his theories, although not always consistently. He did not engage in empirical research and only rarely does he quote his sources: however, he is clearly influenced by many people, not least his wife Joan, who was his companion, spokesperson and editor. His students described how 'his ideas always passed through Joan'.[34] Behind his writing on women must lie her experience, which has its own validity as I 'hear' her story in his pages.

In the next few paragraphs, I will discuss and critique his writing about women and menstruation, and highlight his understanding of women's spiritual capacity. Later I will draw in part on his artistic imagery to shape my own analysis of girls at puberty. I turn to Erikson despite rejecting, as other feminists do, his psychosocial theory that a woman is determined by her anatomy, so that the monthly menstrual 'emptying' leaves a void to be penetrated and 'filled' physically and symbolically by a woman's male lover for and with whom she will find her identity as home-maker.[35] For Erikson, a woman cannot complete her ego identity formation without a male sexual partner. 'Anatomy is destiny', fixed and unchanging, sexual difference 'parallel(ing) the morphology of genital differentiation'.[36] This view denies a woman the freedom to develop her personal (ego) identity through choice of relational others, who may be neither sexual nor male.

In his 'Eight Ages of Man', Erikson sets out his epigenetic sequence of stages of personality development, each of which is attained through resolution of a crisis, leading to a radical change of perspective as new achievements are negotiated. In adolescence, he says, identity is formed prior to intimacy, the order which, as we have seen, Gilligan rejects. Erikson describes intimacy from a male perspective as 'the capacity to commit himself to concrete affiliations and partnerships and to develop the strength to abide by such commitments';[37] although he develops the idea in relation to the social significance of genital sexual relationship, he envisions for men fulfilment in other forms of intimacy, 'commitment' being an accompanying achievement in successful negotiation of this ego state. In this respect, Erikson's treatment of women is qualitatively different from men, which Gilligan cites as one of many examples in developmental theory of a hierarchical dualism in which men are 'outward' (for example, active, competitive, logical, autonomous) while women are 'inward' (for example, passive, relational, diffuse, interdependent). Girls suffer in particular, she says, citing Bettelheim's concurrence with Erikson, growing up with fairy tales: Snow White and Sleeping Beauty are examples of characters whose 'first bleeding is followed by a period of intense passivity' which perpetuates weakness and dependence, deemed to be inferior to

---

34   Robert Coles, 'Remembering Erik', in Hoover, *The Future of Identity*, pp. 19–20.
35   Erikson, 'Womanhood', p. 278.
36   Ibid., pp. 285, 271.
37   Erikson, *Childhood and Society*, p. 255.

the norm, which is constructed according to male characteristics.[38] Walkerdine, like Hess, takes this further in her analysis of a wider range of girls' texts (story books and comics) which encourage passivity, and the resolution of conflict by silent suffering and selfless action.[39]

The 'sexual revolution' of the 1960s strained Erikson's developmental theory when women began to choose careers and find fulfilment through the delay of marriage and childbearing. He attributed this to a 'psychosocial moratorium', a foray into the 'outer space', when woman experiments with being the counterpart of the 'phallic-ambulatory male'; in this temporary phase which he describes in language of playful seduction, she 'selectively invites what seeks her'.[40] He takes little account of how a woman's career assists in her self-definition. For all his determination to locate development within a social context, Erikson's vision is culture- and time-bound within the North American context of the mid-twentieth century, a society which 'may not reflect the cultural norm for the majority of the world's teenage population'.[41]

While rejecting Erikson's basic schema regarding women's development, there are two aspects of his thinking which relate to my study. Firstly, spiritual awareness underlies his thinking. Zock sees this interest deriving from the 'existential climate' of Europe of the 1930s,[42] and Friedman assigns it more specifically to the influence of Kierkegaard whose works he studied,[43] and Tillich, a colleague and friend.[44] As a result of a conversation with Tillich, Erikson intimates the beginning of a deconstruction of Enlightenment's striving for progress, in which 'the Ultimate has too often been visualised as an infinity which begins where male conquest of outer space ends'; he recognises that that renders Being '"even more" omnipotent and omniscient', also expendable. In 'Womanhood and Inner Space', which can be read as a philosophical as well as psychosocial reflection on living in a nuclear age, he sandwiches his reflection on women between an awareness of the effect of radioactive fall-out on the unborn child in the womb (representing the destructive results of historic male dominance), and the inwardness of women (connecting with Tillich's ultimate concern which Erikson interprets as feminine).[45] The Ultimate, he says, 'may well be found also to reside in the Immediate, which has so largely been the

---

[38]   Gilligan, *In a Different Voice*, pp. 13–14.

[39]   Walkerdine, *Schoolgirl Fictions*.

[40]   Erikson, 'Womanhood', pp. 282–3.

[41]   Kroger, 'Identity in Formation', p. 33.

[42]   Hetty Zock, *A Psychology of Ultimate Concern: Erik Erikson's Contribution to the Psychology of Religion* (Amsterdam, 1990), p. 24.

[43]   L. Friedman, *Identity's Architect: A Biography of Erik H. Erikson* (New York, 1999), pp. 448–9.

[44]   L. Friedman, 'Erik Erikson: A Biographer's Reflections on a Decade-Long Process', in Hoover, *The Future of Identity*, p. 27.

[45]   Erikson, 'Womanhood', p. 262.

domain of woman and of the inward mind'.[46] In the intervening argument, he sees the only solution to men's competitive and nationalistic use of technological advance to be women's intervention in the political sphere bringing their gifts of householding, peacekeeping and healing, that is, 'an ethically restraining, because truly supranational, power to politics in the widest sense'.[47] In places, his argument contradicts his somatic view of women ('no woman lives or needs to live only in this extended somatic sphere'),[48] and he castigates women for their failure to contribute their caring and caretaking gifts to society 'to balance man's indiscriminate endeavour to perfect his domination over the outer spaces of national and technologic expansion'. He in turn fails to acknowledge the patriarchal structures which limit her freedom so to contribute. In the context of his awareness that women's creativity can and should be applied in a leadership capacity to curb the 'ruthless self-aggrandizement' of men which has brought the world to the brink of extinction, he values and elevates women's intuitive and cognitive capacity.[49]

His thinking is limited by the discourse of his day, but his experience brings a contradiction he cannot satisfactorily resolve.[50] Although inadequate as an analysis of women's 'development', he identifies a spiritual yet embodied dimension to women's contribution to public life. About religion itself, Erikson was ambivalent: he saw it as the institution which in his day offered a coherent worldview undergirding the trust which was the foundation of his epigenetic system, while at the same time associating it with surrender and control which militates against the growth of identity. Although he 'disavow(ed) any intention to call religion as such childish or religious behaviour as such regressive' he was aware that 'large-scale infantilisation is not foreign to the practice and the intent of organized religion'.[51]

This leads me to make two points about the significance to Erikson of the onset of menstruation as an expression of his artistic imagination. Firstly, he suggests it may birth in a girl an awareness of her interiority and potential for creativity/ generativity. Such creativity is, from a feminist perspective, generic, and not confined to the physical in childbirth. Thus, when Erikson defines generativity as 'primarily the concern for establishing and guiding the next generation',[52] I opt for the broader definition: 'capable of producing or originating'.[53] I prefer 'symbolic interiority' to Erikson's 'inner space', which physiologically is a misconception:

---

[46]   Ibid., pp. 293–4.

[47]   Ibid., p. 262.

[48]   Ibid., p. 289.

[49]   Ibid., pp. 292–3.

[50]   A description and discussion of the feminist response to Erikson's essay and his own reaction to being, as he perceived it, misunderstood, is found in Friedman, *Identity's Architect*, pp. 423–6.

[51]   Erikson, 'The Life Cycle, Epigenesis of Identity', in *Identity*, p. 106.

[52]   Ibid., p. 138.

[53]   As in *Collins English Dictionary*, 5th edn (2000).

women do not have 'spaces' to fill but elastic muscles designed to expand to accommodate penis or embryo in vagina or uterus (a different 'place' for each, indicating biologically and symbolically that the 'fulfilment' of sexual intercourse is of a different order from that of childbearing). This does not concede to dualism; in addition to their opportunities in the 'outer' world, it validates girls in the caring roles welcomed by many of those whom I interviewed (whether in childbearing or other spheres of service) and the deeply creative inner life of spiritual relatedness they revealed. In her later writing, Irigaray offers us another way to connect the physical/sexual with the spiritual. She holds out as an ideal a relationship between the two genders devoid of power differential and as a 'type' of our relationship with God. Regretting that '*gender has become inseparable from genealogy*', she argues for the rediscovery of '*love within difference*, love that is neither possession of the one by the other, nor exploitation of the one by the other in order to satisfy personal or even procreative instincts'. For her, these are steps towards 'the spiritualization of humanity'.[54]

Secondly, Erikson introduces the idea that grief is in some sense intrinsic to puberty: 'each menstruation ... is a crying to heaven in the mourning over a child', and he speaks of women's pain in menstruation, as well as motherhood, in a theologically nuanced way as a 'dolorosa'.[55] Although rejecting such an interpretation of each monthly cycle, at a deeper level I have already identified grief as a present emotion in girls' conversation as they reflected on the way life was changing for them, of which the monthly repetition of blood loss is a regular reminder.

Consumerism and Body Image

The girls whom I interviewed presented themselves in a wide variety of ways with regard to the attention they paid to the externals of clothes and personal care. For some it was either not important how they looked, or they had not yet reached the stage where they wanted, or were allowed, to spend time and money on clothes and cosmetics; for others it was of some importance or it mattered a great deal.

Among those for whom image was important were Mary and Michelle; they felt under pressure from, and made vulnerable by, external influences:

> Girls more have to have their hair the right way
> and get, I don't know, like
> I think if someone compliments them, they feel happier. (Michelle)

They have 'manicures and pedicures and just mak(ing) ourselves feel really good about ourselves'. Georgia represented the opposite view: commenting on the girls

---

[54]   Irigaray, *Luce Irigaray: Key Writings*, pp. 179–80. Author's italics.

[55]   Erikson, 'Womanhood', pp. 278, 284.

she was in charge of as a Cadet, she observed they were 'hardly ever happy' about their body image:

> they're always upset there's something wrong,
> they think they're either a bit too short or a bit too big.

She noted the sadness of desiring the unattainable, imposed by external pressures.

When Bethan, for whom at just 12 looking sophisticated was important, spoke about shopping and her phone as being important in her life, the others in the group laughed, and they made it clear to me that this predilection on Bethan's part was the subject of regular banter with a negatively critical undertone, as if it was not appropriate for these things to be important to a Christian girl. I wonder how honest they were being. In Brierley's survey, shopping was the third most popular 'outdoors' pastime, scoring more highly among girls than boys.[56] Victoria endorsed this:

> shopping's more of a girl's thing ...
> lads can't admit that they do [like it].

Is Bethan speaking with an honesty the others feel inhibited to do, because they know that to admit in a church context to enjoying it would not receive approval? This is the church in which I felt the girls wanted to give me 'right' answers. If shopping is indicative of a preoccupation with materialism and conformity to fashion, and if these are real issues for Christian girls, then to face the tension set up between this facet of contemporary society and a Christian ethic of restraint or, at its extreme, asceticism is crucial. Indeed, Mercer wrote her 'practical theology of childhood' intentionally to help girls/boys to 'oppose the destructive identities consumer culture offers today'.[57] How, then, do the girls hear and interpret Jesus' teaching, 'do not worry about ... your body, what you will wear. Is not ... the body more than clothing?' (Matthew 5.19–33 and Luke 12.22–31). Unlike the gospels, the O.T. is full of examples of fine clothes and jewellery bedecking the human person, especially the virginal bride; although the prophets prefigure Jesus when they condemn flagrant extravagance, there is approval of lavish bridal adornment when the bridegroom metaphor is applied to God.[58] These sit alongside Jesus' acceptance of the extravagant gift of perfume poured on him out of love, and his habit of feasting, not fasting.

Concern with the body is often seen as vanity, and to enjoy human beauty is to take pride in something other than God. It is a 'classic' theme of feminist theology

---

[56]   Brierley, *Reaching and Keeping Tweenagers*, p. 92.

[57]   Mercer, *Welcoming Children*, p. ix.

[58]   Ruth's preparation for seducing Boaz (3.3); the love poetry of Song of Solomon (for example 4.9–10); Ezekiel's description of YHWH's bride (16.8–14). Prophetic condemnation includes Isaiah 3.18–24, Amos 6.4–7.

to note male theologians' preoccupation with condemnation of the sin of pride and its corollary, the commendation of self-denial. Theologians from Valerie Saiving onwards have argued how spiritually destructive this view is for women.[59] Body theology plays an important part in feminist theology, offering an alternative to the dualism which associates God only with spirit and goodness, and the body, especially women's bodies, with fallen humankind and therefore with sin. To answer her struggle to relate humankind and God, Bryony ended up finding only in the soul any manifestation of the image of God.

Among my interviewees, Mary appeared to have been offered a way forward in integrating self-care with her faith. She spoke of a local group for girls, recently started, which enabled them to explore a biblical basis for paying attention to looks and the body, as well as offering various 'therapies'; Esther was the character who provided the inspiration, and Mary felt encouraged by the idea of a biblical role model who shared her experience and whom God valued. Until recently, Esther has not rated very highly in feminism, in contrast to Vashti who has become a symbol of resistance to male domination.[60] Hess is ambivalent about Esther; on one level she sees her conscription into Ahasuerus' harem as conforming to the dehumanising sexism typical of society today but she also offers her as an alternative model of resistance to it, 'a vision of girls and women empowered in the household of God'[61] as she defeats Haman and rescues the Jewish people from annihilation. Mary is at odds with Hess here, for she is seizing on Esther's presumed enjoyment of her cosmetic treatments and massage as justification for her own pleasure in it, a sensation she shares with other women in her church, including the minister who is a significant role model. There is no sense in which Mary thinks she is doing it to gratify men, but for her own sake, to enjoy the bodily sensations and the admiration of others to build her self-esteem. To feel and look good, however that is defined (it does not necessarily follow that everyone's model is *Cosmopolitan*[62]), and to be admired does not necessarily mean to be dehumanised by submission to patriarchal definitions of femininity, even though the desired image is culturally constructed. Julie and Martha also enjoy being with other girls to 'do each other's hair and other things and talk about clothes and stuff, and massage'. For them, it is intrinsic to being 'girlie'.

Could Esther be used more constructively as a role model? I do not know how far hermeneutics informed the teaching Mary received on Esther, but she had taken from it what she needed for that moment in her life. The story does lend itself to

---

[59]   See for example, Ursula King, *Women and Spirituality: Voices of Protest and Promise* (Basingstoke, 1989), p. 164.

[60]   Timothy Beal discusses Christian ambivalence to her in *The Book of Hiding: Gender, Ethnicity, Annihilation, and Esther* (London, 1997), p. 44.

[61]   Hess, *Caretakers of our Common House*, p. 150.

[62]   Beattie uses *Cosmopolitan* magazine as the symbol of manipulation of women towards vacuous consumption and away from 'feminist activism and radicalism', *Woman*, p. 43.

further support of girls and women as they face these cultural and personal issues. Although Esther submitted to the beauty treatments, she really had no choice as she was a conscript. However, she is not the 'bimbo' she is often thought to be to contrast with Vashti, although Brenner dismisses her as such.[63] Each woman, in her own way, refused to submit to male dominance. Each took a risk with her own safety to resist male oppression for herself and for others. Esther wanted to win the competition (although competition is not a stereotypical feminine trait, even Karen admits that they do compete sometimes, 'but it's just with other girls!') or else there would be no point in her subjection and imprisonment. She craftily sought advice on what to take with her into the king's presence from someone who should know what would please him. It worked. Later, Esther dared to come into the king's presence unbidden, in a rebellion as audacious as Vashti's. The plan to expose Haman is one of Esther's own choosing, using her feminine power over the king against Haman. Hess, despite his suspicion of Esther's compliance, notes that 'Esther uses her beauty to overturn his (the king's) capricious laws'. And through the actions of both women, 'a woman's right to possess her own beauty has been vindicated'.[64] In her commentary, Bechtel finds a particular relevance for girls and women today in the story of Esther, the challenge to 'remain faithful in a cultural context that is not similarly committed and that, in fact, may be openly hostile to the life of faith'.[65] She explicitly relates this to the 'aggressively individualistic, consumerist culture' of her North American context, and suggests three possible responses: to deny the tension and 'become like the nations'; to cut ourselves off from contact with outside influence; or to seek some critical compromise 'adapting to our culture wherever possible, while still straining to maintain the integrity of faith'. I suspect that even subconsciously, many churches and children's and youth workers behave as if adhering to the second while the more realistic – and biblical – approach is the last, which requires the development of skill in evaluating where and when to compromise, and on what grounds; this is the skill of theological reflection. An added relevance in using the book of Esther in our current context is in the apparent absence of God from the narrative. To Linda Day, the story 'permits actions to remain in their theological ambiguity' because it reflects the common human condition that God does not speak directly, but leaves it to us to discern either hiddenness or absence.[66]

---

[63]   Athalya Brenner, *The Israelite Woman: Social Role and Literary Type in Biblical Narrative* (Sheffield, 1985).

[64]   Hess, *Caretakers of our Common House*, p. 24.

[65]   Carol M. Bechtel, *Esther* (Louisville, 2002), p. 10.

[66]   Linda M. Day, *Esther*, Abingdon Old Testament Commentaries (Nashville, 2005), p. 18.

Living in Transitional Space

What I have detected in the girls has resonance in their own context with the crises others have identified, and the images they offer are helpful in understanding the experience. The girls are at a threshold of a new way of being human and woman, one which they cannot escape. In this borderland, they grieve the loss of childhood's freedom, and face the future in which they must determine their identity insofar as they are free to do so, as girls and as Christians.

Interpreting it as a 'threshold' invites another perspective on it, as a liminal place, a border crossing. Insight on this comes from studies of others at points of liminality. Erikson is one such person. It was Tillich who, through an autobiographical essay in which he described his life as one of boundary dwelling, helped Erikson find a way 'to understand aspects of his own life in a special way'. Tillich, like Erikson, had travelled across many boundaries, national, political, intellectual and spiritual, to become the person he was and knew that the 'unrest, insecurity and inner limitation of existence' of boundary dwelling 'made for neither serenity, security nor perfection "in life as well as in thought"'.[67] This may partly explain the 'authority' Erikson thought he had to write about girls on the boundary or threshold of womanhood.

Another kind of threshold is faced by people who are terminally ill, and in a study of their spirituality, Stanworth has found the language of liminality rather than marginalisation appropriate, in its evocation of a borderline place, a frontier between the past to which there is no return and the future which cannot be escaped. The use of the metaphor in this way illuminates further the transitional place which girls inhabit. The 'letting go' necessary to cross the threshold takes courage, a quality which Martha identified as necessary to get through situations as life-threatening in her recent experience of the London bombings of 2005. Since a threshold would not be such if there were a void on the other side, it implies a future, thus symbolising creativity and power. Liminality has, then, a future orientation, involving a 'leap of faith', for 'although experiences of liminality lie beyond the individual's control, they sometimes induce an expanded consciousness of what life is ultimately about and what really matters'.[68]

In a different context but sharing powerlessness in extremity, Raphael investigates the role of women in Auschwitz, who stood in a liminal place and mediated life and death, accompanying the dying by being present to them and uncovering the face of the living out of dirt and degradation to restore what humanity they could.[69] In these actions of maternal presence, Raphael suggests, the God whom male-constructed theology holds to be at best silent, at worst absent

---

[67]   Friedman, *Identity's Architect*, pp. 343–4.

[68]   Rachel Stanworth, *Recognizing Spiritual Needs in People Who are Dying* (Oxford, 2004), pp. 115–20. See also C.S. Lewis, *The Last Battle* (Harmondsworth, 1956), chapter 14ff.

[69]   Raphael, *The Female Face of God*, p. 51.

(in Stanworth's terms leaving a void which thrust humanity to the margins), was revealed as maternal love.[70] Liminality implies or encourages agency even where there is an inevitability about a future path: there is choice about the way the threshold is crossed. This has potential as I begin to identify ways girls can be supported by people of faith as they move holistically through adolescence.

Jairus' daughter was in both a liminal and a marginal state. She was at the threshold where life meets death, possibly had just crossed it. Her status in life had been marginal, assigned to the edge of sacred space by adult men at the centre of religious power. She had no agency over her future pathway. Jesus met her in liminal space, and by touch in an act of mothering called her into life, and anticipated her own and all people's calling forth to resurrection life after his own border crossing outside Jerusalem. A girl's life, death and rising to womanhood, it can be argued, is imbued with christological significance.

---

[70]   Ibid., p. 120.

Chapter 5
Theological Reflection 1: Lucy

Introduction

Having explored what it means physically, emotionally and theologically for girls to live on the threshold of adolescence, I turn to analysis of their faith lives in the next chapter. As an introduction, however, I am giving voice to Lucy who, in her struggles to articulate faith, demonstrated an ability to identify and discuss some quite sophisticated theological arguments. Lucy was one of the youngest girls in my sample and this analysis is of part of the conversation in our third meeting. My initial reaction to her contribution was dismissive as, in contrast to other girls', it appeared to lack both coherence and substance. However, analysis of her 'thick description'[1] revealed a depth of insight into the nature of God, the world and humankind as she reflected on her experience of them. As I engage in the analysis, I suggest areas of alignment with theological argument from a variety of sources.

By the time of this interview, we had developed a rapport; Lucy had confidence that I would listen, and she spoke freely and with assurance. In the first interviews, she had shown a yearning for the genuine and for the exposure of falsehood and artifice. She was aware that God could not be pinned down but met us in ways that addressed our need at that time: 'a bit like a shapeshifter sort of thing: it can be whatever you want it to be' (she used 'it' to designate God in this section on the theme of God and gender: at all other times, she referred to God as 'he'). Lucy's faith showed signs of being still at the affiliative stage, not yet fully 'owned';[2] she was capable of abstract thought about God, but did not articulate any personal experience except through her cognitive processes. She distanced herself at every opportunity from engaging at a more personal level, aligning herself with the words and actions of others. Lucy was 'held' by their witness, but was 'starting to realise that he does make a difference'. Remembering an adult's 'testimony' to God's presence from two years previously, she recognised that: 'now I'm getting older, when I think about it I know what she means, because it's not like he was there but he *was* there'. There is no doubt that she thought about these things deeply, and was on a spiritual journey, as she tried to make sense of issues at the interface of the religious and the ethical.

---

[1] C. Geertz, *The Interpretation of Cultures* (New York, 1973), pp. 3–30. It denotes the richness and variety of the everyday detail a 'conversation partner' offers in the interview process.

[2] Westerhoff, *Will Our Children Have Faith?*, p. 95.

Stage 1

To open this conversation, I asked Lucy to tell me more about how she thought
and felt about God. This triggered an answer determined by her experience of
relationships with people whom she found 'not very good at understanding
things' and not to be trusted with secrets. She was resisting the anthropomorphic
God-language she heard around her and was searching for images which more
adequately reflected the God who is beyond human imperfections. She found
partial answers in animal metaphors (animals were important to her as the
evidence of attachment to her pets showed). For her first resource, she drew on
the Narnia stories of C.S. Lewis which offered her the image of a lion (Aslan),
a fictional creation intended as an allegorical representation of Christ; although
she recognised this is not the whole story, in reality or in the character, she
identified the paradoxical qualities of gentleness and strength as most closely
approximating God's.

Her second choice, a whale, was set alongside the lion as being more
consistently positive towards humans, but also awesome in size and beauty, as
reflected in her tone of voice.[3] Animal figures are sometimes used in the bible
as representations of or metaphors for the divine. However, in theology, their
usage is more ambiguous in that, as creatures subject to human 'dominion', they
are part of an inferior order; indeed, in patriarchal thought, as Jantzen points
out, animals are often linked with women as belonging bodily to the earth, in
contrast to the superior culture and rationality belonging to the male.[4] Lucy was
reclaiming metaphorical use of animal imagery for the divine, but wild animals
lack relatedness, so she then chose a third image, a teddy bear, which although
inanimate, when used in combination with living creatures, contributed the absent
qualities of nearness, trust and personal attention.[5] Lucy showed here a practised
understanding of the use of metaphor.

Stage 2

Lucy moved the reflection on by giving reasons for her use of these metaphors.
Here she introduced the contradiction between the theological concept of God

---

[3]   This association may be generated by drama as she had seen the film *Whale Rider*
shortly before this interview. Unlike the Lewis story this is based on real animals; in the
narrative, girl and whale save one another, the whale's size belying its gentle treatment of
the girl.

[4]   G. Jantzen, *Becoming Divine: Towards a Feminist Philosophy of Religion*
(Manchester, 1998), p. 151.

[5]   Gilligan et al. quote an 11-year-old girl's explanation of this: 'talking to stuffed
animals or things; it just helps you get out your pains': *Women, Girls and Psychotherapy*,
p. 17.

as creator and her experience through local, national and global news bulletins of human wickedness which to her emptied of proper meaning anthropomorphic language for God. She didn't mention any specific incident but the town in which she lives had seen serious race riots three years previously, and the second Iraq war was in its early stages and regularly in the news. 'People', she said, 'do all this really bad stuff to the world so why would God be a person?'. She was struggling at the boundary of her linguistic and discursive skills, which did not yet suffice to express her thoughts. She solved the dilemma by returning to the animal image and setting up an imaginary narrative pursuing the metaphorical image of God, to create a correlation which in its contrasting imagery nourished her theological reflection.[6] She called on a biblical story as a new resource, Noah's command to take all the animals into the ark when 'people did all the terrible things'; she used this to justify her use of the animal metaphor (God takes care of God's own kind against the human enemy), but also noted its shortcomings because in the end God cannot be reduced to, or fully described by, any figurative language. God is 'a spirit sort of thing. I just don't think of him as a person'.

She took 'personhood' to denote a 'metaphysics of substance'.[7] Lucy will not be the only person of any age in her church to understand God's personhood in this way. Yet she was clear that it was for their particular qualities that she had selected animal metaphors: she cited here a self-conscious assertiveness (strength) and care (gentleness). She was seeking an underlying morality as a fundamental characteristic of deity, against which she could evaluate human behaviour.

Stage 3

Having introduced human wickedness, she turned to wider evils affecting the world's people that God might be accused of causing, drawing on the 2004 tsunami as an example. It was not a problem to her to see God as in some way behind this disaster, but she asserted as a theological and moral principle and as a statement of her faith, that God is consistent and not arbitrary, and despite all appearances is both just, and biased towards humankind: 'God wouldn't just hurt somebody for the sake of hurting them, there has to be a reason ... he's got his reasons why he's done it'. I probed a bit further on this connection between God and the tsunami, and in answer she drew on a fresh resource, a school RE lesson about the Egyptian plagues, where wholly natural explanations were

---

[6] Such correlation in the process of theological reflection, inspired by the theology of Tillich, is explored by Howard Stone and James Duke, *How to Think Theologically*, 2nd edn (Minneapolis, 2006), pp. 30ff.

[7] 'Despite the postmodern critique, the pull of the Enlightenment – which identifies a "person" with an individual center of consciousness – has not been overcome', David S. Cunningham, *These Three are One: The Practice of Trinitarian Theology* (Oxford, 1998), p. 27.

suggested. Although Lucy could understand the chain of events as natural, she couldn't accept what would amount to chaos theory, but wanted instead to place God at the heart as initiator of the sequence, so that there was a 'first mover' (but not 'unmoved' as we see later) who acted out of choice, but with good reason: 'If God wanted to stop it, God could stop it … but he didn't so he must have had his reasons for doing it'. That God has the power to do anything is another theological truth she wanted to uphold by faith. For her, 'God made nature' means that God has the power of choice over its fate.

This presented Lucy with the problem of finding an adequate reason for suffering on such a large scale. She suggested two reasons:

1. Although seeing ancient and contemporary disaster as a sign of God's impatience with human wickedness, the anger is directed at those with power and wealth: the poor suffer disproportionately, but may benefit from a fresh start, an equalisation reminiscent of biblical jubilee. There is thus a benevolence underlying God's intention. Lucy understood global interconnectedness as she began to align herself with the power and wealth of the west which drove her to explore another explanation of suffering in her second reason.

2. A classic answer to theodicy, that God is testing us. We could shrug our shoulders and deny connection, but people cared enough to respond and not only with money. Drawing again on a biblical example, she named Noah as not being able to prevent all the suffering, but doing what little he could, which did help. This is not easily dismissed as immature reasoning; as in the story of Abraham and Isaac in Genesis 22, if people pass the test then they can be trusted.

As she pursued this line of thinking, Lucy returned to the model of animals, but her metaphoric construction became a little confused, and her argument fell apart. She had stretched the metaphor too far, and had lost her way.

Stage 4

Lucy would not, however, be satisfied without a resolution to the argument, so sought a way of bringing order to it. Again this is theologically based, and builds on her prior designation of God as creator and merciful judge. A moral order governs creation which its creator will not ultimately transgress; God places time-boundaries around acts of judgement, turning towards the world in mercy because 'he is bothered about what happens'. This is a kind of redemption. The human response reflects God's care (she might have said that by this we pass the test), in campaigns about environmental concerns, the final resource upon which she draws.

Although tempered in this way at the conclusion, Lucy's stance here did not primarily display an ethic of care as identified by Gilligan, in contrast to other girls whose argument demonstrated a similar dialectic to that noted in the Harvard research where the awareness of the need for justice is tempered by the sheer awfulness of human suffering experienced in the tragedies which motivated a care for the victims.[8] Lucy's starting point was not, however, acts of evil in themselves but the very character of God, and her emphasis on 'otherness' dictated her attitude to human imperfection. Her goal was not to find an answer to evil but ultimate meaning for herself within a human community which seemed to defy the *imago dei*.

Lucy was attempting to construct an objectively logical argument, but lacked the empathy of other girls' expressions of concern about suffering: she admitted at a later point in the interview that she had lived a sheltered life in the sense that God had 'never done anything bad to me', so she had never had to face these issues at first hand. She did, however, on an earlier occasion show a depth of concern about others' suffering, and expressed a real sense of injustice when people, who ridiculed her for her concern, expected her to sympathise with them in their own difficulties.

I turn now to themes which emerged from analysis of my interview data in the 'space' in the girls' lives to do explicitly with God and their faithing, starting with a biblical example of a girl 'thinking outside the box'.

---

[8]   Gilligan, *In a Different Voice*, p. 73. Although most of the subsequent research by Gilligan and her colleagues undertaken with adolescent girls is in the area of peer and family relationships, girls' care for the wider world can be found in, for example, *Making Connections*, pp. 127ff.

Chapter 6

Girls in Godspace

Naaman's Wife's Slave Girl[1]

This girl, anonymous like her mistress, is given no more than a passing mention in commentaries. She plays a 'bit part' in the Elisha saga, but is a significant 'agent of change amid international conflict'.[2] To begin to engage in anything other than a sentimental reading of her brief story, I will suggest a context in which her plight may better be understood. The background is of war between Israel and her neighbours, in which in a border raid, the girl had been taken captive. We find an equivalent social context in Judges 19–21, the story of the Levite's wife or concubine. Writing on that passage, Lapsley sets it in the context of the whole of Judges and the author's narrative intent, concluding that, when seen in this way, the woman's fate stands as a judgement on ethical ills resulting from and contributing to social breakdown and a cycle of violence including that against women:

> The progression of the story from violence against a lone woman to civil war, in which women and men are killed, and the eventual wounding and fragmentation of all Israel, offers some suggestive theological avenues for reflection.[3]

It thus becomes, Lapsley concludes, a 'trenchant critique' of war, of which the bodies of raped women are a sign.

If we apply Lapsley's critique to the study of the story in 2 Kings 5, it can become an avenue for fresh learning about YHWH. Its background is likewise a turbulent political period, of the divided kingdoms and their frequent armed disputes with their neighbours, in which women and children were innocent victims, sometimes of tribute with its sexual implications for women (1 Kings 20.1–7), at others of siege (2 Kings 6.24–31). This girl is such a victim, in her case of forced removal from home into a life of servitude: her young age may have protected her from the sexual slavery expected for an older girl (Judges 5.30) but the injustice of her exile is not mitigated by the apparent humanity of her mistress. While hostility remains between Aram and Israel, the author asks the theological

---

[1] 2 Kings 5.2–3.

[2] Esther M. Menn, 'Child Characters in Biblical Narratives: The Young David (1 Samuel 16–17) and the Little Israelite Servant Girl (2 Kings 5.1–19)', in Marcia J. Bunge (ed.), *The Child in the Bible* (Grand Rapids, 2008), p. 351.

[3] Jacqueline E. Lapsley, *Whispering the Word: Hearing Women's Stories in the Old Testament* (Louisville, 2005), p. 64.

question: 'how can we live together in peace as neighbours?', a question which in itself threatens to undermine the dominant theology of Judah and Israel as the chosen people whose God will side with them as they try to extend their power ruthlessly over those who are not YHWH's. Structures and people embedded in entrenched oppositions offer no way out.

So the narrator introduces a character whose 'forthrightness allows us to imagine her as spirited and bold',[4] who cuts across these fixed positions, a 'little' person set against the 'big' people and powers in play here.[5] Reinhartz points out that the preponderance of servants in the books of Samuel and Kings are at royal courts, so the role of a girl, in an army household, has added significance. Faced with Naaman's illness, her wish to call upon Israel's prophet counters theological paradigms: a young girl, and her deportation, are both of concern to YHWH, and YHWH's interest and healing purposes extend beyond national boundaries even to enemies. Obedience was expected of servants; it was unusual for them to give counsel. Through the intervention of her mistress, the girl becomes the one through whom the voice of YHWH speaks and the reader must listen – as also must the alien army commander. The theological significance of his hearing and heeding *her* voice to receive the healing YHWH offers through Elisha is normally missed. In the new thing which comes about through her (the humbling of the powerful, and the 'translocal' nature of YHWH) lies the potential for peaceable living which the kings' warlike projects are denying the ordinary people. Her insight can only be 'birthed' for us when we hear the whispered voice of the least significant person, the young female victim, who dares to speak of home and her faith in the prophet who implacably opposed, in YHWH's name, Israel's kings who 'did what was evil in the sight of the Lord'. Lapsley calls to mind the words of Rowan Williams after the September 11 destruction of the World Trade Center, that choosing to respond to violence in a different language is not an endorsement of passivity, but 'trying to act so that something might possibly change, as opposed to acting to persuade ourselves that we are not powerless',[6] which is the contrast between the girl's action and that of Israel's king.

Jesus chose Naaman's story to demonstrate in his Nazareth manifesto (Luke 4.27) his understanding of his mission as the incarnation of YHWH's word rejected of old. Here in Luke's gospel Jesus knows from the beginning what in Matthew and Mark he learns through encounter with the Syro-Phoenician woman that God's power and purpose transcend human boundaries. She was driven to desperation by the sickness of her young daughter, a girl who 'is for all practical purposes non-existent'.[7] In the gospels, the agent of new theology is a woman; more strikingly in the O.T. narrative, the agent is a girl.

---

[4]   Adele Reinhartz, *'Why Ask My Name': Anonymity and Identity in Biblical Narrative* (Oxford, 1998), p. 38.

[5]   Menn, 'Child Characters', p. 344.

[6]   Lapsley, *Whispering the Word*, p. 66.

[7]   Mercer, *Welcoming Children*, p. 57.

Into Godspace

The voices of Lucy and of the anonymous servant lead into exploration of both the processes of these girls' faithing and the theological understanding they are developing as they live by that faith, approaching the same material therefore from two directions. These girls inhabit 'Godspace', a sacred place and time in which their spiritual inheritance meets and often clashes with lived experience, and they wrestle with the God with whom they want to relate. Their doing of theology in this space is indeed 'faith seeking understanding', so studying both their faith and the understanding it seeks, helps us create a more comprehensive picture of:

- the *meanings* faith has for them as they explore the things of God in simplicity and complexity; and
- the *strategies* of faithing they adopt at their life stage, and with their particular gendered self-awareness.

Fowler says of faith that it is 'trust in another and … loyalty to a transcendent center of value and power', the content of religion being 'relative apprehensions of our relatedness to that which is universal'.[8] What is relative for the girls is the particular needs they have at this period in their lives which faith can serve. Their ability to do theology does not necessarily correlate with the limitations determined by their psychological needs or brief life experience; in contrast to Slee's discovery that the women in her study 'had ready access to more conceptual and analytical discourses, but nevertheless chose, on the whole, not to employ them',[9] I suggest that girls are capable of more conceptual thinking than their needs, expressed in their faithing strategies, would indicate. Although lacking the sophisticated level of articulation of an older mind, there is evidence of serious attempts at doing theology, located in their life experience, which needs to be heard and valued. The analysis of Lucy's reflection demonstrates this.

Other Research on How Girls 'Do' Faith

As I explore girls' faith and theology, I shall set it in the context of existing research on girls' faithing, creating a framework from the findings of Tamminen, Heller and the NSYR, particularly in those areas where gender differentiation is significant.

Their findings were broadly consistent with the view that girls are more positive than boys in their attitudes and beliefs. Heller drew out 'gender themes', and Tamminen also isolated gender difference for discussion. Although not all their research set out to be comparative, they found a greater level of

---

[8]   Fowler, *Stages*, pp. 14f.
[9]   Slee, *Women's Faith Development*, p. 79.

sophistication, complexity or nuance in girls' spiritual understanding than in boys
of similar age. Both found girls had a more aesthetic view of God, often domestic,
even docile, oriented towards intimacy, while boys favoured performance and
power, rationality and activity. Both uncovered in girls a higher incidence of
religious experience which emphasised the closeness of relationship with God,
and God's guidance of them. Among most girls in both Tamminen and Heller,
security was an important feature of the relationship, and belief in a caring God
who loves and forgives. Prayer was more relational for all girls, who engaged in
conversation with God, with thanksgiving featuring strongly.[10] Their prayer was
less petitionary, but overall attitudes were very positive; Heller found that girls
expected prayer to work.

Just as Tamminen found development in his longitudinal study beyond the
age of 12, so Heller found older girls in his sample willing to stretch traditional
boundaries and try new ideas as they connected faith with experience. He cites,
for example, 12-year-old Lorraine who saw God as androgynous but was reluctant
'to say this out loud' for fear she will be treated as 'stupid'; she is already aware
that deviance may be demeaned as a mark of immaturity. Her unwillingness to
articulate her thoughts publicly resonates with the decision of 13-year-old Jane to
suppress her independent view on abortion, as told by Brown.[11]

Twenty years after Heller, the NSYR research project was carried out in the
United States in response to the awareness that spirituality and religion were
omitted from studies of adolescents while other evidence suggested faith still
played a part in young people's lives through a wide variety of traditional and
postmodern forms of spiritual and religious practice in which they were engaged.
The subjects were grouped into three categories for a representative cross section
of American society: religious, spiritual but not religious, and disengaged. The
resultant report pays some attention to gender, and the findings support some
of those of Heller and Tamminen, for example, girls' more regular attendance
at religious services, frequency of prayer, and their felt closeness to God.[12] In
their religious thinking, they found girls worked with concepts at an earlier age.
In general, American teenagers were not clear about basic religious beliefs;[13]
the researchers were surprised by the vagueness of the respondents about the
person and work of Jesus and his relationship to God; 'these were not throwaway
comments of teens, these were their main answers to our key questions about their
basic personal religious beliefs'.[14]

The findings in these studies led me to look for evidence from the girls that
a relationship with God who loves and cares for them is important to them; that
they have an ability to think conceptually, and may not be afraid of divergent

---

[10]   Tamminen, *Religious Development*, p. 219.
[11]   Heller, *The Children's God*, p. 74; Brown, *Raising their Voices*, p. 107.
[12]   Smith with Denton, *Soul Searching*, pp. 277, 279.
[13]   Ibid., pp. 131–7.
[14]   Ibid., p. 135.

beliefs although may be reluctant to name these publicly for fear of negative reactions from others, whether friends or parents, which might break relationships. I wondered how far they could articulate some basic Christian beliefs: if I encountered formulaic expressions of theology, would they reflect the stance of the church, or the influence of a leader, minister or the learning material used? At the time of my visits, two churches were using lesson material published by Scripture Union, two were not using published resources in their work with the girls, and in one church, worship and learning were integrated for all, and based loosely on *Roots* material.[15]

I turn first to the girls' theological understandings, then later to their processes of faithing. Throughout, I shall also suggest some correlation between what I judge to be significant theological insights by the girls, and writing on the same themes by a range of systematic theologians.

Girls' God-talk

In asking the girls the question: 'Who is God for you?' I was not asking them to engage in abstract theory or systematic theology, but to narrate or to reflect on how and where in their own experience they had encountered God. This might be directly, through a spiritual experience, or mediated through a relationship, a conversation, an odd musing, a book, or a picture. In their answers, they drew on all of these. Much of their talk was stimulated by particular experience, and remained at the level of particularity. Many were also, like Lucy, reaching beyond and drawing on wider knowledge – from tradition of family and church, from the bible, from moral precepts or just sound common sense – to engage in a dialogue between life and faith. These girls have not all yet chosen to commit themselves publicly to a life of faith, and may not do so; so their search for 'truth', taking place as it does from within a faithing community, is not a search for intellectual satisfaction, although it is that, but for what both makes sense and feeds their yearnings for meaningful subjective relationship with the divine at this transitional stage in their life. It is a dialogical process which grows in breadth and depth as knowledge and experience increase, one ideally open to renewal and re-evaluation as new experience encounters new knowledge. This is the definition of practical theology which Veling describes as wanting to

> keep our relationship with the world open, so that we are never quite 'done' with things; rather always undoing and redoing them, so that we can keep the 'doing' happening, passionate, keen, expectant – never satisfied, never quite finished.[16]

---

[15]   *Roots* worship and learning resource material for the whole church based on the *Revised Common Lectionary* is supported by Churches Together in Britain and Ireland.

[16]   Veling, *Practical Theology*, p. 7.

In the spirit of the prayer, 'Thy Kingdom come', he claims for practical theology a 'passion for what could yet be, what is still in-the-making, in process, not yet, still coming'.

When in my analysis of the girls' responses, I asked of the interview texts 'Who is God for the girls?', I was not doing it in isolation from their relational experience of God; in fact it was hard to separate out their God-talk from their relational talk, and relationality and caring underlay all that they said. However, for the sake of clarity, and to emphasise their facility at doing theology, I am attempting to let their God-talk be heard in and for itself, as in the two discrete passages of theological reflection I have selected for more detailed analysis. The contents of each subsequent section in this chapter will be interlinked.

1. Talk about God

The God whom they knew and sought was unequivocally 'on their side'. They expressed a desire for divine consistency, manifest in love, in equal care regardless of gender or wealth, in justice, and for Martha in the balancing of life and death (when one person has died another is born). God lived in enigmatic personhood in Godself, but was trustworthy, active on behalf of humankind in the natural world, which was the place of encounter and the making of relationship. Karen perceived the contextuality of belief, the dissonance between different views according to who is doing the believing, and the ambiguity of her own situation at a formative life stage:

> God can be something that you're just brought up to believe in
> and then there could be something else which people would say is God
> but I think that God is something else
> because that's what everybody seems to think,
> and it's like having two things,
> one that you've been taught to believe and one that you do.

Although, according to Fowler, anthropomorphic images can be expected at Stage Two ('mythic-literal faith'), I found no evidence to support his claim. The two girls who did use anthropomorphic images[17] also described experiences of God as a living presence, so did not betray the limitations of concrete operational thinking. In his work on the 'theologizing' of children, Büttner refers to research which reveals that 'the childlike tendency to express theological content by anthropomorphic images is not that childlike but absolutely a dominant feature of human thinking in general'.[18] We should not take one linguistic feature alone

---

[17]   'A big cuddly man in heaven wearing a brown robe', Amber contributed humorously, and Holly's 'wearing a white ... not a dress, like an overshawl' was, we decided together, how Jesus is portrayed in pictures, and God is being imaged in that way.

[18]   Büttner, 'How Theologizing with Children can Work', p. 138.

out of its wider context to determine (im)maturity of faith. The ability of most of the girls to operate on different levels, literal and metaphorical, mirrored the combination of embodied and abstract thinking of most adults.

2. Talk about God, the Creator

Creation good The starting point of much of the girls' theological reflection was that God is creator of a world, which is:

> dead good,
> because it's like this big massive thing like God made …
> it's just a wonder how someone could just make that. (Rosie)

Mary was deeply in tune with the natural world and found evidence of 'God's wonder through creation and nature'; so of the 2004 tsunami, she said:

> if you put aside all the bad things that come from that,
> the amazing thing is the earthquake and the massive wave,
> just how majestic is that to show God's power!

A picture of earth seen from the moon's surface evoked a sense of wonder at God's creation, for Ruth putting the earth and human life in perspective:

> I think … how small earth is compared with everything else!
> It makes me think of how powerful God is to make the world,
> and every single thing in it.

This sense of wonder at the world and the power God must have was also reflected by Julie, who attributed to God a pride in creation, generating a 'good feeling'. Mary, looking at a picture of a peaceful lake scene, felt herself swimming in the water as she did from a holiday beach in Wales:

> it's massive and I swim around and it really shows God's wonders
> and it's peaceful with the mountains,
> seeing the waves just move in and out,
> it's just really, it gets to me a lot
> 'cos I find it a lot easier to see God's wonder
> through creation and nature.

Knowing God through creation thus strengthened her faith. Mary had been baptised as a believer, and used similar language of her baptism.

As Lucy, several girls affirmed that God was in 'control' in a variety of contexts, that is, God had a purpose for creation and a plan for humankind. How girls understood the operation of that control differed: some credited God with direct action to manipulate people's behaviour, others were more aware that God does not dictate every detail of the execution of the plan, but allows us the freedom to seek a way to fulfil it by learning to be in tune with God. Ruth recognised that:

> in some ways
> I think he is (in control of the world),
> he knows exactly what we're gonna do,

but then, realising that God's foreknowledge does not always determine positive outcomes, she qualified it by saying:

> he's not, like, controlling us,
> thinking you must do this now,
> like he tells you what to do,

but that if we are in tune with God through prayer, as she tried to be, we would act as God guides us. Julie on the other hand spoke of a more direct divine control:

> God is someone who controls the day and the night
> and all the birds and everything in it
> and he controls you.

That control of our actions is more simplistic and lacks the subtlety Ruth comprehended. It is God's purpose to improve human life on earth so, for Julie again, God's control of Jesus' life was to direct him to use his skills for other people's benefit, to improve their lives materially ('to make better houses for people') and spiritually (to 'help people and die for them and heal them').

Several girls recognised the 'independence' of the natural world while still being filled with the presence of God. Beneath Ruth's hesitancy of speech was a search for God's immanence through a unification of scientific theory and theological understanding:

> I've had this feeling before about creation.
> I wonder if the Bible and the scientists' theory and all the different theories,
> I think they all seem to make sense in different ways to me
> but God is still in there somewhere
> and he's the cause of whatever's happening,
> so ... they're never going to know what really happened,
> so I just know that God is in there somewhere.

There are resonances here with Cunningham as he differentiates between the world in general to which God gives life, and humankind within that created order.[19] Julie has not yet understood, as other girls seem to be on the way to, that living according to their created nature means that everything is 'returning the gift to God ... of its own accord, not as the result of divine pulling of various strings ... the created order glorifies God by being what it most fully is'. Cunningham separates out human life from the rest of the created order since 'although created to come into communion with God humankind has also been given the choice to turn away, so like a parent who does not fully "control" a child, builds into the relationship the means by which the child may return and be taken up once again into the divine life'. In very different ways, two girls expressed a similar thought. Martha understood life's difficulties as opportunities to

> grow stronger so they'll believe in God stronger
> then that's how they become good Christians
> and follow the teachings of Jesus,

while for Rosie, God was no interventionist. Using her relationship with her parents as a model, she said that 'it's like with God, he'll always be there and always stand by you like a parent with everybody ... and like he doesn't interfere when you don't want'.

Creation flawed Reflection on God as creator was not naïve or sentimental. Although the natural world testifies to God's creative beneficence, it contains inherent violence, in which sometimes humans are caught up. It is because God has created a world that is good that harm caused, naturally and through human agency, is a problem. This is true for other girls who expressed unease or dis-ease at human fallenness: injustice, enmity, inequality on the basis of wealth or gender were a source of ambiguity in the created order.

Most girls introduced the flawed nature of creation, drawing on tragedies affecting their immediate families and the global community, with both human and natural causes. Memorable natural disasters and acts of terrorism, national and international, had occurred in the months immediately prior to the interviews, one in close proximity to the church attended by Julie and Martha. The girls' reflections fell into two main categories which echoed standard theological interpretations.[20]

1. The cause of natural disasters is a mystery known only to God whose omnipotence they did not question. Many concurred with Lucy that we can trust that God has reasons for allowing them to happen. Only one girl suggested God caused disasters and that was not unqualified; this, therefore, is no tyrannical deity. Omnipotence was governed by the character of God, following in love the divinely ordained moral order which from the

---

[19] Cunningham, *These Three are One*, p. 75.

[20] As outlined, for example, in Alan Richardson and John Bowden (eds), *A New Dictionary of Christian Theology* (London, 1983), pp. 193–6.

perspective of eternity works for human good. Martha believed we are all held in God's loving plan, that although *we* grieve, those who have died are in a better place. Lucy was alone in suggesting God's testing, but others tentatively suggested that divine punishment might be operative, this time for disbelief as well as sin, but natural disasters could birth trust in God's care. None of this was said without a struggle, recognising the depth of human suffering. Rosie, facing the same issue, saw the punishment theory as problematic since the equal distribution of the effects of disaster was unjust: 'there'd be good people he'd be punishing as well'. Having weighed up different views, each girl was content to accept ambiguity here, all placing absolute trust in both God's benevolent purposes, and presence within the suffering.

2. Several girls also explored an alternative view, based on God's chosen self-limitation in relation to the created world. Natural forces follow their own laws, which are neutral. God does not surrender all power, but is present alongside those who suffer and those who are bringing aid. Many saw the hand of God in the response, and the reconstruction in devastated areas, so Mary said 'I really believe he's in the middle of it and he's with all those charities', and Holly, 'he looks after the families of those who've died'. God was 'just waiting for someone to ask him for help'. We are never outside God's plan and purpose:

> you've really got (to) put your total faith in God
> that you know you're either going to get saved from the situation
> or if not then that's what God planned
> and, emm, however hard it is to take in. (Michelle)

God cannot prevent disasters caused by human will. Although recognising that suicide bombers, for example, must be 'brainwashed', Martha did not let that suffice as an excuse; people retain moral responsibility for their actions. Here, too, God has ultimate power; to account for the non-proliferation of acts of terrorism and natural disasters, Julie, like Lucy, suggested God places a temporal boundary round such acts.

These views, combining aspects of moral theory and process theology in their original responses to the 'problem of evil' were found across the spectrum of theological position of the churches represented. They indicated clearly both a desire and a facility the girls had to make sense of the world's complexity in theological terms, and to do so in a way that preserved relationship with God and with humankind. An ethic of care, divine and human, was central.

Two girls, both from the same evangelical church, spoke of evil in dualistic terms, as the devil's work. Neither wanted to develop her thinking, but chose instead to talk further about personal sin. Bryony explained that the idea was not her own: 'I think I read (it) in a book'.

3. Talk about God, Transcendent and Immanent

God's transcendence, which permeates much of the girls' awareness of God's creative activity, is not perceived as remoteness, but as qualitatively 'other' while still in relation to humankind. Otherness cannot be absolute or there can be no mutual self-discovery. The girls' sense of transcendence has more in common with a biblical understanding than a philosophical one deriving from Hellenistic thought forms which has characterised much systematic theology across the ages, by which 'he is sundered from the natural universe by the transcendent exclusivity of his being'.[21] There is broad concurrence between the girls' ideas and theological thinking that rejects the two substances theory opposing God and creation; their ability to know God is in connection, formed through divine creative agency.[22] Although Bryony struggled to acknowledge this, most saw humankind made in God's image. Keller argues that discourse of exclusivity, separation and individualism is inherently gendered. Transcendence as otherness of being is exposed as projecting the male ego, while the female desire for intimacy strives towards connectedness reflected in the relational interplay within the Trinity. Tanner, drawing on both Schleiermacher and Rahner, argues that human God-consciousness is dependent on divine initiative. In their different ways, both Tanner and Keller agree that the desire for 'loving intimacy' lies at the heart of the relationship between God and the created order, where transcendence and immanence converge: 'predicates affirming the free transcendence of God should be used to characterise God in the very same respects as predicates affirming loving intimacy'.[23]

Supporting Keller's argument above, it is through such relational awareness that several girls spoke of God's transcendence, awareness that was rooted in experience which could sometimes be described as mystical. This is evident in Karen's heightened self-awareness in the presence of 'something else', in Amber's sense of 'working presence' and insights through experiences seemingly mystical in nature, and Ruth's awed tone as she spoke of the wonder of her own salvation through divine kenosis enacted by the one experienced relationally 'like your best friend sat next to you'. Although this relational awareness is an 'experienced reality', it is rooted in an 'otherness' which human language and thought form struggle to articulate – at any age. These features of spiritual development are supported by Hay, Reich and Utsch,[24] alluding to Watts' helpful

---

[21]   Catherine Keller, *From a Broken Web: Separation, Sexism and Self* (Boston, 1986), p. 37.

[22]   For example, Kathryn Tanner, *God and Creation in Christian Theology* (Oxford, 1988).

[23]   Ibid., p. 80.

[24]   David Hay, K. Helmut Reich and Michael Utsch, 'Spiritual Development: Intersections and Divergences with Religious Development', in Roehlkepartain, *The Handbook of Spiritual Development*, pp. 46–55.

distinction between Implicational and Propositional systems of cognition. Watts argues for a better appreciation of the former, in which meanings are felt before any codification: 'it is not unusual for important but difficult insights to be glimpsed initially at the level of inarticulate meanings before being recoded in a propositional form capable of articulation'.[25] He is sensitive here to the development of religious consciousness, 'especially in the apophatic tradition of the unknowability of the transcendent God'. The danger for the girls is that the environment offers rigid propositional formulae for interpretation of experience. Hay, Reich and Utsch recognise that girls/boys draw on worlds of imagination and of fantasy in bringing to speech their spiritual experiences, and acknowledge the harm that can be done to spiritual growth when adults fail to take it seriously either by not entering sufficiently into their world or arguing with it from an adult perspective. In analysis of the conversations with Lucy (Chapter 5) and with Rosie (Chapter 7), I explore how they handle relational awareness of transcendent reality on their own terms.

4. Talk about the 'Godness' of God: One or Three?

Many of the girls used language of both transcendence and immanence, and of spiritual presence, which suggested in their God-talk a rounded trinitarian awareness. Fiddes, citing the difficulty and limitations of communicating the doctrine in church teaching, acknowledges the popular view that the 'doctrine of the Trinity is a highly speculative topic, detached from everyday experience and best avoided by those whose concerns are largely pastoral'.[26] However, Amber responded to my question about her imaging of and relationship with God by setting out a profusion of thoughts and experiences of the three persons of the Trinity:

> sometimes when I think of the Holy Spirit
> I think of it just more like a mist,
> like a working presence without hands emm
> like that can comfort you,
> like has all the senses but just like a mist, do you know what I mean?
> like a presence, sort of thing, that like can hold you,
> like gives you feelings like a person.
> And then emm, the Father, God,
> I think of em just like a big man …
> like one person up in heaven with his arms out,
> he's really lovely and everything …
> And Jesus, I think of him as Son of God, obviously
> and as a person who's just, like, did good works,
> it's a good idea to follow him.

---

[25]   Fraser Watts, *Theology and Psychology* (Abingdon, 2002), p. 87.
[26]   Fiddes, *Participating in God*, p. 13.

Amber recognised the individual 'functions' and 'persons' of the Trinity, the Father of the incarnate Son who is still present in the Spirit who comforts and supports. She spoke expansively of experiences of the Spirit which appeared to be synonymous with experiences of God. Although there was some confusion between Father and Son (the God who came to earth 'was not necessarily a "he"'), she was also at pains to explore how God as creator is beyond human imagining, defying our understanding: in the end language was inadequate to make her point clearly so she described God in the language of 'excedence' or dissimilarity: 'God can think about things more; we can't see all the molecules, like, or speak in long words'. Likewise when Julie spoke of God as 'a very powerful man' this is more than a figure of speech as she later made a clear distinction between the human Jesus and God who is with us 'mentally'.

As adults, we are not always clear in our God-talk whether we are speaking of God as one person or three-in-one, the father/creator or the one whom we know simultaneously in creation, redemption and ongoing presence. We assume some awareness that when we speak of God we understand the complete story of God's historic and perpetual out-going in creation, God's perpetual self-giving in the historical life, death and resurrection of Jesus the Christ, and God's perpetual presence by the power of the Spirit bringing all things to consummation; that is, of God's triune life and of perichoresis between the divine 'persons'. McIntosh comments that not 'all Christian spirituality is inevitably self-consciously trinitarian, nor (must) all Christian spirituality be fully analyzable into trinitarian terms'.[27] For Cunningham, the 'persons' cannot be differentiated since 'God is *wholly constituted* by relationality ... Three participate in one another in a profound way, undermining any attempt to understand them independently of one another'.[28] Yet teaching in churches employs many pictorial devices to teach three-in-oneness, of which water/ice/steam, a triangle and cloverleaf are examples. Such talk fails, Fiddes believes, because they are 'attempts to *observe* God', rather than focus on the experience of relating to God, and, following his thesis, participating in God.[29] In the girls' God-talk, I found evidence of relational experience: I did not find a clear delineation of three distinct roles nor a full representation of the relationship between the divine persons. Cunningham notes how relationality has now 'achieved the greatest amount of consensus among scholars'.[30] Rosie said: 'I don't think of him as father, son and holy spirit or like that, I just think of him being just there', (she paused) 'he's just *there*!'.

---

[27]   McIntosh, 'Trinitarian Perspectives on Christian Spirituality', in Holder, *The Blackwell Companion to Christian Spirituality*, p. 179.

[28]   Cunningham, *These Three are One*, p. 165. Author's italics.

[29]   Fiddes, *Participating in God*, p. 12. Author's italics.

[30]   Cunningham, *These Three are One*, p. 25.

5. Talk about God: Where does Jesus Fit?

Amber's summary of Jesus in the previous section is indicative of a less assured view of Jesus, and leads me to explore the other girls' discussion of him. They placed more emphasis on his divine-human nature, the 'Second person of the Trinity incarnate ... through whom we come to the Trinitarian God',[31] than on soteriology. Although traditional understandings of the salvific work of Christ were in evidence, more prominent was a relational understanding with both the Jesus of the gospels and the Jesus of contemporary experience, which although largely individualistic, had some resonances with strands of feminist theology which understand Christ not as a heavenly manifestation of the man Jesus but as the community of those who, with Christ, bring healing and liberation.[32]

Such movement between the historical and contemporary figures is evident in the following exchange: Michelle struggled to describe how she saw Jesus, and how he relates to God, but in the end said: 'it's this huge thing that God sends to show us the way to live ... and it's amazing to think how, emm, one man could do so much difference'. Mary followed this by speaking of her personal relationship with him, and this in human metaphor. He was like a brother:

> you know, he's been through these situations and emm
> yeah, it's like hanging out with a brother and your dad, you know,
> your dad's always the amazing person
> who you'll look up to and protect you and things
> and then a brother's like someone emm
> you can like talk to and have a laugh with
> and he'll support you and things
> so yeah I see Jesus like that.

For Michelle, though, Jesus could not be a dad because she 'never had a strong father figure'. His maleness may have been a barrier to empathy. Her experience gives rise to a similar question to that of Ruether: 'can a male saviour save women?'.[33]

Jesus' identity and function within the Trinitarian relationship often coalesced with those of the Father and Spirit. Ruth saw God as initiating the work of Jesus: using language of kenosis, God was

> prepared to give it all up and that's the sacrifice ...
> I mean that he's king of all the earth

---

[31]   Maurice Wiles, 'Christianity without Incarnation?', in John Hick (ed.), *The Myth of God Incarnate* (London, 1977), p. 9.

[32]   As, for example, Rita Nakashima Brock, *Journeys by Heart: A Christology of Erotic Power* (New York, 1988), p. 52.

[33]   Ruether, *Sexism and God-talk*, chapter 5.

and he could come down in such a humble way,
bring himself to such a low level and be born in a stable.

She made no reference to Jesus' ministry. While she echoed biblical and doctrinal language which included by implication the pre-existence of the Son, Julie understood the meaning of the incarnation in relational terms. She saw Jesus, God's creation through human conception, both as the icon of God to us, and as the icon of humanity to God sharing a knowledge which enables God to empathise with humankind:

God only created Jesus so that
he could come to this world and see what it's like
and tell God how it is …
he made a man, a clever man and that a hard-working one
to make houses far better for people …
and Jesus, he's this one that he would be like,
he would be powerful but not as powerful as God
so he'd come to this world and help people and die for them and heal them,
do things for them.
God would do the same but much more for people.

Here, Jesus is the 'parable of God',[34] in whose incarnation 'the self-giving, the becoming-man, the suffering-love were not just additions to the divine experience … In becoming man, God revealed the meaning of what it is to be God'.[35] Martha continued the theme picked up by Julie: 'Jesus was like a symbol of how it was, like, before your eyes, like …' (Julie completed her sentence) 'to see him'.

Julie's insights into the humanity of Jesus had been deepened by her dramatic writing and performance. By this she had identified with Jesus' power and strength in healing, and his emotions as he approached the passion; taking the part of Jesus in her own play, she felt his sadness when she said:

It was like my last meal,
and I knew I was going to, like, be put on the cross
but (I was) kind of happy
because I knew like that I was going to be taken away,
that my life was going to be put back and
I was going to be taken away from the cross.

---

[34] Sallie McFague, *Metaphorical Theology: Models of God in Religious Language* (Philadelphia, 1982), p. 165.

[35] A.M. Ramsey, *God, Christ and the World: A Study in Contemporary Theology* (London, 1969), in D.F. Ford and M. Higton (eds), *Jesus* (Oxford, 2002), p. 505.

Through this personal experience, the Jesus of history became also the Christ of faith. The marked difference in understanding of the person of Christ between Julie and Martha, and girls from white British backgrounds may be related to their African heritage. Their ideas share resonances with African feminist Christology as identified by Oduyoye: Christ as liberator brings freedom from oppression by his sacrificial life and death. For both girls, he liberates from poverty and sickness, in this life and in death.[36] That Christology 'takes the form of appropriating the Christ-event, seeing oneself in the daily drama that Jesus lives from cradle to cross and beyond'[37] may account for Julie's depth of insight into his self-understanding evident in her dramatic presentation of Jesus' life. The nuance may be African but feminist theology more broadly sees 'through the dynamic life of the risen Christ, the varied beings of the cosmos gather into one living whole in God, in which all that is good, beautiful and true is nurtured and grows in the unending life of God'.[38]

For all girls, God is the originator of the work of Jesus, but they showed mixed understandings of the connection between Christ and the healing of flawed humanity. There was limited understanding of atonement as the work of Christ: the two who introduced the doctrine did so in very different ways. For Ruth, it was instrumental in achieving her personal salvation, Christ's sacrifice being the price God paid for her sin, as Stott says: 'the righteous loving Father humbled himself to become in and through his only Son flesh, sin and cursed for us, in order to redeem us without compromising his own character'.[39] Although a formulaic evangelical response, Ruth was deeply moved by the personal affirmation she received in the condescension of the Son. It was

> absolutely amazing that he could come down
> and die for us on the cross ...
> wow! God would do that for me!

Rosie's use of substitutionary atonement theory was not personal but a resource she drew on in wrestling with the problem of suffering. Proof that God, who loves all people, is innocent of causing human suffering is found for her when 'in the bible (it says) that he killed his own son for all the bad things that we did, so he must be like that (loving), otherwise he wouldn't have killed his own son for all the people'.

We should not expect of girls, any more than of most adults, more than a broad understanding of the sweep of God's story, but when we intentionally nurture their

---

[36] Mercy Amba Oduyoye, *Introducing African Women's Theology* (Sheffield, 2001), p. 55.

[37] Ibid., p. 64.

[38] Patricia Wilson-Kastner, *Faith, Feminism and the Christ* (Philadelphia, 1983), p. 155.

[39] J.R.W. Stott, *The Cross of Christ*, 2nd edn (Leicester, 1989), in Ford and Higton, *Jesus*, p. 436.

faith through regular exposure to the gospel narratives, we should take note of what is held in the memory and integrated with their experience.

6. Talk about God: The Spirit

Of the persons of the Trinity, the Spirit's nature and role are on the one hand the most elusive, on the other the most deeply powerful. Whereas the Father and Son can at least be identified metaphorically through their relationship to one another, the Spirit, as Fiddes and others suggest, appears as 'God anonymous, God incognito'; the 'idea of the Holy Spirit (is) curiously hard to pin down',[40] to which centuries of doctrinal disagreement bear witness. In biblical writings, the metaphor of breath or wind is used to express the experience of God's activity both within and beyond people. However, without a more substantial metaphor, the girls struggled: where Bryony regarded its invisibility as a cause of its being forgotten, Michelle adopted the cross she wore as the symbol of its encompassing presence.

The Spirit's activity in human life is summarised by Fiddes as the 'living presence' in our lives for which we may use the language of being 'filled',[41] inseparable from the image of being taken into the flow of the Sprit. This is evident in the girls' direct 'spirit talk'. Six girls, from two of the churches, described their personal experiences of the Spirit; they also saw it at work more widely in community.

Personal experiences of the Spirit were associated with special events, such as youth weekends or evangelistic services. Manifestations were similar to those identified with a charismatic 'baptism in the spirit'.[42] For two of the girls, it was associated with their baptism as believers. The girls who described such experiences showed no cognitive awareness of theological or credal formulations: indeed, Ruth initially said she'd 'never really been told much about the Holy Spirit'. Nevertheless it is an expected manifestation of faith in two of the churches, and the girls recorded a rich experiential knowledge. Common to all were physical feelings (washing inside and out, filling, breathing fresh air) and images connected with the elements (mist, oxygen), temperature (both warm and cool), emotions (happy, excited), and a heightened awareness of bodily sensation. Observable manifestations involved loss of bodily control (shaking, falling, jumping, uncontrollable laughter or tears); more private were receiving visions, and developing skin reactions. Both of the girls who had been baptised testified to an accompanying experience where feelings of fear were set aside by the Spirit's surrounding presence which was 'overwhelming' but comforting with 'the Holy Spirit there just around you'. The 'work' of the Spirit in the recipient was seen by all girls as deeply personal, in comforting and holding. Water baptism, following conversion, was followed by measurable change in the

---

[40]   Fiddes, *Participating in God*, pp. 252–3.
[41]   Ibid., p. 257.
[42]   Michael Green, *I Believe in The Holy Spirit*, rev. edn (Eastbourne, 2004), chapter 8.

present: 'My mum saw me being happy', 'God's helping me a lot more' (to make faith public where she used to hide it), and for future direction: 'I just want to let God decide' (about a career pathway). Although other girls did see some change in their lives after an experience of the Spirit, it was largely restricted to imprecise desires ('I want to do things for God and Jesus') and personal evangelism, setting an example to other people.

For girls who did not share these personal or charismatic experiences, the Spirit was everywhere, caring, helping, giving courage and perseverance in distress, associated with the caring supportive nature of God. This was most clearly expressed by Martha for whom the Spirit was 'everywhere, like in the room, he's looking after everyone, even the poor, he's still with them'. It was the Spirit that gave them strength and courage to persevere in distress: it was therefore life-giving, but faith was necessary to access it, so it was operative in the context of relationship with God. Martha understood faith to be rooted in the earthly physicality of Jesus in whom God was present by the Spirit, but whom we can no longer see but 'hear (him) in your heart'.

Discussion of the Spirit gave Karen the opportunity to locate the feminine in God. It may have been the contrast between the evidence of masculine power in her Roman Catholic school and the inclusive practice in her Protestant church that drove her to seek it: the comment that 'the priests are all men', led her to make a connection with an earlier part of the conversation: 'going back to what we said earlier ... I always think of the Holy Spirit as female', supporting her argument by noting the interdependence of men and women, implying that the mutual interdependence of the creatures must reflect a complementary plurality within the creator.[43]

Girls' Styles of Faithing

It is clear that the girls' conceptualisation of God, although often couched in the propositional language of their context, was based on and filtered through their own relationship with God, characterised by varying degrees of closeness. The features of their contexts, home, school, church, peer group and wider society, encountered at the liminal place they inhabit, result in particular styles of faithing which I have identified from their conversation, common strategies to create safe spaces to live, and to test out new ideas. In order to bring out the complexity and nuance of these styles, I have identified categories, which again have close internal connection.

---

[43] Examples of the Spirit's femaleness in theological writings can be found in Elizabeth Johnson, *She Who Is: The Mystery of God in Feminist Discourse* (New York: Crossroad, 1992), p. 130.

1. Safe Faithing

I have shown how some girls expressed their vulnerability, both as girls and as Christians. Consistent with this, I identified as a feature of every girl's conversation the desire for safety in and protection by God, in line with Tamminen's findings[44] that God represents sanctuary, because God knows, understands and protects. Turning to God in prayer, the girls sought and felt God's presence, and drew upon or rested in a power beyond themselves which would comfort, protect and shelter at least for a while. This would often happen, called for or unbidden, in some special 'place'; it was a happening both in space (a small room, reminiscent of the small curtained off 'holy place' of tabernacle and temple) and time (an experience), therefore a relating contained in and by intimate space. Because God is known as creator who controls the world and orders it according to a purpose based on justice for and love of all people, God could be trusted as the girls' protector.

The creator cares   Creation is not for its own or for God's sake alone, but 'for us to live in'. Creation's wonder is completed in the intimate knowledge and care of the creator for the created: Ruth completed her creation eulogy by saying 'He knows everything about us all, which is so amazing', and Suzanne '(he) made things and made us and knows everything'.

To be in relationship with God is to be treasured as special: this helps build a sense of self-worth. Mary named the assurance she received from others that she is special to God as a source of her own faith, which supported her through the many difficulties she encountered, not least being a Christian. She remembered when she was aged seven, someone said to her: '"Mary, I want you to be prayed for because you're special", and I became a Christian that night'. This assurance remained with her, but needed regular reinforcement in the face of recurrent self-doubt:

> When people say how special you are to God
> and things like that, it makes you feel,
> you know, wow,
> it just makes that (vulnerability) go away.

God protects   Several other girls showed a lack of self-esteem, although none but Mary and Michelle spoke explicitly of feeling vulnerable: others implied it in expressing their need for protection. Amber's extrovert nature revealed a person of volatile emotions, highly imaginative, and locating authority in external role models. She spoke of the Spirit holding her 'without hands' and giving her 'feelings like a person' meaning self-esteem and wholeness, the equivalent of being special that Mary and Michelle longed to feel. This was 'emotionally comforting'. She

---

[44]   K. Tamminen, 'Gender Differences in Religiosity in Children and Adolescents', in L.J. Francis, W.K. Kay and W.S. Campbell (eds), *Research in Religious Education* (Leominster, 1996), p. 174.

had a strong sense of the power of evil and 'visions' which scared her, so that, influenced by an older girl, Amber had developed a ritual by which she clothed herself in the 'armour of God' to give her protection. As with her physical reaction to spiritual experience above, Amber's sensitivity suggested some connection with the ecstatic experiences recorded of girls and young women in history.[45] There was similar emotional intensity in Mary's reaction to the pressure she felt at school, but her strategy for protection was either to listen to or to create music, when 'I can feel God a lot closer to me'. Tamminen found that experiences of God's closeness were more frequent and positive for girls at puberty in situations of fear and loneliness, and they were 'more positive about the possibility of experiencing God's presence in different situations'.[46] These three girls expressed by far the most intensely emotional responses both to the hostility in their environment from which they needed protection, and the support they received in different ways from God.

Others did not own to the same level of insecurity and so relied less on emotional reassurance, but that did not lessen their need to know that God was with them, valuing them for themselves. Karen's daily ritual of talking to God was one example, together with her experience of standing encased in a beam of sunlight and feeling 'something else was there'. That it is safe to trust God was borne out in their own experiences and in the testimony of others; this enabled their faith to grow.

> When I was quite young
> all I knew about was God created the world
> and I knew that he was just powerful
> but I didn't know the things that he could do ...
> but when I've been like in church and listening to Martin (the minister)
> and I feel like God is a very powerful man
> and I feel, I respect him a great deal,
> and feel like I believe in him and I trust him to do things for me. (Julie)

> When you grow up you know more and then, like,
> God comes when you're really in trouble
> and if you really like believe in him,
> you know that he's there,
> but you've got to have faith in him,
> you know that he's there. (Martha)

In the face of evil, the questions arose as to whether God gives preferential protection to 'good' people and people of faith, and whether faith itself protects.

---

[45]   See, for example, Susan Hardman Moore, '"Such Perfecting of Praise Out of the Mouth of a Babe": Sarah Wight as Child Prophet', in Diana Wood (ed.), *The Church and Childhood* (Oxford, 1994).

[46]   Tamminen, *Religious Development*, p. 63.

Both Martha and Mary suggested this operates in disasters; Ruth denied this, voicing the struggle faith has with a God of love in the face of loss. Victoria told of her father being mugged and her prayer for him for protection from further danger; Julie was sure God kept her friends safe when the London bombs exploded in 2005, and her prayer for further protection was that others would be deterred from such acts of terrorism in the future. Some found resolution in the belief that God's presence with us is for eternity and therein lay safety.

2. Empathic Faithing

Empathy which arises from being heard and understood by those who recognise shared experience is a significant feature of girls' faithing. People can be God's agents for safety because they too have experienced similar issues to those of the girls. Some mothers are looked to for empathy over the physical and emotional side of adolescence as when Bethan spoke of valuing her mother as a gift from God because 'she's been in the situation of developing and things like I have ... I think that's a gift God's given to help us'. Support from other Christians can help girls remain true to their faith and stand against antagonism or indifference from a secular society, especially in school which can be an exposed and unprotected place for Christian girls. For Mary, 'talking with other Christians really helps cos like they understand what we're going through'. For Georgia, being at church in an intergenerational context with 'everybody like 50 or, er, a young age ... everybody knows you', helped put life back into perspective.

That God, too, can empathise, contributes significantly to the safety the girls find in their faithing. The closeness of their relationship is based on God, too, sharing their experiences. For Martha, this was a key purpose of the incarnation, where God learned empathy with our losses through the risk of becoming human: in response to a picture of an adult holding a child's hand, she said:

> I'd like to say like, God and Jesus, cos Jesus as a baby ...
> it's like letting go, to let go of him to go to Mary,
> he's saying I'll see you later
> but then, but when he got crucified it's like hard to let go
> cos he knows what's going to happen in the end
> but then he doesn't really mind
> until he finds out eventually what the end is like;
> he's letting go
> but they know they're going to meet up in the end.

Mary explained the importance of Jesus' role:

> it means that we can relate a lot more to Jesus
> because he walked on the earth
> like we do.

Michelle believed so strongly in God's capacity for empathy that she defended God:

> some Christians that I've known
> have said that they don't know
> he could have gone through what they've been through,
> because what is happening to them is so big
> but it says in, emm, the gospels and everything
> that he has been through it
> and that he knows what you're going through.

The image of the pioneer as in Hebrews 2.17–18 fits the model girls were seeking in their desire for empathy. Ruth sees God empathising as a friend:

> You've got your best friend sat next to you
> but you're not, like, talking to them
> you just understand each other,
> you know everything about them,
> they know exactly what I'm thinking.

She was able to relate to God as she would with her closest friend, with the empathy of identification. Although there is a suggestion here of the 'easy empathy for one's own kind' against which McFague warns in the use of the friendship model, there is also a sense of the 'mutuality, maturity, cooperation (and) reciprocity' which for her makes the metaphor of friendship 'ideally suited to express certain dimensions of a mature relationship with God', that is, it exceeds the 'hierarchy, subordinationism and patriarchal authoritarianism' of parental imagery.[47] In the light of the importance of peer relationships to the girls, to see God as friend, something Slee found among women, too, has a significance which I explore further below.[48]

Did gendered language for God affect empathy? For Rosie this was an important question. Empathy was located in the qualities of the Godhead, beyond the limitations of an identity structured according to gender traits. So, to empathise with all humankind, God must be beyond gender. Despite the temptation to think of God as female, 'because like, women give birth and bring new life', she saw any gender attribution as excluding the one not chosen:

> if it was a woman
> then people would think that cos she's a woman
> she wouldn't know things that men know
> and if she's a man

---

[47]   McFague, *Metaphorical Theology*, pp. 179, 177.
[48]   Slee, *Women's Faith Development*, p. 140.

then she wouldn't know what … women know
but I think it's more likely to be a 'something'
rather than 'he' or 'she'.

Although all girls used the masculine pronoun, God was 'not necessarily a he' for Amber. Neither girl wanted to define or relate to God as female, but both resisted maleness as the norm for speaking of God. They were striving after a similar idea pursued by Gerstenberger in his study of the development of maleness as the dominant gender attribute of YHWH; exploring traces he finds in the O.T. of a female co-deity in pre-exilic Israel and Judah, he affirms the figurative nature of gendered language for God since deity is not circumscribed by language: 'Whatever the deity's gender, its powers surpass human understanding and make it able to appropriate the functions of both genders'.[49] For Rosie, this language does not in any way diminish the 'personhood' of the God who cares for her, but emphasises the fundamental need to be able to relate to God unhindered by gendered imagery; drawing on McFague again, who sees the root-metaphor of Christianity as relationship, Rosie can be understood as rejecting models which describe God at the expense of potential 'images of a relationship'.[50]

Empathic faithing is significant to girls who often feel a lack of understanding on the part of others, in church and in their social contexts. On Kegan's model, girls at the Interpersonal stage will be accommodating their own views to those of others to maintain relationship, and there is evidence of this, but also in some cases a desire for affirmation of the individual identity construction. For Hess, empathy is one dimension of caring which enables girls and women to grow in faith; she bases her advocacy of 'conversational education' on the empowering of girls and women by leaders exercising 'passion, empathy and wisdom'.[51] A dimension of conversational education is honest dealing with God, facing God with the questions thrown up both by the bible and by life; what Hess does not develop is the 'Godward' side of the dialogue, or, in confining her approach to the cognitive, the need girls have for relationship at the affective level.[52]

3. Daunting Faithing

The girls in my study had all made a conscious decision to continue coming to church. They all came from Christian families and had been brought to church in the past by parents or grandparents, but had freedom to choose, as Karen said: 'I wouldn't even be forced to come any more because I'd be allowed to stay at home'. Rosie still chose to come but said, 'I don't know when I'm older whether

---

[49]   Erhard H. Gerstenberger, *Yahweh the Patriarch: Ancient Images of God and Feminist Theology* (Minneapolis, 1996), p. 5.

[50]   McFague, *Metaphorical Theology*, p. 166.

[51]   Hess, *Caretakers of Our Common House*, p. 225.

[52]   Ibid., pp. 209–12.

I'm going to go to church'. In a variety of ways, each girl 'owned' her Christian faith, choosing for herself to take up the mantle of discipleship. Bethan chose to go to the weeknight bible study at a different church, and enter into all that that entailed in terms of being taught to follow a Christian lifestyle, while still worshipping with her family at a church of another denomination on Sundays.

In the harsh world of secondary school, it is a brave thing for any young person to admit to an active Christian faith, although there is a higher church attendance rate among girls. Its acceptability as a pastime for girls and thereby its association with traditional female identity may, however, make it harder for girls who are trying to break out of old-fashioned female stereotypes. It is not 'cool', indeed it is counter-cultural to attend church.

Three of the girls I interviewed attended church schools, two Roman Catholic, one Church of England. Although we might expect that there it would be more acceptable to practise a Christian faith, this was not uniformly so. Each of the three named a particular spiritual experience that had happened in a school context (an assembly, a retreat and a church visit), but two of the girls also experienced antagonism from their peers.

Because they encountered hostility, girls needed courage to hold to their faith. They must decide if or how far to make their allegiance public. For those who attend a more confessedly evangelical church, it is an expected dimension of their discipleship to make it known they are Christian and to influence others, or actively to evangelise. This took different forms among the girls. Bethan had no other Christians in her RE class so she kept putting up her hand to answer questions 'to show people my faith'. Bryony repeatedly asked a friend to come with her to church. Amber openly told her friends of her faith as an essential mark of her Christian discipleship, which laid on her the responsibility for their eternal destiny. Recounting a lesson containing that message, Amber concluded:

> You got to tell non-Christians.
> You got to tell people.

Michelle and Amber both invited school friends to their respective baptismal services, Michelle admitting the hostility she and Mary were subjected to because of their faith, but hoping that the baptismal service would show them how welcoming church can be. On a day-to-day basis, they tried to overcome their isolation by seeking out other Christians with whom they could talk and find support:

> I also find it really encouraging
> being with Christian friends than non-Christian friends,
> I find that's sometimes easier to talk to than my normal friends. (Ruth)

> I've discovered more and more people
> who are Christians as well
> and started groups and things like that

to support each other.
It's becoming easier
and God's helping me a lot more. (Mary)

Julie asserted that God gives us friends to help overcome the isolation and to manage the pressures, so the picture she saw of two friends talking to each other set off a web of connected thinking about girls giving one another mutual support to endure these pressures:

I think, like, God created friends
because we have company
and (you're) not always by yourself and give up,
if you're lonely and someone should be there for you ...
when you're sad and angry.

The girls' testimony was consistent with the findings of Pearmain in her research among older teenagers, for whom 'an alternative group of friends could be a refuge from other school-related groups where other pressures and tensions may operate'.[53]

Being a Christian involves more than going to church and youth events. It is following a lifestyle and adopting values which are contrary to the prevailing culture, or what it is perceived to be. However far young people are influenced by their faith, the preoccupation with celebrity and the hedonism around them, especially among their peer group, will affect them. This is not to say that a Christian should be an ascetic and eschew contemporary music, technology and fashion, but there will be a tension between these things and Christian values, which each girl alone or within her peer group must negotiate. That many girls are willing to take a stand against the prevailing culture, risking isolation, is clear from their conversation, and is consistent with Baker's finding that girls were 'quietly employing their spiritual selves in whatever acts of resistance to mainstream culture they are able to muster'.[54] This is not only in taking the risk of making their faith public, as already seen, but of going against majority views when conflicting with Christian values. Lucy expressed this with vigour in reflecting on the contrast between her own empathic response to suffering and the lack of concern by her peers: 'if they've got all the things that they want, they're not fussed about what's going on elsewhere'.

The language girls chose also betrayed how daunting they found the prospect of the life of faith: they described the responsibility they felt for others as a dimension of their Christian calling, and their need for God's help. Julie made frequent reference to the need for strength and the courage to persevere.

---

[53]   Rosalind Pearmain, 'Transformational Experiences in Young People: The Meaning of a Safe Haven', *International Journal of Children's Spirituality*, 10.3 (2005): 284.

[54]   Baker, *Doing Girlfriend Theology*, p. 13.

Martha wanted God to help her 'grow stronger'. Implicit here is fear, of a large or dangerous task ahead, combined with a sense of inadequacy for it. Rogers notes that 'courage' means something different for men than for women: for men she says it refers to 'an absence of fear and an overcoming of vulnerability – a psychological and physical disembodiment'; however, she holds that for girls it means to 'speak one's mind by telling all one's heart', that is, an 'embodied courage'.[55] Although of slightly older girls, Tamminen also finds girls need 'inner power and courage', to survive, for example, 'ridicule and teasing at school'.[56] To speak or live by faith involves the whole person and cannot be compartmentalised. Michelle expressed her fear of criticism in bodily terms: 'you just want to crawl into a corner'. For her and for Mary, God's supporting and comforting presence was tangible.

The evidence from my study suggests that as they become less certain about their emerging womanhood, girls also lose confidence in their ability to perform in a competitive environment, despite the statistical evidence which shows that girls do better in public exams than boys. Brierley claims that 'confidence in spiritual things is linked with confidence in other areas'.[57] My research did not endorse this for the girls: even those sure of their faith in a safe Christian context were daunted by the hostile environment of school. It is also hard for girls outside the church to step out of their comfort zones (the milieu of family and peer group) and into a faith group; this supports Kegan's designation of this evolutionary balance as 'Interpersonal', where they are particularly dependent on support structures and shared subjective experience in which the development of identity is caught up with peer relationships. 'Not being aware of this', Kegan says, 'makes us vulnerable to unforeseen losses when we make choices, however wholesome such choices may be, that cost us these supports'.[58] Any reorientation at this stage needs a strongly supportive alternative individual or social group. Hess acknowledges this when, citing Marge Piercy, she discusses 'the courage to leave the place whose language you have learned'.[59] Both Besag's and Hey's research projects into the dynamics of girls' friendships uncover the power of conformity to secure inclusion within friendship groups 'to make sense of their own identity. They are almost compelled to position themselves against girls who appear to be what they are not'; normality is what they mirror to one another.[60] Both Bryony and Michelle showed sensitivity to this in their dealings with non-Christian friends. The friend Bryony brought to church

---

[55] Gilligan et al., *Women, Girls and Psychotherapy*, pp. 21–23.

[56] Tamminen, *Religious Development*, p. 61.

[57] Brierley, *Reaching and Keeping Tweenagers*, p. 162.

[58] Kegan, *Evolving Self*, p. 193.

[59] Hess, *Caretakers of our Common House*, p. 55.

[60] Hey, *The Company She Keeps*, p. 132.

can't decide whether she wants to be a Christian,
but it's like when she's with Sally[61] she says she is
but with everybody else she'll say she's not.

Bryony herself is quiet and knew that on her own she was not strong enough to support her friend, but Sally and those around her might be able to offer her an alternative friendship group to help her make the move. Michelle commented on one of the friends she invited to her church, that she seemed to

follow other people and be them,
so we brought her here
to try to let her be herself
and have the courage to be herself.

This shows insight on the part of a 14-year-old of the operation of the Interpersonal stage; although at one level, the friend would be exchanging one set of relational influences for another, Michelle is testifying to a spiritual understanding that there is more freedom to find one's real identity in relationship with God than in human friendships alone.

Following a Christian lifestyle may mean taking up a career or vocation of service, which appears at this stage to be beyond human strength or skill. Michelle's awareness that her aspiration to be a nurse would demand courage, again reflected Rogers' interpretation. Some studies show a general fear of success among girls and women,[62] which may be symptomatic of girls' loss of self-worth and confidence, as Gilligan holds, which follows the loss of voice in adolescence. In Michelle's case it may be more complex, as she lived with the consequences of her parents' divorce. I wonder how far values explicit in Christian faith drive or attract girls into caring professions whether or not they are suited. Some had unformed notions of working overseas as missionaries. Julie and Martha approached the future with more confidence and saw success allied to academic achievement which would rely on their hard work of which they were not afraid. Julie's aim was to 'help people' by becoming a doctor or a scientist.

4. Relational Faithing

If, following Kegan's stage structure, the girls are entering the Interpersonal stage, then their relating to others will be of a different quality from the command relationship of the Imperial stage which typifies a younger child. I explore here how they work out their faith as they relate to others.

---

[61]   An extrovert 14-year-old, a 'leader' among her peers.
[62]   Kroger, 'Identity in Formation', p. 36.

Caring   In selecting care as a mark and foundation of relational faithing, I am following Gilligan's understanding, extended to a Christian context by Hess, that care involves nurturing relationships with others in which women combine self-assertion and self-giving. In the ways in which girls express their desire to care, some clearly show an awareness of the challenge of self-sacrificial living but also choose an active caring role for themselves which fosters agency. The social climate within which they live, as well as their age, restricts their freedom for self-giving in that pressures to succeed educationally are exerted by parents: Mary voiced this tension between wanting 'to do something practical, to do with my faith' and her mother's opposition to it until she had left school. Brierley finds a correlation between church-going children of this age and educational motivation and achievement.

Within those limitations, they recognise that relationships bring responsibility to care for the other, responsibility which extends beyond family and friends to the wider community both local and global. It has both practical and spiritual dimensions, although neither is mutually exclusive.

Practical care for friends included being a peacemaker when there was a quarrel, responding to overtures for friendship from unlikely sources (Karen), and going shopping and giving fashion advice (Michelle).

Concern for the wider world was shown by most of the girls, who introduced it into the conversation. Although largely powerless to help materially, some girls showed a deep care for people suffering as a result of poverty or disaster. They may have been aligning themselves with the focus given in some of the churches to the work of aid agencies and to political campaigning on issues of poverty or climate change, but the consistency of their mention suggests a self-authored interest. Moreover it was triggered by a variety of stimuli: Martha made the connection between the drops of water she saw in the picture exercise and the 'Make Poverty History' campaign;[63] Lucy used, as an illustration of genuine care, her reaction to stories of the hardship of life in the First World War trenches. Some identified human with divine action; fire-fighters and doctors are agents of God's care. Martha expressed her own desire to become actively involved, helping to do God's work, by giving her old toys and clothes to a charity shop: for her, giving money was too impersonal: 'I would like to give it actually to the people'. Against a background of international tension, relationships created with victims by people involved in relief work is a by-product of disasters for Rosie and for Martha, and a model of co-operation between peoples.

Some girls saw care as a responsibility given to women, particularly as their specific gender role, named by Julie, Martha and Amber, is to bear and nurture children.

Spiritual care was evident in a deep desire among some girls to share faith so that others, including family, might come to know God and share in their own happiness. Ruth felt deep sadness that her father hadn't joined them at the new church, to discover 'how good it could be'. Whatever trouble had caused them

---

[63]   Third world debt cancellation was a major theme at the time of the interviews.

to leave their former church had created a barrier for him, and this brokenness within the family caused her deep sorrow and determined prayer. For others, care for family included praying for quarrelling parents, and for their safety when perceived to be in danger (when travelling in areas of high risk; through a mugging). Inclusion within a wider caring community enabled the girls actively to participate: in her extended family in which her mother was godmother to many children, Martha had a role where children as godbrothers and godsisters cared for one another. Prayer was integral to this caring and Julie valued the opportunity she had as part of the faith community to pray for sick people. This extended beyond the immediate context: for Martha, prayer created a perspective on suffering, that God's way of caring is not limited by time but stretches into eternity, so death is transformed from disaster to new life in a 'better place'. Not all have this breadth of vision in understanding suffering, but in struggling with it, as discussed above, several expressed empathy with the sufferers, and explored where support may be available for them even in extremity. Through a visit to South Africa, Karen felt a new and vital connection with people in poverty, whom she held in her thoughts: she was uncomfortable with language of prayer.

Being cared for Relationships with people of all ages within the church community play a part in faithing, a feature valued by Georgia who found relationships with girls of her own age difficult, sensing she had a different set of values. For her and for others, God's presence and love were mediated through positive intergenerational relationships. People creating a loving atmosphere in the church 'wowed' Michelle when she first walked in. Bethan felt cared for when her grandfather died, and in text message exchanges with Amber was helped to understand he had 'gone to a better place'.

5. Sensual or 'Girlie' Faithing

In their relational faithing, the girls were not shy of expressing very openly their feelings, with one another, their families, friends and God. Karen for example was intimately aware of her self and her emotions in her relationship with God. Her mood and need dictated the gender she attributed to God: 'if I'm angry it's "he", if I'm really upset, it's "she"'. Others, feeling vulnerable, wanted to know God was 'bigger, stronger'. Some were overtly physical in the expression of the intimacy they sought or experienced, for example expressing their feeling of loving and being loved by God in tangible language: they were excited or happy in their faithing, and one needed a 'massive hug' from God.

For some, this was an expression of being 'girlie'. This could denote escapism, such as entry into a fantasy world, either of the lifestyle portrayed by 'girlie mags' or of romantic love in 'girlie films' (that such a film will have 'some cute love in it' suggests that at the conscious level, the relationship portrayed *is* fantasy). Or it could refer to girl-only pastimes, which were intimately relational, involving talking, personal care and sensual physical activity (dancing, playing music) which they felt their gendered identity permitted ('if a boy tries to act like a girl, they get bullied').

My findings suggest there is a consistency between the way they identify themselves as girls and the way they 'do' their faithing. The creation of a fantasy world in a boundaried space serves as a sanctuary where there is goodness, love and perfect understanding which the world appears to contradict. I explore this further in Chapter 8. Other girls testified to finding sanctuary in the world of their own imagination stimulated by literature, art or nature, or in music used as an expressive means of releasing pressure and transforming sadness, or in fantasy worlds created through other media. The relational element is sometimes reinforced by the use of tactile or even romantic language, 'feeling the Holy Spirit's presence around you', and 'we look to God and like fall in love with him'. Such expressions were only in evidence among the girls in the more evangelical churches where the sensual side was experienced particularly through intentional exposure to stimuli likely to induce such subjective experiences, as in youth weekends.

It could be argued that such experiences are the stuff of fantasy, not reality. Indeed, this is the contention of Walkerdine from her research into pre-teen fiction: she concludes that cultural practices produce in girls romantic fantasies, inscribing also selfless behaviour by which they can overcome adversity. Her analysis of the effect of schoolgirl fiction, in dialogue with both Freudian and Lacanian psychoanalysis, has potential implications for interpreting the way girls express, and possibly experience, their faith particularly in an evangelical/ charismatic context. How far girls' relationship with God is influenced by the 'relation between the psychic production of feminine desire and cultural forms and practices' is, however, beyond the scope of this book.[64] Many girls did testify to a relationship with God which supported their Christian life in hostile circumstances but this God was far from being a Freudian illusion.[65] The God whom they met in these moments was the lens through which they interpreted the real world, giving them hope and courage to pursue their life of faith in the face of opposition. That this was expressed as intimately relational was also a mark of 'girliness', a characteristic which is retained into womanhood and which Slee has concluded from her research is a distinctive pattern of women's faithing.[66]

6. Biblical Faithing

Although I have drawn out the biblical base of some of the girls' theologising, I want here to reflect specifically on their knowledge of the bible, and the way they used it.

---

[64]	Walkerdine, *Schoolgirl Fictions*, p. 87.

[65]	I follow Jacobs here in a positive understanding of illusion as a form of faith, 'an example of the intermediate space in which I try to make sense of the relationship between me and my internal and external worlds'. *Living Illusions*, p. 26.

[66]	Slee, *Women's Faith Development*, chapter 7.

The bible teaching they experience will tend to emphasise narrative, and draw meaning, and moral and spiritual application, largely from the gospels and epistles: the group I joined on several occasions in one church used Scripture Union material, and the passage and moral lesson were from the Sermon on the Mount. Bible passages formed a significant part of both worship and teaching programmes, reinforced or engaged with through drama, creative activities and discussion. There was little evidence, however, of a deep knowledge of biblical stories; the girls summarised them vaguely and largely inaccurately. Knowledge of biblical women was particularly hazy even in churches with women in leadership positions. Awareness was largely at a cognitive level, with little understanding of the stories' potential for personal meaning.

Yet for a few there was an openness to being transformed by the stories, by entering into the feelings of the characters: Ruth 'always knew' the story of Mary, but in the interview became surprised and amazed as she identified through her own experience how much Mary must have loved God to have accepted her role as Jesus' mother. Her deepening understanding of characters through growing human empathy parallels that gained by Julie in dramatising biblical narrative. The stories did not always come alive, however: Karen now rejected those used intensively with children, such as Noah and Joseph, preferring her own choice based on contemporary relevance, and openness to mystery which sparked her imagination. Her favourite book at the time of the interviews was Revelation.

Direct reference to stories does not reveal completely the bible's importance to the construction of their faith. As I have shown in analysis of Lucy's reflection, they mined its resources to construct faith dialogue, both in the interview, and in reporting their thought processes in other contexts. As Amber developed her explanation of God's complete otherness and our human struggle to understand, she drew analogically on Genesis 1.3, 'Let there be light', and for Mary, Jesus' teaching on the poor in Mark 14.7 helped her argue a case against God's direct intervention to prevent disasters.

Faith was to a lesser extent shaped by Pauline teaching, but examples were: sin and atonement (the atonement as sacrifice, punishment and gratuitous gift – as in Romans 3.25, 5.8); incarnation and exaltation (Philippians 2.6–9); the equality of all people (Galatians 3.28); and spiritual warfare (Ephesians 6.11–17).

Biblical material was sometimes treated critically. Whether through direct teaching or the absorption of values of justice and equality in their churches, many girls revealed a nascent 'hermeneutic of suspicion' when approaching the gender inequity in the biblical text. Some were fully aware of the low participation rate of women in biblical narrative (Hannah commented that 'in Christmas plays there are more boy parts than girls") but assigned it to the social context of the day, with which Jesus had to conform. Several were confident that in contemporary contexts the picture would be different. Out of their own reasoning, they were adopting a stance similar to that taken by Fiorenza, which sees the texts as 'historical prototype open to its own critical transformation' rather than '"timeless archetype" whose word is binding for all time'.[67]

> I wonder if it's that ... in that time it was all about,
> the girls were the wives and the mothers
> and they would stay at home and
> cook and things,
> but the boys would be the people who would get noticed
> and people would listen to them and take in what they were saying
> but if girls say it, it's like 'whatever' so ...
> and if Jesus was around like how he was then, like now,
> then I don't think it would be just all boys
> because it doesn't really matter whether you were a boy or a girl,
> it would be equality. (Rosie)

There is a danger that the bible's androcentrism may cause the girls to dismiss it as irrelevant: Lucy, Karen and Sarah all agreed that it is more of a story for boys since most characters are male, and 'women are not listened to or given important jobs like we do now'. The majority stance, however, was that it is foundational for faith, and those who have questioned its relevance based its redemption on its contextualisation and their own authority to interpret it according to the knowledge gained from their relational experience of God.

Corroboration

Although of an older age group, I note here significant correlation between my findings in this chapter and those of Baker and Mercer in their separate research programmes. Both studied girls in very different contexts, drawing together in intentional settings groups who opted in to their structured research processes. Some conversations grew out of residential events and all took place away from their regular places of worship, if indeed they had one. Similar themes emerged from their data as from mine, although with heightened sophistication and clearer articulation attributable to wider vocabulary and greater life experience. So the themes Baker identified from the stories her girls told were around violence and suffering, friendship and embodiment, each resourcing reflection at the place where God met them in their experience. In Mercer's data, too, girls related to God in conventional as well as creative imagery, and they were aware of the risks faith involved, although in their North American context more from the consequences of independent thinking within conservative church structures than from wider

---

[67]   Nicola Slee, *Faith and Feminism: An Introduction to Christian Feminist Theology* (London, 2003), p. 23 quoting from E. Schüssler Fiorenza, *Bread not Stone: The Challenge of Feminist Biblical Interpretation* (Boston, 1984).

society. Both authors premised their research on the 'loss of voice' theory and the diminution of girls' self-esteem during adolescence; it may be that the girls whom I studied have not yet felt the full force of the silencing of their mothers' generation, but in twenty-first-century Britain, 'girlpower' has constructed a different and hopefully more empowering narrative for many girls as they grow through adolescence, although silencing is still an issue in some churches. There is, therefore, sufficient commonality in these areas between my own research and that of Baker and of Mercer to offer some external corroboration of my findings.

Chapter 7
Theological Reflection 2: Rosie

Introduction

As with the previous chapter, I am prefacing my final discussion of an aspect of girls' faithing with another example of theological reflection. For Rosie, the communities in which she was being nurtured and which encouraged her to exercise a concern for others on both a local and a global scale were of particular importance. Her contributions, in conversation with Suzanne, lead into the next chapter which focuses on nurturance within the Christian community.

I had one extended interview with Rosie for which Suzanne joined us after the church service in which I'd shared. Suzanne's family is Roman Catholic, but she often attends Rosie's Protestant church. By the time we reached the section of conversation I am analysing, they had begun to speak freely and interact a little with each other. It quickly became clear that Rosie's main concern was the overcoming of inequality and difference leading to harmonious living, her anxiety being caused by evidence of tension and violence around her on a local and global level. Her family lives in a deprived inner-city location, home to many members of immigrant and refugee communities, and Rosie attends a multicultural church school where she meets practising members of other faiths. Both girls had already emphasised the universality of God's love to which the bible and hymns testify, and Rosie had summarised the Pauline doctrine of the atonement, so they approached the issues with a working knowledge of Christian doctrine. Rosie showed evidence of being drawn by the 'mysterium tremendum et fascinans', and was aware of the significance of her small, struggling church community on her faith journey.

Stage 1

In this part of the interview, I invited them to explore how they pray, or communicate with God. Rosie immediately spoke of an experience of communal not personal prayer, in a worship setting; it was an assembly for the whole of her school, which she remembered as different from other assemblies of smaller groupings which are 'boring'. Here she experienced 'otherness', illustrating the power of a crowd united in one activity: participation was key to filling the experience with the wonder of transcendence. That atheists and people of other faiths also participated heightened the feeling: it had the potential to be a glimpse of the kingdom of God, and the anticipated harmony between peoples of all races, religions and generations.

If this was so, consonant with her deepest values, it drove Rosie to think of experiences where it was not the case, firstly when worship was passive and divorced from real life, and when hierarchies created boundaries between people. Her examples were the divisiveness of racism, and non-participatory worship. A narrative illustrated her desire for inclusion: in Black History Month, which gave her a resource for her reflection, staff and pupils were engaged in a joint learning activity. This mirrored her experience of worship in her own church where there was much sharing, and a minimum of evident leadership; 'in our church it's like the minister sits with everybody else and like gives us things that we can do ... and then if he gives us things to do then we remember what he's saying – or she'.

Stage 2

Suzanne introduced a note of dissension when she introduced her own contrasting experience, thus broadening the scope of the discussion. She recognised that such experiences don't necessarily originate in a 'religious' setting, but are universal signs of human relating, reflecting the will of God. Since 'talk about the world' is not confined to RE lessons but applies equally to geography, Suzanne spoke of the necessity of integrating faith with life. Her thought was rooted theologically in the greatness of God and the incapacity of humans to have all knowledge. God is more than a large scale human, however; there is a difference in kind. She emphasised that God cannot be confined to our limited ways of thinking. As with Amber, she was expressing in her own way the thoughts of Deutero-Isaiah.[1]

Stage 3

For Rosie, this was still too vague; she wanted to pick up on the idea of the 'bigness' of God and shape it more firmly into a universalist theology. Her starting point again was narrative but this time imaginary, a 'what if', created around her four-year-old sister, which built on the innocence with which young children can ask important questions which Rosie suggested she would be now be too embarrassed or inhibited to ask.[2] There were two important things she wanted to foreground here:

1. however different the tenets and customs of a religion are, what unites all is a belief in one God;

---

[1]   Isaiah 55.8–9.

[2]   Gilligan et al. call this silencing the 'closing down of childhood' when a girl can no longer engage honestly with the world around her, *Women Girls and Psychotherapy*, p. 19.

2. (with some admiration) others who carry observable outward marks of faith, like Sikhs, are not afraid publicly to own their faith.

Stage 4

Rosie's driving force, like Lucy's, was a concern over the dis-ease of the world. Recognising and valuing the importance in religion of tradition (here her resource was her learning about those religions in RS lessons and through school friendships), she wanted to believe in an underlying God-given moral consensus in which people can live their different lives in harmony. However, she found the reality of the society she lives in reflects different values: she showed by her use of the nominative 'we' that she identified with that society as part of its dominant grouping (white, British, educated, relatively affluent), but was resisting the evils of racism and war it perpetrates (local racially motivated killings and, again, the war in Iraq were part of the political and social background to the interview). To her, it would make God glad if all people lived in their differences but in peace, mirroring the external differences but internal coherence in God.

The girls were drawing widely on a range of resources: personal experience, the arts, the media, school, the bible and Christian tradition, although Rosie in particular was able to formulate her own original theological expression. The tentative speech and lowered voices with which they both often spoke were signs they were moving into new territory which stretched their previous understanding.

Both girls conveyed a disquiet with a world of disharmony, and a desire to live in relationship with all other peoples, in their differences, in a world of peace and justice. It was a desire for a fuller life, which overcomes, or transforms, the destructiveness of severed relationships, war and death. Full and harmonious living comes about by accepting and valuing difference. This includes a difference of gender which does not have to be obliterated politically any more than theologically or spiritually.

Chapter 8
Girls in Nurturing Space

Moses' Sister

In this narrative,[1] the girl is not named, but is generally understood to be the same sister who features later in the Moses saga; I will therefore name her Miriam throughout.

Miriam's initiative and role in the rescue of Moses is, as with other stories I have highlighted, commonly overlooked both in writing on biblical children and in feminist exegesis.[2] Her part in the story is treated as a narrative backdrop to the 'real' events where power lies, with Pharaoh's daughter and the male child. In contrast to some feminist rejection of the story as contributing to the reinforcement of patriarchy through its focus on the salvation by women of a male child, the narrative can be interpreted as a reversal of, and maybe for the reader a conscious protest against, stories of abuse by male relatives against women close to them which were almost certainly known to them in tradition. One who is a daughter and sister ironically preserves the life of another who is son and brother.[3] Discussing the story, Lapsley notes that of the women in the encounter, the princess has the power and Miriam has none, yet the girl manipulates the princess into keeping the child, sensing that her emotional and ethical response to a crying baby will take precedence over obedience to her father's edict: 'Miriam has on her side rhetorical power, the power to mold the moral response of someone more privileged and powerful than she'.[4]

Interpreted in this way, this story could become for contemporary girls an example of defiance against a feminism which has resisted association with the nurture of children. Yet while Lapsley focuses on this story's strength standing not as a precursor to the deliverance in the Exodus but as a template for 'the divine liberation of all humanity that is yet to come' in its transgression of gender, ethnicity and class,[5] she too overlooks the further dimension of its subversion, that

---

[1] Exodus 2.1–10.

[2] For example, C. Mathews McGinnis, 'Exodus as a "Text of Terror" for Children', in Bunge, *The Child in the Bible*; Luise Schottroff, Silvia Schroer, Marie-Theres Wacker, *Feminist Interpretation: The Bible in Women's Perspective* (Minneapolis, 1998), p. 157.

[3] There is a double irony here as the narrative suggests Moses is the firstborn: Miriam's very existence is ignored until she earns some significance by playing a part in the boy's rescue.

[4] Lapsley, *Whispering the Word*, p. 78.

[5] Ibid., p. 79.

of generation. We have no evidence that the initiative to act to save her brother did not lie entirely with the girl. Others have drawn attention to the Hebrew word for 'standing' in verse four, interpreting it as signifying 'having a clear stance of one's own' and connecting it with the girl's 'expectation of a saving event in the future'.[6] It also introduces a measure of independence to her action. So I add 'generation' to Lapsley's list when she claims that 'the stories of deliverance told in the early chapters of Exodus both rely on human constructions of identity (ethnicity, gender and class) and simultaneously undermine those very categories through the transgressive acts of deliverance performed by women'.[7] It might be counted an invalid criterion since childhood is a modern construct. Yet at that time, a girl would only enter the world of women at puberty: until capable of bearing children, her status was even more marginal. Miriam's action here is risky, needing real courage, as there is no certainty that the daughter of Pharaoh will listen to a child, a daughter of the Hebrews. I have shown how 'courage' featured regularly in the vocabulary of the girls I interviewed, denoting their seizing of the future, and making it work for them. They know it will not be easy in a world which is still male dominated, and where they fail to credit themselves with skill and ability. Living faithfully is a daunting prospect, now as then.

Miriam serves as an example of a girl shaped by her context, acting to re-establish family relationship as well as to save life, but using her own initiative, and her interpretation of events, to create the desired positive outcome. Her story thus creates for us a pathway from girls' understanding of and relationship with God in the previous chapter to a more explicit exploration of the nurturing function and capacity of the spaces in which girls are growing through puberty as faithing subjects. From my analysis of the texts I will identify some of these girls' needs and expectations, and assess the environment's contribution to their healthy growth as they explore ideas, experiment with identity in this liminal place, and negotiate the crossing of the threshold into womanhood.

Each girl is inhabiting these spaces in ways which offer her secure connection, while at the same time exercising a limited freedom in expressing herself (physically, emotionally, verbally) in chosen relationships. She needs secure attachment within these given contexts, but as she attains greater independence, she assesses the health-giving value of each attachment to her development of self and agency. Some individuation is evident as she negotiates the growth of her own identity.

In this chapter, I interweave my analysis of the girls' experience of their nurturing space with discussion of the categories I identified from study of their texts, to enable me to integrate ways of seeing their experience with some suggestions of biological, psychological and philosophical ideas which facilitate

---

[6]   Kim Elli, Jung-su Kim and Yeung-mee Lee, *Women of Courage: Asian Women Reading the Bible* (Seoul, 1992).

[7]   Lapsley, *Whispering the Word*, p. 69.

interpretation; the discussion, however, is still held within a framework of a theology and spirituality that take account of girlhood.

Finding a Guiding Metaphor

In the search for a balance between freedom and connection, it was a combination of the work of Trible and of Kegan that suggested the images I have adopted, to express in graphic form what I was hearing from the girls. Kegan describes as an 'amniotic environment' the space which holds without constraining the re-organising of 'who the person is' in the next step of growth. Trible follows the semantic journey of the womb (*rechem*) metaphor 'from a physical organ of the female body to a psychic mode of being ... from the wombs of women to the compassion of God'.[8] As for Kegan, so for Trible: 'the womb protects and nourishes but does not possess and control'.[9] From analysis of the interview texts, I suggest that the growth of identity for a girl at this stage in her life, in the interplay between autonomy and connection, developed by a variety of scholars in different disciplines, is most creatively constructed and informed by the metaphor of the womb.

To introduce the theme, I explore the role of the holding environment particularly as it operates in times of transition. By extending Winnicott's original concept, Kegan directs our attention to the cultures in which girls are growing. An 'amniotic environment' imagines both embeddedness and transition, the uterine waters of human gestation picturing the optimal environment for 'hold(ing) without constraining'[10] and for letting go, the 'twin functions of confirmation and contradiction'.[11] All those in Kegan's transitional stages are described as 'floating' in amniotic waters, or conversely if not well supported, of growing 'without the protection of the amniotic shield':[12] the subject is still held by its context 'where holding refers not to keeping or confining but to supporting ... the exercise of who the person is'.[13] This analogy, then, holds potential for imaging the transitional process of female puberty. As the foetus within the womb, so the girl is secured (embedded), and embeds herself, receiving nurturance while re/creating her maturing identity. It is the safe space which offers retreat, nurture and holding, in which she actively engages in the gestation and birthing of herself, experimenting with identities, transitional and multiple. Biology and psychology cohere as she moves within the trusted space as agent to exercise, to explore and test her motor

---

[8]   Hebrew for 'compassion' is *rachamim* or *rachum*: Trible, *God and the Rhetoric of Sexuality*, pp. 33–4.

[9]   Ibid., pp. 33–4.

[10]   Kegan, *Evolving Self*, p. 162.

[11]   Ibid., p. 140.

[12]   Ibid., p. 156.

[13]   Ibid., p. 162.

abilities, to stretch her cognitive skills, find and test her own and her environment's boundaries, in the process of birthing her emerging womanhood. This metaphor has particular poignancy for girls at this age in the analogous relationship it sets up between the physical maturing of her uterus and her psychological and spiritual growth. I stress that my use of the image is limited to analogy, in contrast to Erikson's assertion that a woman's 'physiological functioning and ... to an extent personality configurations ... reflect the ground plan of her body'.[14] I shall develop the metaphor in more detail as I explore the girls' own stories.

'Holding' through puberty is more than a physical process; it has a spiritual dimension which heightens the significance of the role of the church in girls' growth. This uterine space of gestation where she is 'mothered' in love, accepted unconditionally for who she is, is a place of sacred trust where the mothering host nurtures new life. For Trible the adjective *rachum* describes the mercy and compassion of YHWH which Stevenson-Moessner translates as 'womb-love as expressed by God is not biologically based (but) that yearning from the very center of being (which) describes the tenacious compassion in God's desire and mercy'.[15] Winnicott acknowledges the spiritual dimension of the growing space: 'The potential space between baby and mother, between child and family, between individual and society or the world, depends on experience which leads to trust. It can be looked upon as sacred to the individual in that it is here that the individual experiences creative living'.[16] Keller suggests that what Winnicott means by separation of child from mother is in fact differentiation which allows the subject to 'experience' for itself while remaining connected. Her argument woven from psychology, mythology and theology, moves towards a 'connection without constriction' in the development of a 'true' female self.[17]

Spirituality, then, is intrinsic to the process as the girls in my study affirm: this is a dimension of the holding environment that Kegan overlooks. By calling it 'sacred', Winnicott recognises the spirituality of the process that connects the experience of trust that environments generate, and the creativity necessary for the flourishing of life. Sheldrake agrees that spatial experience represents something critical as we 'pass through the stages of life and become the person we are potentially'. We need 'a place that offers access to the sacred (however we understand that term) – perhaps, crucially, relates us to *life itself as sacred*'. Although from a different starting point he, like Winnicott, sees the spaces

    [14]   Erikson, 'Womanhood', p. 285.

    [15]   Jeanne Stevenson-Moessner, 'The Practice and Theology of Adoption', *The Christian Century*, 24 January (2001): 10–13; Trible, *God and the Rhetoric of Sexuality*, pp. 38–9.

    [16]   D.W. Winnicott, 'The Location of Cultural Experience', *International Journal of Psychoanalysis*, 48 (1967): 368–72.

    [17]   Keller, *From a Broken Web*, pp. 143–54.

as being located in communities which are open to the world of people and to the natural order.[18]

These images of the processes – psychic, relational, spiritual – taking place within such 'spaces', symbolise that growth takes place not in a vacuum, but in relationality and embodiment. It is not, according to Keller, that 'I am here at this point alone, and everything else is in its proper place'. Were that so, space would 'prevent our overlapping'. She follows Irigaray in assigning our existence in individual points of time and place to an 'external grid' imposed by patriarchy which isolates each of us 'in the solitude of a pure present'.[19] Likewise she denies the 'inner space' concept of Erikson. Instead, just as in physics 'there exists no empty space … (but) more like a continuum of greater and lesser densities of matter/energy', so space 'comes to be through the events of relationship', a dynamic process of interaction with others or an-Other in a physical or a spiritual relationship. Just as the uterus, by nature elastic, becomes spacious as it hosts the foetus, so an environment offering hospitality to a growing person can structure a relational place to encourage and facilitate growth to occur; but the growing child will also create her own inner spaces as an agent facilitating her own 'processes of becoming'.[20] Kuang-Ming is another philosopher who adopts the wombing/birthing metaphor to describe the dynamic relationship between self and other. As we grow into the 'home' of our own personhood, he says, 'our ontological resonance lets you become – come to be – yourself, and enables me to become myself'. His 'void' differs from that of a psychologist such as Erikson. It is the space our being needs to become itself, a hospitable space, found in formative relationship:

> Home is where I both was born and am continually being born within that womb called other people, in their being not me … Every human relationship worthy of its name is a mothering and wombing – your being vacuous draws me forth, lets me become as I am.[21]

This has further links with Irigaray, who writes from her experience of 'that which has been repressed and denied in the making of Western culture and ideas of subjectivity'.[22] For Irigaray, being born a woman puts a girl in a 'privileged position with respect to the forming of subjectivity and inter-subjectivity'. Such

---

[18]　Philip Sheldrake, *Spaces for the Sacred* (London, 2001), p. 10. Author's italics.

[19]　Keller, *From a Broken Web*, p. 240, referring to Irigaray in *This Sex which is Not One*. Tina Beattie also writes about the patriarchal circumscription of women's spaces of spiritual becoming in *Woman*.

[20]　Ibid., p. 243.

[21]　Kuang-Ming Wu, 'The Other is My Hell; the Other is My Home', *Human Studies*, 16 (1993): 194–5.

[22]　Beattie, *God's Mother*, p. 28.

relationship-building in girls is the psychological counterpart to a bodily capacity for giving hospitality to another within her womb:

> The girl's creative precocity and cultural vigour ... are undoubtedly caused by her more rapidly developed relational identity, the result of having been born of one the same as she, and of her intuition about her hospitable role in taking, in love and in maternity, the other into herself.[23]

The other is not engulfed within hospitable space; loving 'does not exclude respecting the other as other than the self'.[24]

A girl's 'wombing' enables the growth of her own identity symbiotically with the holding environment. Especially at puberty, this is a relationship which oscillates between autonomy and connection, a movement familiar in feminist theology as well as psychology and philosophy. A theological motif can be found in the search to fathom individuality and communion within the Trinity. I choose this image on the basis that the relational dimension of trinitarian theology holds within it a rich potential for the exploration of the divine resonant with female subjectivity. Beattie makes reference to Irigaray's suggestion that 'a trinitarian god is potentially more suited to a female morphology than a monotheistic god'.[25] For Johnson the three persons are in 'eternal and hypostatic distinction ... constituted by their relationships to each other, each unintelligible except as connected with the others'.[26] To seek relation and autonomy is, for a girl, to assert individuality and power, while acknowledging that in relating, she need not sacrifice her will or her identity. Keller suggests 'we need not be misled by pairs of false alternatives like "self" versus "relation". Relation can either foster dependency, or test and nurture freedom'.[27] Yet, as we have seen, girls can be so acted upon by their environment that they 'lose voice', or through peer and cultural pressures take on an identity or identities not their own. So I reflect further here on the growth of identity in the interaction and sometimes conflict between self and other, autonomy and connection.

To return to Kegan, he assigns to alternate stages, appearing as they do at his spiral's extremities, the 'preferences' associated in psychoanalysis with male and female, autonomy, separation and exclusion being the male (paternal) characteristics, intimacy, dependence and inclusion being the female (maternal) ones. He argues that this image allows for fluidity between the two, and although men and women may have a preference for and therefore remain longer in

[23]   Irigaray, *Luce Irigaray: Key Writings*, p. 178. For further discussion of the charge of essentialism against Irigaray, see Toril Moi, *Sexual Textual Politics: Feminist Literary Theory* (London, 1985), pp. 139ff.; Joy, *Divine Love*, pp. 30–32.
[24]   Irigaray, *Luce Irigaray: Key Writings*, p. 157.
[25]   Beattie, *God's Mother*, p. 186.
[26]   Johnson, *She Who Is*, pp. 215–16.
[27]   Keller, *From a Broken Web*, p. 3.

inclusive or exclusive stages, within each of us there is a desire for both, and Freudian dualism is overcome.

Likewise Irigaray speaks of different relationships for girls with those of each gender. She urges the strengthening of singularity within friendships with others of the same; and to a girl becoming adolescent and beginning relationships with one who is not the same, she advocates 'keeping one's virginity (which) means not losing oneself in the attraction of the other nor letting oneself be ruled by the other'. As she uses it here virginity

> should in no way be confused with the existence of part of the human body ... (but) could be the name for a return of the feminine to the self, or a spiritual interiority of woman, capable of staying woman and of becoming more and more woman.[28]

Her more recent explorations into female subjectivity have moved towards the theological and spiritual, and therefore are of particular interest in my own search for deeper understanding of girls' spirituality.[29] The task to love the different while staying ourselves 'probably corresponds', she says, 'to the most spiritual task of human becoming'.[30]

Jantzen develops Irigaray's writing on spirituality so that it resonates with the theme I am pursuing. In identifying the 'assumption constitutive of the western symbolic' found in individualism, progress, rationality and developmentalism, she indicates its necrophilic obsession, arguing instead for an alternative symbolic in natality, 'its repressed other', which is temporally prior, 'always already material, embodied, connected with other human beings and with human history'.[31] Jantzen draws on Irigaray's challenge to Lacan's (Freudian) contention that subject positions are 'inherently masculine' and little boys grow into them by the repression of unacceptable desires, while girls must become masculinised. In this thinking, girls have no symbolic of their own, for they desire, and desire must be repressed. The male symbolic is therefore dominant, defined by language which demands rational discourse. In its terms, as Freud and Lacan maintain, women have nothing to say. How then, Irigaray asks, can a woman speak? Her aim here is to advocate a strategy for women to achieve their own subjectivity, by finding voice, in the distinctiveness of 'otherness', 'a language ... of their own',[32] which is 'not a bid for separationism, but a move towards the possibility of creative exchange in which women have something of our own to give, something which

---

28 Irigaray, *Luce Irigaray: Key Writings*, p. 161.

29 This perspective is adopted by Morny Joy who reflects on Irigaray's earlier work and its influence on philosophers of religion such as Pamela Sue Anderson and Grace Jantzen; *Divine Love*, pp. 142–60.

30 Irigaray, *Luce Irigaray: Key Writings*, p. 161.

31 Jantzen, *Becoming Divine*, pp. 129, 141.

32 Luce Irigaray, *Sexes and Genealogies*, trans. C. Gill (New York, 1993), p. 79.

is more than the reflection of the male'.[33] Her contention is that the masculinist imaginary which drives the dominant discourse is phallocentric and as such denies any representation of the maternal body. Jantzen sees this as privileging in the western intellectual tradition an obsession with death and other worlds. She has an unexpected ally in Erikson whose motivation for his essay 'Womanhood and Inner Space' was exposure of the 'typologies and cosmologies which men have had the exclusive opportunity to cultivate and to idolise', which have brought the danger of annihilation to 'the unborn in the wombs of women'. For him, hope lies in women's capacity for 'building and of bringing up rebuilders' where man's 'adaptive imagination' has reached its limit. This translates easily into the language of natality.[34] Jantzen argues for a discursive transformation from necrophilia to natality which, I argue, has particular relevance to girls' growth in faith.

In my data, I found evidence from the girls which suggested three dimensions of the experience of being in the womb, whose physiological counterparts relate to the process of foetal gestation. They offer girls both the connection they seek and the freedom to grow and explore in individuality, the two qualities I named as constituting an optimal environment for growth. They provide protection from the buffeting of the outside world, to which they are also organically connected.

The uterus consists of two linked membranes, the *chorion* and the *amnion*, each functioning separately but inextricably to attach and to contain the growing infant, together embedded through the *placenta*.

The *chorion* is the outer membrane, which forms part of the complex connection to the mother through the placenta. It circulates oxygen between mother and child, exchanging deoxygenated for oxygenated blood, and capillaries carrying foetal and maternal blood respectively remain separate. I adopt the chorion as a metaphor for that environment which is responsible for the secure attachment of the immature life.

The *amnion* is a 'tough, transparent, non-vascular membrane' which forms the wall of the amniotic cavity. It acts like an expandable bag, holding the baby in the circulating amniotic fluid to protect from injury and allow freedom of movement; it also provides fluid to drink and keeps it at an even temperature. The rate of renewal of the amniotic fluid is high, estimated at one-third of the volume each hour. Thus it does not stagnate.[35] It acts as a 'protective cushion against external injury' and the pressure exerted on the baby by the uterine contractions prior to birth. I use the properties of both membrane and fluid in my analogy. The delicate interweaving of dependence and separation in the uterus lends itself significantly

---

[33] Jantzen, *Becoming Divine*, p. 60.

[34] His assessment resonates with Irigaray's 'masculine vision of the world'. Erikson, 'Womanhood', pp. 261–2; Irigaray, *Luce Irigaray: Key Writings*, p. 159.

[35] Richard Snell, *Clinical Embryology for Medical Students* (Boston, 1972), p. 37.

to the adoption of the analogy for the process of girls' growth and maturing in a faith community.[36]

The *placenta* is the organ formed where the umbilical cord, itself formed out of the fusion of amnion and chorion, embeds within the uterine wall. It is the organ that carries out respiration, nutrition and excretion for the embryo. The image suggests the interaction between mother and child, where each participates for good or ill in the life of the other, but the major responsibility for foetal health lies with the host, in whose lifestyle and relationship with the child lies the baby's flourishing.

These physiological images, then, offer a metaphorical framework for discussion of the girls' dependence on, independence within and participation with their environment.

Chorion – The Protecting Membrane

The chorion is both the source of nourishment and forms the boundary to the space within which the girl grows. The boundary is only temporary, for this is a liminal place and time, from which border crossing, birth/natality, will follow.

For the duration of transition, it marks out a place of safety, a 'home space'. I have already shown the importance of home space for girls' healthy growth, and I draw additionally here on empirical research undertaken by Rosalind Pearmain. Among an older age group, she identified a need for a 'safe haven', 'the holding of a spiritual space in which they could be silent, reflect, feel connected and allow deeper insights to surface'. Drawing on Bachelard's philosophical reflection, she proposes a connection between 'home space' and the opportunities for young people away from pressures of commercialism and 'cynicism and denigration of spiritual and human values' in which they can 'return home again to the Self within'.[37] This is consistent with the need I have identified from girls to find a refuge from the threatening world of non-faith. For Bachelard, the concept of 'home space' is key: 'all really inhabited space bears the essence of home', where 'the imagination build(s) "walls" of impalpable shadows, comfort(s) itself with the illusion of protection'.[38] I understand Bachelard to use 'illusion' of the home's protective function, in the sense explored by Jacobs in the context of faith. For him illusion is a positive and necessary 'intermediate space' which we inhabit as we

---

[36] Ibid., pp. 41–5. Where a medical textbook such as this uses embryo and foetus for the unborn child, I choose 'baby' and 'infant' to remind the reader of the analogical purpose of the exploration. Foetal is used where appropriate only as an adjective.

[37] Pearmain, 'Transformational Experiences', p. 289.

[38] Gaston Bachelard, *The Poetics of Space* (Boston, 1969), p. 5. Bachelard also recognises home may threaten and the imagination may 'tremble behind thick walls, mistrust the staunchest ramparts', reminding us that home may also be a place of betrayal and abuse.

attempt to make sense of reality. In it, we use 'objects, fantasies, words and ideas as ways of mediating and interpreting realities which we can never fully either know or understand'.[39] The reality is that nothing can offer total protection from the danger, but what we want to give girls is the framework to enable them to trust where they (and we) do not yet see. Jacobs again is helpful here in seeing that trust 'includes the integration of negative experiences', being able in Jungian terms to hold together light and shadow, and in religious terms responding with 'healthy ambivalence' to the contradiction between good and evil.[40] I have already shown how much of girls' faithing takes place in the space where good and evil collide. The 'containing' membrane or holding environment therefore has a role not completely to shelter girls from the real world but to create a space where, together with trusted people and values, they do their faithing.[41] The language of poetry and metaphor best serves this purpose.[42] So again Bachelard helps us to picture the importance of the image of 'home' for the protective function of the holding environment: using house and home as interchangeable metaphors, he sums up his purpose as to 'show that the house is one of the greatest powers of integration for the thoughts, memories and dreams of mankind'.[43] Bachelard's 'home' imagery speaks to Sheldrake in his exploration of 'sacred space' which enables us to 'pass through the stages of life and become the person we are potentially'.[44] From Grey's feminist perspective, that potential can only be realised through a tougher journey, of which the girls already have some intimation; that is, dislocation of the dominant (patriarchal) narratives and re-location in a home space which 'redeem(s) the fragmented self' and becomes a place of connection with one's own body, with a faith community, with the earth and with God. Grey sees this 'home-coming' as the goal towards which feminist theology and religious education work together to actualise these for women.[45] Jensen, also recognising the pain of childhood, emphasises the quality of safety offered by the church and links it to the Old Testament concept of sanctuary, which

---

[39]   Jacobs, *Living Illusions*, p. 16.

[40]   Ibid., pp. 76–9.

[41]   Reminiscent of Fowler's dynamic triad which he describes as the context for growth in faith, *Stages*, p. 17.

[42]   In using 'poetics' in this static and nostalgic way, it could be argued that Bachelard is not allowing poetic language its 'head' in its capacity to 'jar' with our preconceptions, and introduce new dimensions to our thinking: 'poetic movement is … a ceaseless searching, open-ended yearning and movement towards what is always elsewhere and otherwise, toward what is coming'. Veling, *Practical Theology*, p. 200. In this sense, poetry has to do with awakening, with birthing.

[43]   Bachelard, *Poetics*, p. 6.

[44]   Sheldrake, *Spaces for the Sacred*, p. 10.

[45]   Mary Grey, '"Sapiential Yearnings": The Challenge of Feminist Theology to Religious Education', in J. Astley and L. Francis (eds), *Christian Theology and Religious Education* (London, 1996), p. 88.

'provides the space for physical safety and a harbor for emotional and spiritual growth, in the midst of God's holiness'.[46]

The girls I interviewed identified spaces which represented safety to them in the protective environment of home or church, and these usually corresponded with actual physical space. To be truly safe, these spaces must be imbued with affective significance and fulfil a function both psychological and spiritual to promote mental health and sanctuary. Lucy captured the essence of this when, reflecting on a school Remembrance Day assembly where they were shown pictures of men in the trenches, she said, 'the thought of just lying there with no blankets or duvet or anything like that' was 'horrible'; Sheldrake might accuse her of reflecting the 'tendency in the West ... to idealise domesticity as the shaping symbol of a satisfactory life',[47] which betrays an Enlightenment view where the body and soul, private and public, are arranged hierarchically. Lucy was, however, bringing a female insight to counter the 'glory' of war: context is everything in understanding her elevation of domestic comfort over wallowing in mud, and any presumption of 'hierarchy'. Mary found comfort in the familiarity of her bedroom, alone or with a trusted friend 'if I've had a bad day'. Amber found friendship made the church a Christian 'home':

There's lots of young people here,
you can be with your friends, but they're not just your friends,
they're like your Christian friends.
And you can have fun with them and share your faith with them,
and share God with them and talk to them about God.

The security offered by mutual understanding through shared experience is a quality of the relationship not just between friends but between mothers and daughters as both Bethan and Amber, resonating with Irigaray, affirmed:

My mum, she's been in the situation
of developing and things like I have (Bethan)

and

with my mum it's different
and I can relate to her,
talk to her about things more
mum went through
like all adolescence and everything,
Well, my dad did

---

[46]   Jensen, *Graced Vulnerability*, p. 113.
[47]   Sheldrake, *Spaces for the Sacred*, p. 10.

but my mum did
the same stages that I've been through. (Amber)

Most girls attended mixed schools, but for Karen moving to the more protective environment of a single sex secondary school where she need not confront older boys of whom she was scared, gave her renewed confidence. There were other challenges in a girls' school, but there was at least shared gender if not interests and values to connect with other girls.

It is therefore the quality of relationships within or around the space, not the space alone, which brings the protection. These relationships also have an integrating, healing effect when other spaces, which should offer safety, fail to do so. The environment cannot effect a 'rescue' from danger, but the very act of being heard and understood encourages an objectivity and realism in their approach to the situation, and offers hope in embodying an incarnational theology where 'goodness is stronger than evil'.[48] Michelle felt neither home nor school offered her the sanctuary which she found in church, where she was conscious of:

> having all the love round you
> cos … my mum and dad got divorced
> so I felt that my home was a bit,
> there wasn't a lot of love there
> cos my mum got depression,
> it was like my second family,
> … yeah it's just a home environment now.

Here the cause of Michelle's discomfort was beyond her control. Like other girls, she had chosen a lifestyle which was stressful, living by Christian faith and values. What she was 'going through', cited earlier, was being the subject of gossip at school, where religious faith and practice were derided. Mary described the vulnerability she felt at school, as if 'the whole lot's falling in on you'. The crushing experience in one environment was countered by the safety of the other where affective attachment (being in the church music group) secured her. For Georgia, too, the church and all it stood for enabled her regularly to earth herself away from the contradictions around her:

> when you get down and stuff,
> sometimes I come to church not on top of the world
> and I just like looking out cos there's that window out there
> and I just look where everybody's walking in the street
> and just think 'what are they doing?'
> and I just get on with my life
> and I just feel like it's helping get on with my life.

---

48   Words of Desmond Tutu.

Another coping strategy could be described as withdrawal. To disappear into a small space has universal appeal, to find a niche or corner into which you can crawl as a child might do to hide in a dark corner, or nestle as on a parental lap when frightened. Michelle longed for a safe corner to crawl into as a refuge from school gossip, and Karen, naturally quiet yet non-conforming, described others seeing her as sitting silently in the corner, but this represented her own place of safety and personal autonomy. Bachelard helps us to see the importance of such close physical containment which brings security; he finds what he is looking for in the complementary picture of the nest, which, he suggests, we remember in daydreams as the place of warmth, security and trust to which we return when we have ventured far from it.[49] Rosie reflected on the growing independence she had as a young teenager, but she still 'nests' at home, and recognises that her confidence to adventure depends on the security her parents gave and still give her:

> when you're little, you've always got your parents,
> and they're always there ... whatever happens to you
> and they'll always like believe in you, and things that you do
> and they'll help you, when you need their help they'll help you,
> when you want to do something on your own,
> they'll stand back and let you do it.

Rosie here touches on something which Bachelard also picks up when he says: 'When we examine a nest, we place ourselves at the origin of confidence in the world, we receive a beginning of confidence, an urge towards cosmic confidence'.[50] So he takes us from ornithology 'out' to the cosmos, and reminds us that the division between physical and spiritual is artificial. Winnicott recognised, and Erikson affirmed, the foundational nature of the development of trust in children as we find it expressed by Rosie, and the necessity of its successful negotiation for the foundation of religious faith. Fowler attributes the development of his faith stage theory to Erikson's 'account of the crisis of the first stage, basic trust vs. mistrust, (which) avowedly deals with the foundations of faith in human life'.[51] Karen created in her home space a place in which she could transcend physical boundaries. In her early morning walks alone, secure in the knowledge that her family was asleep in the house, she followed a self-made ritual to earth herself, to exert some control, a regular rite in which she took on a quasi-priestly role: she designed what she did in the space, but it was in order to abandon herself to 'intervention' and communication with Otherness or God. Only trust in her environment enabled her to do this:

---

[49]   Bachelard, *The Poetics of Space*, p. 99.
[50]   Ibid., pp. 102–3.
[51]   Fowler, *Stages*, p. 109.

I like to have half an hour or so downstairs on my own
before anybody else gets up …
there's some really odd things like
I always go out to get the milk when the milkman's delivered it …
and I go out like … I end up walking down the garden and just talk …
Not out loud, not too loud anyway!
If I was too loud someone might hear …
I don't feel like I'm talking to somebody but they don't answer,
they listen.

For Karen, this space in which she feels accepted and 'known' is a sanctuary for her, one which 'witness(es) God's holiness and welcom(es) the vulnerable'.[52]

Amnion – The Containing Membrane

In the inner sac, the foetus floats in amniotic fluid. I have shown that Winnicott and Kegan employ this image appropriately to illustrate the need for connection to the holding environment while growth and change are taking place in safe space towards the eventual separation that each new 'birth', with its reconfiguration of relationships, will bring. Kegan, however, loses sight of the dynamic activity of the foetus in the space the sac enfolds. As I read Kegan's description of the child '"floating" as in an amniotic environment', my body and my emotions react as a mother, recalling the moments in each of my own pregnancies when I felt the first flutter of movement of the new life growing within, and how the relationship I had with my child changed as for the next weeks they explored their growing skills, and the boundaries of their containing vessel, turning and twisting in joyous play. The child's own agency is biologically limited, but is inherent in that each is a unique individual to whom the mother is offering the hospitality of her body. Irigaray describes how a woman 'welcome(s) the other in her soul, not only in her body'.[53] For a short while, she offers the 'felicitous space' of Bachelard's 'home'.[54]

In this section, then, I discuss girls' agency in their own nurturance through seeing the amnion as playroom, their activity as play. Berryman, following Winnicott, states that from the psychological standpoint, 'playing takes place in the intermediate and overlapping area of experience between the "me" and the "not me"',[55] which describes not only the process of early identity formation but of self-discovery at subsequent stages, too. From a sociological perspective, and in her

---

[52]   Jensen, *Graced Vulnerability*, p. 112. Jensen ascribes sanctuary only to the church, but these girls show how certain conditions can render other spaces holy.

[53]   Irigaray, *Luce Irigaray: Key Writings*, p. 167.

[54]   Bachelard, *The Poetics of Space*, p. xxxv.

[55]   Jerome Berryman, *Godly Play: An Imaginative Approach to Religious Education* (Minneapolis, 1991), p. 11.

study with children aged nine to 13, Mayall finds young people define play as what happens in free time, time out of adult control. In accordance with the sociological paradigm that children are active participants in constructing their lives, play is seen as acquiring and working up their identities; it 'has a developmental and social function; (and) performance in play is engagement with real life'.[56] Thus, in describing as play the girls' exploration of their psychological and spiritual identity, I am not belittling the activity but seeing it as formative. Play, then, denotes activity which serves the purpose of that self-discovery and orientation (or re-orientation) in the face of increasingly independent life experience; this includes experimentation with identities, responsibilities, relationships, beliefs and ideas on the path to living authentically in a community which offers girls support towards wholeness, physically, emotionally, cognitively and spiritually. Although I will focus predominantly on play as I interpret it happening within the church context, where the girls show themselves to be 'playing' in other contexts, I will draw on those, too.

Play is serious business, but it also allows for fun, relaxation and laughter. Although my interviews were about serious issues, both in the individual and group contexts, they were filled with laughter as we talked and interacted with each other in different ways. Each interview ended with the sharing of chocolate! Physical play was an intrinsic part of the normal group time together in two churches. The weeknight activity in one church began with a half hour of games: while most boys joined in, not all the girls did, many preferring their own 'play' between themselves, talking in small groups and with a noticeable degree of physical contact – handholding, hugging, preening one another. Sociological analysis of girls' friendship makes us aware of the complexity of this behaviour as a cultural phenomenon[57] and raises the question of whether the behaviour displayed in the play space was a tacit submission to patriarchy, its objective being to bring themselves under male surveillance, or evidence of a defiant homosocial feminism (sub)consciously resisting hetero/social pressures. Hey comments that 'it is between and amongst girls as friends that identities are variously practised, appropriated, resisted, negotiated', and McRobbie that 'girls negotiate a different leisure space and different personal spaces from those inhabited by boys'; their tight-knit friendship groups in the immediate pre-teen years 'can be viewed as responses ... to their anxieties about moving into the world of teenage sexual interaction'.[58] Where I met with girls in single gender groupings I noticed that public display of friendship was not evident, but most girls talked of similar activity with their friends in private spaces.

Sociological analysis as above has strayed into psychology, and Winnicott contributed substantially to the recognition that 'playing facilitates growth and

---

[56]   B. Mayall, *Towards a Sociology for Childhood: Thinking from Children's Lives* (Maidenhead, 2002), p. 133.

[57]   For example, A. McRobbie, *Feminism and Youth Culture*, 2nd edn (Basingstoke, 2000), pp. 12–25.

[58]   Hey, *The Company She Keeps*, p. 30; McRobbie, *Feminism and Youth Culture*, p. 24.

therefore health'.[59] The ability to play is, according to Winnicott 'intimately connected ... with the ability happily to be alone in the presence of somebody'.[60] On this foundation, Berryman builds his 'Godly Play', which although systematising play, recognises the importance of spontaneity to encourage new experience. He says: 'the significant moment in such experiencing is when a child ... at play surprises himself or herself with a glimpse of the true self. Godly play is growth-enhancing, because it is a place where one can be not only with the true self but also with the true self of others. Moreover, it is a place that also includes being within the earth and with the Creator God'.[61]

Berryman thus points us to a crucial role of the church to offer a safe space within which girls can not only chill and have fun, but experiment with ideas, with different identities, alone or with others. Miller-McLemore reminds us of the implications of the experimental nature of such play for girls/boys: 'they need a certain protected sphere of irresponsibility that allows them to play with words, actions, and commitments for which they do not yet have to answer'.[62] It is in the amniotic playspace that ideas about God are tried out, as discussed in the previous chapter, and the awareness of the presence of God nurtured and enjoyed. To return to Karen, she named just such experience, not in the church building, but as she walked in her garden in the early morning, and felt close to 'something'. She was reluctant to name God, as she was developing her own understanding and relationship, which she preferred not to be limited by the lessons she had been taught. Speaking out in one's own voice as she was doing is seen by Brown and Gilligan as an act of resistance to being defined by the given speech, 'the established story' of the lives of women who influence her within her context; psychological wholeness stems from authoring one's own feelings and views. Brown and Gilligan note the inherent relationality of speech (it is to be heard by another) but also how the sound changes in resonance depending on the 'relational acoustics'.[63] What Karen needed in order to continue to experiment with her own words was to be heard by God and to know she was heard.

Play serves another psychological function which supports the spiritual quest at times of transition. While transition can be positive in the benefits it can bring through 'a freeing up of one's internal life, an openness to and playfulness about oneself' resulting in new insights and transcendent experiences, Kegan notes that 'the same loosening up may be experienced as boundary loss ... and the experience of not knowing'.[64] Watts, Nye and Savage see play as having a supportive

[59]   D.W. Winnicott, *Playing and Reality* (London, 1971), chapter 3.

[60]   A. Newman, *Winnicott's Words: A Companion to the Writings and Work of D.W. Winnicott* (London, 1995), p. 333.

[61]   J. Berryman, *Godly Play: An Imaginative Approach to Religious Education* (Minneapolis, 1991), pp. 11–12.

[62]   Miller-McLemore, *Let the Children Come*, p. 131.

[63]   Brown and Gilligan, *Meeting at the Crossroads*, p. 20.

[64]   Kegan, *Evolving Self*, p. 231.

functioning through the losses involved in transition, giving us 'comforting access to old ways of seeing things … recharging our confidence to face new learning challenges' and making it 'easier to respond positively to cognitive conflict as schemata begin to crumble'.[65] So Karen, Sarah and Hannah all agreed, in response to pictures I showed them without human images, that they fed their imagination which could then play in a free rather than a 'real rushed world'. We have seen in the reflections of Lucy, Rosie and Suzanne, a strong creative edge which leads the girls to play confidently with new ideas, stretching their grasp of mystery through image and word play. However, others also gave examples of having their roots in old ways of seeing God. Julie looked back to

> when I was quite young
> all I knew was that God created the world,
> and I knew that he was just powerful,

and contrasted this with the complexity she now found in understanding God in the face of the evil she was becoming more personally acquainted with. Although she assigned playfulness to childhood innocence, Julie had not outgrown play but tussled with her new questions in the dramas she wrote. By playing the part of Jesus, she gained profound insight into the passion, for example. Mary, in her own mode of playfulness in her relationship with Jesus, saw him as a companion, 'someone you can … talk to and have a laugh with and he'll support you'.

Some of the girls' contexts fostered playfulness more than others. Julie's drama was encouraged through public performance; the girls' group in another church also experimented with drama, and they valued the freedom of making posters 'about God and the Kingdom of God'. Lucy explained that 'there wasn't a set thing, we could just paint the board with anything we wanted to doodle with' but through the conversations that ensued, they began to understand and value their different views of God. In the church where the evening began with games, the group work was prescribed, and there was less evidence of creative thinking and playfulness: the girls seemed concerned as to whether they were giving the 'right' response.

Girls from every context described the importance to their faith growth of times away from church routines, sometimes on family holidays, more often on a retreat or visit organised by the school, or a church camp. Although different, each offered an environment made safe by the presence of known and trusted adults where 'inward bound' opportunities[66] could be enjoyed: all testified to the impact on their growth in self-awareness, faith expression and commitments.

---

[65]   Fraser Watts, Rebecca Nye and Sara Savage, *Psychology for Christian Ministry* (London and New York, 2002), p. 125.

[66]   The phrase is used by Pearmain, 'Transformational Experiences', p. 278. An example of creative material for use in such a context can be found in Donna Humphreys,

Mirroring is another function of the uterine analogy. There is evidence from my data that some girls were not only following models to grow spiritually as with Amber and Bethan, but needed to see an image of themselves reflected back in or by another. This was true of Karen in the example of how another girl offered her a reflection of herself:

> We went on a retreat day
> and we had to write down
> what we thought about certain people in the form,
> and one girl who I've never really like … like talked to her
> because she was always quite nasty to me, em
> said that em she was willing to say what she thought about people
> and when she came to me she said
> that I always listen to her
> even though I wasn't her friend.

Far from agreeing with her own view of herself as a nonentity, this girl, unbeknown to Karen, had observed and valued her ability as a listener, an attribute Karen herself confirmed when describing her mediation skills: when her friends argued, she said,

> it's always me that says
> 'right, come and sit down
> and I'm going to listen to you
> and you're going to shut up',
> and then the same thing (the other way round),
> and everybody talks and sometimes it gets sorted out.

Fowler recognises at puberty a need for others to see and reflect back 'the image of *person*-ality emerging and to get a hearing for the new feelings, insights, anxieties and commitments that are forming and seeking expression'.[67]

Irigaray's mirror, the speculum ('an inner space of reflection')[68] leads us into another aspect of mirroring rooted in philosophy and psychoanalysis. Where in Freudian analysis of the girl there is 'nothing to be seen', the speculum reveals herself to herself, in interior presence not in absence.[69] Irigaray's cave, as explored by Beattie, is the one from which Plato's prisoner journeyed into the light of the sun, which she interprets as an allegory of man's turning away from the 'materiality

---

Gloria Koll and Sally Windecker, *Daughters Arise! A Christian Retreat Resource for Girls Approaching Womanhood* (Cleveland, 2002).

[67] Fowler, *Stages*, p. 151. Author's italics.

[68] Luce Irigaray, *Speculum of the Other Woman*, trans. G.C. Gill (New York, 1985), p. 255.

[69] Irigaray counters Freud in *Speculum*, p. 47.

and bodiliness of the womb with its own fire to the wider horizon' where the 'functioning of representation' supersedes, indeed eradicates, the 'originating role of the womb',[70] the foundation of phallogocentrism and patriarchy. Irigaray rejects patriarchal discourse which has shaped woman's identity. In reclaiming the womb as the place of identity formation, Irigaray offers an alternative narrative which enables girls confidently to explore their feminine subjectivity 'in great part still unknown and yet to be cultivated'.[71] She validates, as Gilligan does, the preferred horizontal relationships of girls and women, but sees it as prefigured in the birth of a girl to one of the same. To Irigaray, woman's spiritual becoming is to 'be who I am', working out her own differentiation 'in a relation of dialogue with our own gender'.[72] Mary explored her own embodied femininity through identification with Esther, with whom she felt an affinity; Amber rejoiced in the embodied nature of her relationship with her mother. Keller extracts from Winnicott the importance he attaches to the good enough mother who 'mirrors the infant back to itself with the real empathy that allows itself to be itself, to see and feel itself',[73] a mirroring which Beattie applies to growth 'into a sense of her own being', peculiar to women, 'through living in the gaze of love'.[74] Like Beattie and others who reflect on Irigaray's work, Keller claims for the mother–daughter relationship salvific qualities equivalent or superior to father–son, posing in their connectedness a positive alternative to Freudian separation and individuation which is only achieved, she says, at the cost of matricide.[75] Keller thus affirms the image my analysis has identified: 'the original continuum with the mother (symbolic and literal) need not be matricidally ruptured'. She goes on to muse over the consequences:

> what would it be like if … maturation meant the gradual differentiation and modulation of the empathic continuum. We would know ourselves neither bound to parent figures nor severed from them … If symbols – or better – metaphors – transform, their deliteralising force can be encouraged rather than stifled along with the imagination of the child … Connection without constriction: this is the mystery the rising girl-child may be able to teach us.[76]

[70]   Beattie, *God's Mother*, pp. 90–91.
[71]   Irigaray, *Luce Irigaray: Key Writings*, p. x.
[72]   Ibid., p. 153.
[73]   Keller, *From a Broken Web*, p. 143.
[74]   Beattie, *Woman*, p. 56.
[75]   Keller, *From a Broken Web*, p. 153.
[76]   Ibid., p. 154.

Placenta –The Connecting Organ

To continue with the physiological metaphor, my third image is the placenta where the umbilical cord, formed out of the fusion of amnion and chorion, embeds within the uterine wall. It is 'the organ that carries out respiration, nutrition and excretion for the embryo'.[77] Through the placenta, the foetus receives nourishment from the maternal host and expels waste. Analogically, the image represents the attachment of the girls to those environments which offer them the greatest opportunity for flourishing. As their identities become increasingly individual, they will give priority to those environments which match their character, interests and skills, and represent the values they espouse. Church may be only one of a number of competing environments, but only Georgia spoke of a deep connection to another community beyond family, school and church. In the army cadets, she found her identity through its discipline and its development of her leadership skills, recognised by her promotion to Lance Corporal, which to her was 'pretty big'. With that came a responsibility for younger girls, and a high degree of self-awareness; the cadets provided her with another community through which she could express her faith and which would, she hoped, in future help her to act on it by involvement in relief work as a manifestation of God's response to suffering: 'you can see everybody here (in a disaster situation) working with God ... to help'.

I explore next how attachment to the community works for girls, and how paradoxically they grow in independence and differentiation through its nurturance.

Differentiation, the development of selfhood, happens within attachment, as relationships are adapted both to the girls' changing self and through the effect they have on the environment. To belong is to be attached but in a relationship of mutuality. We not only receive from a host but give in return. This begins in the womb. After birth, a baby, while still dependent on its parents for everything, belongs by giving both delight and response to its carers who are changed in the process; its giving increases as it grows and is able to contribute to the construction of the family's identity (this is true for disabled as well as abled children). The family's strength and the child's healthy psychological growth lie to a significant degree in the level of positive participation in, and ability to influence, that structuring.

In any relationship between adults and children there will be inequality, but Miller-McLemore adopts Carter Heyward's concept of 'transitional hierarchy' which recognises that 'conceptions of mutuality are multivalent or age-, expertise-, and context-dependent, as appropriate for adult relationship with children', moving towards but not yet having reached genuine mutuality because of temporary inequity in wisdom and maturity.[78] Increased control of domestic space and time by demands of parental lifestyle (if both parents work, and at

---

[77] Snell, *Clinical Embryology*, p. 42.

[78] Miller-McLemore, *Let the Children Come*, pp. 130–31.

'unsocial' hours) and school, which expects homework of all ages, inhibits the extent to which children can exercise agency in their home. Mayall found that, despite increasing restriction and prescription, solidarity with and interdependence within the family was enjoyed and valued, but towards the early teen years 'within the broad parameters of parental authority, young people reported that they aimed to exercise some control over activity'.[79] While recognising their need to learn from adults, they expected to share the division of labour but also to negotiate its limits, employing identifiable tactics to gain more control over their use of time and space. In my study, Rosie likewise showed herself to be a skilled tactician: 'if someone says "do something" and you say "no, I can't do that cos I've just done my nails", you can get away with that!'. Girls, then, saw both negotiated participation and learning as functions of their childhood.[80]

If this is the ideal for domestic space, how does the church environment measure up? How far do girls see it as a place of belonging through participation in its life? As participants in wider society, James and Prout are clear that 'children are and must be seen as active in the construction and determination of their own social lives, the lives of those around them and of the societies in which they live'.[81] A prerequisite is that the church understand itself in theological terms as a pilgrim people engaged in a teleological journey (rather than as a fixed structure) and therefore able to receive from and be changed by all people who join the community. In her social analysis, Mayall notes the limits to which in society at large, people have opportunity to effect change; she follows critical realists in exploring the ontological distinction between agent and structure and the process of interaction by which transformation can occur showing both the limitations and possibilities of agency.[82] She avers that as a minority social group, girls/boys exert the least influence on social change in society generally. However, when the church as a social unit is in the business of 'transformation', the possibility must always be open that girls/boys can indeed influence the structure. In interviews with ministers of two churches, I found evidence that girls' initiatives had effected change, in one case in internal structuring, and in the other in the church's profile and mission opportunities in the community.

A church as a voluntary group is more capable of self-analysis and internal transformation through theological reflection than other institutions; indeed it has gospel imperatives so to do. Mayall draws attention to Bourdieu's contribution to the debate about generation, where he proposes the idea of 'social generation', i.e. identification between people of different generations where they share similar experiences.[83] Primarily connected with power relations, it may be appropriate to

---

[79] Mayall, *Towards a Sociology for Childhood*, p. 47.

[80] Ibid., chapter 4.

[81] James and Prout, *Constructing and Reconstructing Childhood*, p. 8.

[82] Mayall, *Towards a Sociology for Childhood*, p. 35.

[83] Bordieu's example is of immigrant families, who bring elements from the culture of their country of origin, so that their young people may find more in common with older

adopt it within a church setting, which in the eyes of society at large is a marginal institution. In my interviews, I found that membership of a cohort was not enough for the girls to feel a sense of belonging. Intergenerational sharing was named as a significant feature in their attachment to the environment. The experience of the womb itself is intergenerational: a mother nurtures a daughter in the womb. Girls regularly spoke of the impact on their faith of older people: Rosie was beginning to reflect on life after death through the elderly Edna who kept alive the memory of her dead sister within the community, and Amber was affirmed by a 'prophecy' given to her by a senior church member as she prepared for her baptism.

Most participation was initiated by adults. Worship in Rosie's church was interactive, and after a service where everyone had been encouraged to paint, she commented: 'there's always things you can do so it's not just sitting around listening to people talking'. She took part in public reading of scripture. In two churches, the girls participated in different ways in the communion service whether they received the elements or not. My initial encounter with Victoria was when she stood alongside her grandmother welcoming people into church. Michelle and Mary were members of the worship group. In one church, the minister drew young people with specific gifts into intergenerational not cohort groupings (music group, sports clubs), although none of the girls was participating in them at the time of my interviews.

Of particular value to nurture was participation as a product of their own creativity, especially when owned by the congregation at large. When Julie's play had been performed by a cast from the church, 'people kept coming up and saying like "that's a good play" and I felt quite proud having them tell me'. By contrast, Karen's experience of not being trusted by adults to organise a church lunch may be more typical of the response to a young person's initiative even in a church with an ethos accepting of girls/boys. This was in contrast to the trust shown in her skills as confidante and mediator by her friends; she was angry that in church she might be invisible, dismissed as 'somebody's daughter' (she belonged to a 'church family') and not seen as a person in her own right, the church was out of step with society's view of her. She likened it to the sexist designation of women by their husband's occupation: 'a while ago it would have been everybody's wife … but everyone else seems to have stopped saying that except in church'. Karen had developed an understanding of herself, and wanted to develop a skill, but feared older women would not relinquish their own position. The holding environment is only as strong as its members, and in analysing it, neither Kegan nor Hess gives adequate attention to the character of the community of which girls are a part, its composition and undergirding ideology. Hess in particular, writing about women's development in communities of faith, focuses her critique on formal structures and overt educational methodologies which still operate by male norms, but she ignores the hidden agendas where women themselves discriminate against girls

indigenous generations regarding for example behaviour and attitudes to work: Mayall, *Towards a Sociology for Childhood*, p. 38.

on generational grounds, reflecting the assumption that young teenagers do not have the capacity or the experience to organise well an all-age event. The adults in Karen's church are implicitly adopting developmental theories of childhood. Generational hierarchy was preventing Karen's voice being heard. As we have seen, sociology reminds us, as theology should, that girls are integral to the community; the environment does not stand outside them but must change as they participate, or foreclosure may result.

Because of the nature of their initiatives, the girls often did need adult help bringing their plans or ideas to fruition. Without the experience of Julie's minister her dramatic contribution to the community's life would not have been seen or heard. In Karen's case, the women may have felt threatened by another generation taking over something they saw as their way of expressing discipleship, so guarded it fiercely. Resistance highlights not only generational tension, but also different understandings of the teaching role of the church. In Mayall's study, she finds that young people expect an apprentice model to operate in the home, a training ground for the development of life skills in which they exercise increasing agency.[84] I explore this model further in my concluding chapter. In four of the churches, the girls were extensive contributors to the life of the church, even if to them it seemed limited: there was less obvious participation by the girls in the remaining church even on a Sunday, but in the weeknight activities in which I shared, the apprenticeship model operated to an extent, when the girls themselves led group discussion, although under close supervision. I have noted the conflict evident between working towards academic success and contributing to church life or engaging in Christian service as a mark of a discipleship which envisions self-giving. Appropriate discipleship models, and skills or structures for negotiation of fuller participation in church life, were not in evidence.

Nurturance within Protestant Churches

In many Protestant churches, pubertal transition also marks the point at which young people make a personal decision to own a faith for themselves, made public through the rite of confirmation or baptism. Churches vary as to the extent to which in their ecclesiology they regard girls/boys as full 'members', paedo- and believer-baptists representing the two extremes of view. Regardless of ecclesial status, however, nurture will only be as effective as those who 'hold' the young people: healthy growth does not depend on the size of peer groups, but on the relationship with one or more others, not just dedicated leaders, in the community who have the power of holding, releasing and remaining in place. The danger for any community is of holding too tightly, or of not letting go to allow the exercise of freedom, cognitive and spiritual as well as physical. The owning of personal faith marked by confirmation or believer's baptism is a goal to be striven for, but

---

[84]   Mayall, *Towards a Sociology for Childhood*, p. 47.

nurturance to that end could potentially become a straitjacket which constricts. Faithing conceived in experimental thought forms or new language may not be encouraged.

In discussing the embryonic holding of the girl, I have identified, as does Kegan, that how the holding is effected is as important as whether it is done at all. For him, the test is how existential anxiety connected with times of transition is handled by the 'holder'; where identity growth is accompanied by changes in ways of faithing, there must surely be a temptation to foreclose on her searching and questioning by the provision of 'answers', the doctrinal 'formulae' reflecting the theology of the adult body. Kegan suggests that offering solutions is unhelpful and he advocates provision of a balance, to 'enhance the "good-host" quality of embeddedness culture – providing careful attention, recognition, confirmation and company in the experience ... not (to) tighten a grip by creating a dependence on the host to solve or manage the experiences of disequilibrium'. By standing alongside someone experiencing pain (here, the pain of pubertal transition), he says, 'we testify to our faith in the trustworthiness of the motion of evolution, to our faith in the trustworthiness of life itself'.[85] 'Letting go' is hard to achieve for many when the issues at stake are of ultimate significance, but holding too tightly can lead to unhealthy dependence on external authority, lacking personal validation which Fowler sees as one of the indicators of healthy growth in faith.[86]

What is often missed is the necessity of Kegan's third criterion for emerging identity, for the holding environment to remain in place and to accept the new configuration both of personhood and of faith construction. That will require two areas of reconstruction: firstly in the way the young person is viewed in the community, credit being given for the emergence of new abilities and capacities for responsibility, and secondly in the way the community does its own faithing as it companions girls on their lived encounter between faith and 'world'. This is a challenge to all in a church and a test of their own participation in the pilgrim journey.

---

[85]   Kegan, *Evolving Self*, p. 126.
[86]   Fowler, *Stages*, p. 287.

Chapter 9
Affirming Girls through Transition

I begin my concluding chapter, as the first, with the bible. Two further pre-pubertal girls in scripture help open up a way forward to thinking about and caring for girls in our churches.

The Adopted Daughter[1]

Critical attention has focused on Ezekiel's portrayal of Jerusalem as harlot in chapters 16 and 23, a controversial theme in Hosea, Isaiah and Jeremiah as well as Ezekiel. Ezekiel, possibly taking his cue from Hosea, wants both to locate the origin of the people's faithlessness in an imputed impurity and rejection at conception, and to attribute to God the rescue and special care of Jerusalem (i.e. the people of Judah), imaged here as daughter, at birth. So, YHWH has pity on the girl child, and where parental pity and compassion have failed, gratuitously offers both in, we presume, cutting the cord, symbolically severing her links with her 'godless' birth parents, and legally adopting her, fulfilling the promise of Isaiah 49.15. Without help she cannot survive. The allusion here is to the abandonment of girl babies in other Ancient Near Eastern cultures, which serves as a message to Israel and her neighbours that girls are precious to God. Zimmerli links divine initiative here with that in the creation narratives of Genesis chapters 1 and 2; her innocent nakedness and potential for fruitfulness at the coming to maturity are the markers which differentiate the girl from the whore she becomes.[2]

As in Genesis chapter 1 creation is by divine word, so here her living is commanded. YHWH's word alone saves her: 'Live and grow up like the plant of the field'. Parental rejection at birth was so complete that the amniotic fluid and uterine blood were not washed away. YHWH's word, signifying adoption, then comes 'in your blood', usually a metonymic for death according to Block,[3] but here the word which calls her instead to fullness of life as YHWH's own child, and affirms her generative capacity in the thematic linking of her birth and menstrual bloods. This new connection, between blood, life and God, is suggested by De Troyer: although her argument is primarily about the 'uncleanness' of women after

---

[1]   Ezekiel 16.4–7.

[2]   Walter Zimmerli, *Ezekiel 1, A Commentary on the Book of the Prophet Ezekiel, Chapters 1–24* (Philadelphia, 1979), p. 338.

[3]   Daniel Block, *The Book of Ezekiel, Chapters 1–24* New International Commentary on the Old Testament (Grand Rapids, 1997), pp. 480f.

childbirth in Leviticus, and her discussion of the Ezekiel passage is in that context, she emphasises that 'it is God who gives life to the child, for it is God who says to the person in blood, "Live"'. Looking forward to the girl child's potential for creating new life herself, she goes further and suggests a theological partnership between women and God in the creation of all life: indeed, reflecting the fragility of birth, she claims God puts 'a woman at the border of life and death'. In Ezekiel, then, she sees God's adoption of an infant girl as the first stage of a relationship which culminates in a covenant which comes to its completion 'at the time when she is ready for loving and giving birth'.[4]

There is clearly a problem to be faced here in that girls appear to be valued only for their capacity physically to give birth: my own explorations in the borderlands of puberty are arguing for a metaphorical generativity, signifying their giving birth on many layers, to identity, ideas, relationships and so on. Many commentators see the girl only through the lens of the prostitute metaphor of the chapter, suggesting for example that these opening verses are intended to insult Jerusalem, and allegorise the details of the narrative.[5] Feminist exegesis in its turn deals savagely with Ezekiel for his sexualised treatment of woman both as bride and as harlot, and the opening verses of the chapter cannot be too far removed from the remainder. However there is, I suggest, a theological insight contained here, consistent with the role assigned to girls elsewhere in biblical literature, which associates them with natality; in a variety of ways actually or symbolically by their presence or their actions they signify newness of life.

The Slave Girl

The slave girl in Philippi 'healed' by Paul[6] is treated there only as object. Commentators take at face value her demonic possession,[7] and however they conceive of the place of this story in the wider narrative of the spread of Christianity to Europe through Paul's 'second missionary journey', the girl herself remains a pawn of her owners and her silencing a symbol of the victory of the gospel over inimical pagan forces. Following Musa Dube's work on other biblical women, Staley assigns to the slave girl and to Lydia, whose story immediately precedes this one, a 'border' position, the one receptive and positive, the other resistant

---

[4]   De Troyer, 'Blood: A Threat to Holiness or toward (Another) Holiness', in De Troyer et al., *Wholly Woman, Wholly Blood*, p. 55. See also N.R. Bowen, *Ezekiel* (Nashville, 2010), p. 85.

[5]   Paul M. Joyce, *Ezekiel: A Commentary* (New York and London, 2007), p. 130.

[6]   Acts 16:16–19.

[7]   F.F. Bruce, *The Book of Acts*, rev. edn (Grand Rapids, 1988), pp. 312–14. Bruce Malina and John Pilch argue on the basis of Luke's omission of the definite article in v 17 that Paul concluded it was a deceptive spirit, *Social Science Commentary on the Book of Acts* (Minneapolis, 2008), p. 118.

and negative, both intimately connected politically.[8] It is possible to surmise an alternative interpretation of the story, which foregrounds the girl as subject. Girls' propensity to spirituality and spiritual insight sometimes of an ecstatic nature, such as the experiences named by both Karen and Amber as featuring in their spiritual lives, is regularly attested in history; such a gift would leave the slave girl wide open to exploitation by her owners. In historical accounts of arguably similar phenomena, it appears arbitrary, or dependent on context, whether their utterances are seen as demonic or divine: Joan of Arc's voices, for example, for which she was charged with heresy, and more debatably the Salem 'witches', in contrast to the validity accorded the 'prophecies' of Sarah Wight.[9] The slave girl narrative story raises many questions, but I suggest that she may have had real spiritual insight into the identity of Paul and his companions; her revelation appears to exceed that of Legion whose demons Jesus exorcised, and who became a disciple. Is the divergent treatment meted out to her because she is female and young? The borderlands of oppression she inhabited may have opened up to her a pathway to freedom, a 'way of salvation', but she disappears from the story once her use to her owners has gone, and the focus transfers to their battle with Paul and Silas, leading to their miraculous release. Is this a further case of the silencing of a marginal voice, young, female and foreign, despite Jesus' attention to another such victim in the gospel narrative?[10]

Each of these biblical girls is in a time and place of transition and subject to profound change. In Ezekiel's metaphor, this has a positive outcome, conceived as a new covenant relationship with God with all its potential for reciprocal commitment to the giving and receiving of love and its fruitful outcomes. The opposite appears to be the case for the slave girl, forced into and abandoned in her transition. The liminality of her experience has been named but ignored.

From Gestation to Birth

Like these biblical girls, those whom I studied were in transition, not only moving from one life 'stage' to another, but living through a period resonant with that in childbirth between the first and second stages, the time that immediately precedes the climactic push to bring the crowning and delivery of the newborn. I have imaged this whole period in a girl's life as a wombing, but she cannot remain in the womb, and must make the painful passage through the birth canal. The liminal

---

[8] Jeffrey L. Staley, 'Changing Woman: A Postcolonial, Postfeminist Interpretation of Acts 16.6–40', in A.-J. Levine and M. Blickenstaff (eds), *A Feminist Companion to Acts* (London, 2004).

[9] Moore, 'Such Perfecting of Praise', pp. 313–24.

[10] The Canaanite woman whose daughter was 'tormented by a demon', Matthew 15.22–28.

place she inhabits is 'a difficult and confusing stage leading to new life'.[11] It is a time of patient waiting, of holding back the urge to push when undue haste could damage the outcome, of feeling overwhelmed by tremendous forces which you cannot control. Guenther describes it as 'frightening … of surprising power', and 'a dark, seemingly chaotic period',[12] language reminiscent of some of the girls' own experiences of puberty as my data has revealed.

As we anticipate the outcome of the gestation I have been discussing, we need to remember that childbirth has two essential participants to the experience, infant and mother. I now bring both into my play of imagery as I explore the relationship between the girls and their holding environment which offers the context for their birthing. For a girl is both birthing and being birthed into a new identity; she cannot resist the forces impelling her towards birth, but she is also the agent in the process, enduring the pain and exerting the effort bringing about her own re-emergence in a new form. The application of birthing metaphors to the process of human growth is not new. Kegan describes such transition as we prepare to 'deal with the next chapter of life' in terms of birth, which brings with it a sense of contradiction between what was, and what is emerging: although applying the analogy to an earlier transition, his imagery is equally relevant for girls at puberty, moving 'between the more perfectly responsive intrauterine environment and the less perfectly responsive extrauterine one'.[13]

The Church as Midwife

Birthing should not be done alone: optimally, it requires the companionship of a midwife for assistance and support, the one who understands the desolation of transition as 'a sign of breakthrough and great progress', who can 'encourage and interpret when the birthgiver may feel she has lost control and failed'.[14] The image of the midwife brings rich theological insights. In a biblical context, Claassens explores the role of God as midwife, highlighting Psalm 22 where it generates trust within an experience of desolation and grief for which traditional language 'proves to be wholly inadequate in the current situation'. Two things are happening here, she says. Firstly, the use of the image recognises the dangerous nature of the natal experience (maternal mortality rate then was high; childbirth today is not without risk), so to assign this role to God is to acknowledge the liminality of 'those moments when death and life tend to intersect': the midwife is the companion 'in the midst of suffering and despair'. This takes seriously the danger and grief I have identified as latent features of girls' movement into puberty. Secondly, Claassens

[11]   Margaret Guenther, *Holy Listening: The Art of Spiritual Direction* (London, 1993), p. 102.
[12]   Ibid., p. 99.
[13]   Kegan, *Evolving Self*, p. 123.
[14]   Guenther, *Holy Listening*, p. 90.

draws attention to the creation of a new symbolic order within this process whereby the subject of the experience transforms 'the authoritarian discourse of the past into an internally persuasive discourse ... that breaks open the traditional formulations about God'.[15] Such a movement towards new formulations about God was evident in the voices of the girls whom I interviewed. Among Fowler's seven categories which distinguish people's faith at each 'stage of development', he includes 'locus of authority' and 'forms of world coherence'; steps towards maturity are taken when we move from having an external to a more self-authored source of authority making us 'more self-reliant' together with a 'qualitatively new degree of self-responsibility for the forming system of images, values and stories that constitute the unity and coherence of one's meaning world'.[16]

Guenther adopts the same image for the accompanist in spiritual growth, basing it not only on divine midwifery, but on scripture's wider use of birthing both literal and symbolic; women such as Shiphrah and Puah[17] 'stand guardian' over moments of new birth, which she links with our own 'stories of new life that redirect and transform'.[18] The aptness of this model, to Guenther, lies in the quality of the relationship between midwife and birthgiver, one of trust and mutual respect at a time of utter vulnerability. The midwife may be tempted to act out of experience and professionalism, but that would betray the trust, for she is to do things '*with*, not *to* the person giving birth'.[19] Transposing this into the field of education, and utilising Freire's 'problem-posing' methodology, Belenky et al. similarly emphasise the midwife/teacher's role to 'preserve the student's fragile newborn thoughts, to see that they are born with their truth intact', echoed by Guenther for whom the midwife as teacher 'helps the birthgiver towards ever greater self-knowledge'.[20]

The image also speaks to Baker. 'Girls', she says, 'need companions, midwives who are willing to deal with the messiness of life and to celebrate the clear, shining moments as they come'.[21] Recognising the huge responsibility and commitment of girls' accompanists at this critical time, she develops the thesis put forward by Mercer, to promote 'wholeness and thriving' among adolescent girls, who

---

[15]   L. Juliana M. Claassens, 'Rupturing God-Language: The Metaphor of God as Midwife in Psalm 22', in Day and Pressler, *Engaging the Bible in a Gendered World*, pp. 170–72. That Jesus' cry of dereliction from the (ultimately liminal) cross is drawn from this Psalm heightens the theological significance of the imagery.

[16]   Fowler, *Stages*, p. 300.

[17]   Exodus 1.15–22.

[18]   Guenther, *Holy Listening*, p. 85.

[19]   Guenther, *Holy Listening*, p. 90. Author's emphasis.

[20]   Belenky et al., *Women's Ways of Knowing*, pp. 217–19; Guenther, *Holy Listening*, p. 90.

[21]   Baker, *Doing Girlfriend Theology*, p. 163.

expressed a hunger for in-depth conversation about ethical issues, theology, family relationships, romance, friendship, the future and much more. Girls affirmed the value of simply being listened to for an extended period of time.[22]

Baker and Mercer are here extending the midwife role into that of mentor. Unlike a mother giving birth to a new being, another subject, a girl is birthing her own subjectivity, so additional images must be found to enlarge the scope of the formative relationship to offer her a wider range of resources to feed her spiritual growth. Mentoring for the adult partner, apprenticeship for the girl, are commonly used, although there is danger here of an imbalance of power within the implied hierarchy of relationship. These models may not meet the relational closeness the girls seek.

As mentor, the adult comes alongside not as teacher, but primarily as listener, to hear the often faltering words of the speaker, encouraging her to speak her heart, to mirror back what the mentor has heard, and to share in reflection, maybe drawing on her own experience as in Baker's process,[23] but primarily to provide 'safe space for adolescent women to tell their stories and to probe the emerging horizons of hope in their lives'.[24]

Mayall observes how some young people themselves 'subscribe to the socialization thesis', and, seeing their childhood as preparation for adult life, accept the understanding of themselves as apprentices.[25] Mercer promotes this model for Christian nurture, based on her understanding of a relationship which depends on the presence of a more seasoned practitioner, one who is experienced in practices of faith. Mayall describes apprenticeship in terms similar to Westerhoff's affiliative faith, 'seeking to act with others in an accepting community with a clear sense of identity'.[26] This offers girls a structured learning environment, but must be treated with caution as, typifying faithing of an earlier phase for those who have grown up in the church, it could inhibit their quest (searching) for an 'owned' faith. At this age, they do not all yet have the security of personal identity which can live with too much uncertainty, but some do now recognise that ambiguity and openness are part of the faithing enterprise. I have shown how they all need the security of knowing a God who is worthy of their trust, who loves, cares for and protects them and those close to them. Openness can be fraught with the danger of relativism where truth is seen as dependent on context and interpretation, and fails to offer that security. To close down questioning, however, and to transmit only received tradition of bible and church (all itself the product of interpretation,

---

22   J.-A. Mercer, 'Gender, Violence and Faith: Adolescent Girls and the Theological Anthropology of Difference' (PhD diss., 1997), quoted by Baker, *Doing Girlfriend Theology*, p. 165.

23   Baker, *Doing Girlfriend Theology*, pp. 33–4.

24   Ibid., p. viii.

25   Mayall, *Towards a Sociology for Childhood*, p. 47.

26   Westerhoff, *Will Our Children Have Faith?*, p. 91.

of which the girls are largely unaware) denies the exercise of creativity and generativity in the developing of an enriching personal relationship with God which by its adaptability will develop skills to help negotiate the further changes of increasing maturity and independence. Hess acknowledges the challenge of a questioning approach, but stresses the importance of an education which 'involves handing over to our daughters ... the forbidden fruits of curiosity, inquiry, critical thinking, and voice'.[27]

To be accompanied on this journey by trusted adults could indeed be to enter into something analogous to an apprenticeship, although its adoption as a primary model could inhibit the reciprocity of trust and respect for the other which the midwife image brings. Heidegger uses the analogy of a cabinet-maker who learns from an experienced teacher, but who also develops self-authored skill and intuitive creativity. Not only does the apprentice learn to use tools to practise techniques, but also 'makes himself [*sic*] answer and respond above all to different kinds of wood and to the shapes slumbering within the wood'.[28] For a girl, the goal is to learn the skill of theological reflection which, with practice, becomes similarly intuitive. As a way of doing theology, such nurturance helps her to deal with the disturbance caused by new experience drawing on the certainty generated by tradition, tried and tested but not absolute; it encourages play at 'a place where religious belief, tradition and practice meets contemporary experiences, questions, and actions and conducts a dialogue that is mutually enriching, intellectually critical, and practically transforming'.[29] If this is done within a secure holding environment as Kegan envisages and Hess translates for girls in faith communities, there is the potential for them to live securely with faith while sharing their doubts and questions as they conceive of fresh answers to the question 'who is God for you?'. For Hess, this is achieved in trusting relationship forged through 'hard dialogue and deep conversation', with experience shared between conversation partners, and with scripture in a spirit of critical enquiry.[30]

I observed a kind of apprenticeship in the churches from a more evangelical tradition, and it lacked the fuzzy edges which encourage and accept experimentation. Here, a lesson[31] was the key component of adult/girl interaction, and faith practices were played out in a worship setting. By this means the girls were learning skills for public and private observance, engaging in prayer, in discussion leading and in quasi-liturgical rites in a safe and supportive space. Some girls were gaining in confidence as their leaders attested, and the strength

---

[27]   Hess, *Caretakers of our Common House*, p. 183.

[28]   Quoted by Veling, *Practical Theology*, p. 16.

[29]   Stephen Pattison with James Woodward, *A Vision of Pastoral Theology* (Edinburgh: Contact Pastoral, 1994).

[30]   Hess, *Caretakers of our Common House*, chapter 6.

[31]   Using material published by Scripture Union. It broadly involved a bible passage, questions for discussion around its application for Christian living and a moral message with varying degrees of prescription, accompanied by a creative follow-up activity.

of peer relationships in which this took place gave some of them courage to speak their faith in the more threatening external environments. Their leaders used language of 'progress' and 'development' in describing the girls' faith, a significant goal being its public practice as an evangelistic strategy. This is consistent with the common adherence I found among adults to the developmental paradigm. However, the girls in this church showed less originality of expression and wrestling with ideas when speaking of their understanding of and relationship with God, and of theological engagement with issues around them in the wider world. In another church where there was regular interaction with adults on a more relational non-didactic level and where the girls were encouraged to play with ideas and discuss issues, I recorded some of the most profound insights into the being and action of God, and of their own relationship with God and place in God's economy. Girls such as Lucy and Rosie were certainly influenced by the faith stories of adult women, who might be seen as mentors. The evidence from observation of all the girls suggests, however, that although apprenticeship satisfies an important dimension of faith learning, it is not a sufficient model by which faithing can grow and mature; that is better attained in relationship with 'midwives'.

Mercer recognises the risk of the process bringing change to both parties; accompanists have opportunities 'to reopen and unsettle what has become closed and too settled in their own faith'.[32] In the mutual exploration of issues, adults must be willing to receive as well as to give. Effective accompaniment also demands, on the adults' part, some knowledge of theological themes, ethical principles, and Christian tradition that many have not themselves been offered as intrinsic to their diet of preaching and teaching. While I endorse Mercer's argument that adults do not need to have their own religious lives worked out in order to support girls spiritually,[33] many of those who accompany young people on this journey do not apparently show a willingness to engage in biblical or theological learning for personal transformation. In my work as an adult educator, I experience regular resistance by otherwise committed church members to accessible learning opportunities. I often talk to adults who presume they must always know more than the girls to be able to come alongside them, and feel disempowered by their own distance from the technological world of the young. The generation gap emphasised by the media saps the self-confidence of adults to communicate with young people, and the developmental paradigm discourages the promotion of reciprocity in relationship. To see girls as companions or conversation partners on the way of faith, and adults as midwives with its creative but self-limiting connotations, will not come easily.

If the midwife image, which captures the mutuality and the experiential knowing of the birthing process, is taken seriously as a model for the accompaniment of girls in their growing faithing, then churches might develop

---

[32] Mercer, *Girl Talk, God Talk*, p. 129.
[33] Ibid., p. 28.

more effective strategies for their nurture through the pain of transition. This encompasses the whole of their life, not only those areas overtly spiritual.

My research findings have drawn attention to the way girls wrestle with their growing maturity and negotiate their sexuality in a world which still objectifies them and pressurises them by making judgements according to appearance, and conformity to celebrity culture. Although girls need affirmation of the normality and beauty of their bodies and the encouragement to delight in themselves through the painful period of change, we are generally shy about discussing gendered bodies in a church context, despite the prevalence of sexualised images surrounding girls, and both leaders and girls might suffer acute embarrassment if it were suggested that discussion of the bodily changes which accompany puberty were to become a part of a church 'curriculum'. Awareness of the layers of meaning surrounding this liminal stage and the bereavement which is its companion should, however, be the informed backdrop to effective empathy and care, and the encouragement for secure intergenerational relationship-building with girls. Yet gender-specific programmes to help girls face the issues of self, body, faith and world through a method which encourages open enquiry are rare.

One positive example is found in the North American Roman Catholic 'Voices' project. The purpose of this series of manuals is 'to help girls embrace the true meaning of the phrase "created in the image of God," a profound statement about who they are and who they are becoming'.[34] An exercise, in the handbook on challenging culture,[35] invites girls to write a short note to their body from God with an opening such as 'I'm the God who created your body, and I'd like to tell you that ...'. Most of the girls I interviewed were interested in their bodies and some, like Mary and Bethan, were struggling to find ways of affirming beauty, which they wanted to enhance by an acceptable use of commercial products, in the context of an exploration of Christian values not as a given but to be worked out collaboratively. In a society which promotes sanitised body images, to accept the messiness and moodiness of growth is a mark of a healthy holding environment. Further theological and philosophical study, particularly of the contribution of Irigaray and the corpus of writing inspired by her work to an understanding of the relationships between women and girls, would inform conversation in a space where girls can feel validated, as they reflect on their personhood made in the image of God. Girls are worth the specialist training and reflection effective midwifery requires.

---

[34] Claussen with Keller, *Seeking*, p. 10. Most material in this series is applicable for use in all Christian communities.

[35] Janet Claussen, *Awakening: Challenging the Culture with Girls* (Winona, 2001). Other titles in the series are: *Retreats* (deepening spirituality), *Prayer*, *Church Women* and *Biblical Women*. Although another example of material prepared primarily for older girls, some can be used with or adapted for the younger age group.

A Final Biblical Reflection

In this closing reflection, I return to Jairus' daughter, whose raising signified
her physical birth from the waters of gestation into the natality of womanhood
(daughterhood) and prefigured Jesus' own journey through the waters of suffering
to cross and resurrection, through which all who believe receive new life as
gift. That suffering is primarily pre-figured and eternally symbolised in Jesus'
baptism, sacramentally shared with all God's people as they too make that journey
of re-birth. Jairus's daughter's rising is, then, filled with baptismal symbolism.
More traditionally seen in this light is the Johannine dialogue between Jesus
and Nicodemus, which Jantzen regards as a male appropriation of birth at the
heart of Christianity. She takes it as contrasting physical and spiritual birth, to
the denigration of the former and its dependence on a woman, consistent with
Hellenistic philosophy, which resulted in male domination of the church.

Witherington,[36] in a detailed analysis of John 3.5 and the antecedents in Jewish
and Ancient Near Eastern literature of the connection between water and birth,
argues for Semitic parallelism here. Endeavouring not to perpetuate a hierarchy
which demeans the waters of the womb, he argues for two parallel births, a physical
and a spiritual. If the gospel's author has an eye on countering docetic or proto-
Gnostic views, such an interpretation validates Jesus' human birth as objective
fact, and locates spiritual birth in the physicality of the elements. Fiddes also
explores the physical link between birth and baptism, drawing attention to an early
theological connection between baptismal pool and the waters of the womb.[37] The
consequence for our understanding of the story might then be that Jesus' reply
rebukes Nicodemus' implied dismissal of human birthing, affirming the need for
the water(s) in the process of gestation towards new birth.

I suggest there could be a further interpretation of this passage in relation to
discipleship. Birth, as with an infant, is to a new vulnerability and dependence.
John does not record any of Jesus' teaching on girls/boys, but on this reading
the Nicodemus passage could be their counterpart: for in it we see the humbling
of the adult male religious leader, and learn that the way of true discipleship is
through childhood as Rahner conceived it. To return to Jantzen, the lesson for
and from Nicodemus is that 'the possibility of beginning is rooted in our own
beginning, is always material, embodied'.[38] At puberty, girls are re-born. Their
newly birthed bodily capacity for generation becomes redolent with symbolism
of the life of faith that is opening up before them. Our responsibility is to offer
them nurture towards fullness of life, in body and in spirit.

---

[36]   Ben Witherington III, 'The Waters of Birth: John 3.5 and 1 John 5. 6–8',
New Testament Studies, 35 (1989): 155–60.

[37]   P.S. Fiddes, *Tracks and Traces: Baptist Identity in Church and Theology* (Carlisle,
2003), pp. 109–11.

[38]   Jantzen, *Becoming Divine*, p. 145.

Bibliography

Aapola, S., M. Gonick and A. Harris, *Young Femininity: Girlhood, Power and Social Change* (Basingstoke: Palgrave Macmillan, 2005).

Adams, K., B. Hyde and R. Woolley, *The Spiritual Dimension of Childhood* (London: Jessica Kingsley Publishers, 2008).

Alldred, P., 'Ethnography and Discourse Analysis: Dilemmas in Representing the Voices of Children', in J. Ribbens and R. Edwards (eds), *Feminist Dilemmas in Qualitative Research: Public Knowledge and Private Lives* (London: Sage, 1998).

Alldred, P. and E. Burman, 'Analysing Children's Accounts', in S. Greene and D. Hogan (eds), *Researching Children's Experience: Approaches and Methods* (London: Sage, 2005).

Allen, H.C. (ed.), *Nurturing Children's Spirituality: Christian Perspectives and Best Practices* (Eugene: Cascade Books, 2008).

Astley, J. (ed.), *How Faith Grows: Faith Development and Christian Education* (London: NS/CHP, 1991).

Astley, J., *Ordinary Theology: Looking, Listening and Learning in Theology* (Aldershot: Ashgate, 2002).

Astley, J. and L. Francis (eds), *Christian Perspectives on Faith Development* (Leominster: Gracewing, 1992).

Astley, J. and L. Francis (eds), *Christian Theology and Religious Education* (London: SPCK, 1996).

Atwood, M., *Cat's Eye* (London: Virago Press, 1990).

Aune, K. and G. Vincett, 'Gender Matters: Doing Feminist Research on Religion and Youth', in S. Collins-Mayo and P. Dandelion (eds), *Religion and Youth* (Farnham: Ashgate, 2010).

Bach, A. (ed.), *Women in the Hebrew Bible: A Reader* (New York: Routledge, 1999).

Bachelard, G., *The Poetics of Space* (Boston: Beacon Press, 1969).

Baker, D.G., 'Girlfriend Theology: God-talk Across Religious Borders', *Religious Education*, 95.3 (2000): 320–39.

Baker, D.G., 'Future Homemakers and Feminist Awakenings: Autoethnography as a Method in Theological Reflection and Research', *Religious Education*, 96.3 (2001): 395–407.

Baker, D.G., *Doing Girlfriend Theology: God-talk with Young Women* (Cleveland: The Pilgrim Press, 2005).

Bal, M., *Lethal Love: Feminist Literary Readings of Biblical Love Stories*, Indiana Studies in Biblical Literature (Indiana: Indiana University Press, 1987).

Ballard, P. and J. Pritchard, *Practical Theology in Action* (London: SPCK, 2006).

Balswick, J., P. Ebstyne King and K.S. Reimer, *The Reciprocating Self: Human Development in Theological Perspective* (Downers Grove: InterVarsity Press, 2005).

Baudzej, J., 'Re-telling the Story of Jesus: The Concept of Embodiment and Recent Feminist Reflections on the Maleness of Christ', *Feminist Theology*, 17.1 (2008): 72–91.

Baumgardner, J. and A. Richards, 'Feminism and Femininity: Or How We Learned to Stop Worrying and Love the Thong', in A. Harris (ed.), *All About the Girl: Culture, Power and Identity* (New York: Routledge, 2004).

Beal, T., *The Book of Hiding: Gender, Ethnicity, Annihilation, and Esther* (London: Routledge, 1997).

Beattie, T., *God's Mother, Eve's Advocate: A Marian Narrative of Women's Salvation* (London: Continuum, 2002).

Beattie, T., *Woman* (London: Continuum, 2003).

Bechtel, C.M., *Esther* (Louisville: John Knox Press, 2002).

Belenky, M.F., B.M. Clinchy, N.R. Goldberger and J.M. Tarule, *Women's Ways of Knowing: The Development of Self, Voice and Mind* (New York: Basic Books, 1986).

Berryman, J., *Godly Play: An Imaginative Approach to Religious Education* (Minneapolis: Augsburg Fortress, 1991).

Besag, V.E., *Understanding Girls' Friendships, Fights and Feuds: A Practical Approach to Girls' Bullying* (Maidenhead: Open University Press, 2006).

Block, D., *The Book of Ezekiel, Chapters 1–24* (Grand Rapids: Eerdmans, 1997).

Bohler, C., 'Attending to Alice: The Subjective Aims of Adolescent Girls', in J. Stevenson-Moessner (ed.) *In Her Own Time: Women and Developmental Issues in Pastoral Care* (Minneapolis: Fortress Press, 2000).

Bons-Storm, R., *The Incredible Woman: Listening to Women's Silences in Pastoral Care and Counselling* (Nashville: Abingdon Press, 1996).

Bowen, N.R., *Ezekiel*, Abingdon Old Testament Commentaries (Nashville: Abingdon Press, 2010).

Bradford, J., *Caring for the Whole Child: A Holistic Approach to Spirituality* (London: The Children's Society, 1995).

Brenner, A., *The Israelite Woman: Social Role and Literary Type in Biblical Narrative* (Sheffield: J.S.O.T., The Biblical Seminar, 1985).

Brierley, P., *Reaching and Keeping Tweenagers* (London: Christian Research, 2002).

Brock, R.N., *Journeys by Heart: A Christology of Erotic Power* (New York: Crossroad, 1988).

Brown, L.M., *Raising their Voices: The Politics of Girls' Anger* (Cambridge, MA: Harvard University Press, 1998).

Brown, L.M. and C. Gilligan, *Meeting at the Crossroads: Women's Psychology and Girls' Development* (New York: Ballantine Books, 1992).

Brown, L.M. and C. Gilligan, 'Meeting at the Crossroads: Women's Psychology and Girls' Development', *Feminism and Psychology*, 3.1 (1993): 11–35.

Browning, D.S., *Equality and the Family: A Fundamental, Practical Theology of Children, Mothers, and Fathers in Modern Societies* (Grand Rapids: Eerdmans, 2007).

Bruce, F.F., *The Book of Acts*, rev. edn (Grand Rapids: Eerdmans, 1988).

Bruner, E., *Text, Play and Story: The Construction and Reconstruction of Self and Society* (Washington, DC: The American Ethnological Society, 1984).

Brusselmanns, C., J.A. O'Donohoe, J. Fowler and A. Vergote (eds), *Toward Moral and Religious Maturity* (Morristown: Silver Burdett Co., 1980).

Bryan, J., 'Being and Becoming: Adolescence', in A. Shier-Jones (ed.), *Children of God: Towards a Theology of Childhood* (Peterborough: Epworth Press, 2007).

Bunge, M.J. (ed.), *The Child in Christian Thought* (Grand Rapids: Eerdmans, 2001).

Bunge, M.J. (ed.), *The Child in the Bible* (Grand Rapids: Eerdmans, 2008).

Burman, E., *Deconstructing Developmental Psychology* (London: Routledge, 1994).

Büttner, G., 'How Theologizing with Children can Work', *British Journal of Religious Education*, 29.2 (March 2007): 127–39.

Büttner, G., 'Where Do Children Get Their Theology From?', in A. Dillen and D. Pollefeyt (eds), *Children's Voices: Children's Perspectives in Ethics, Theology and Religious Education* (Leuven: Peeters, 2010).

Carter, M., 'A Preferential Option for Children: The Creation of a Theology of Childhood within the Christian Tradition' (unpublished PhD thesis, University of Exeter, 2004).

Chambers English Dictionary (Cambridge: Chambers, 1988).

Christensen, P. and A. James (eds), *Research with Children* (London: Routledge Falmer, 2000).

Christensen, P. and A. Prout, 'Anthropological and Sociological Perspectives on the Study of Children', in S. Greene and D. Hogan (eds), *Researching Children's Experience* (London: Sage, 2005).

Claassens, L.J.M., 'Rupturing God-language: The Metaphor of God as Midwife in Psalm 22', in L. Day and C. Pressler (eds), *Engaging the Bible in a Gendered World: An Introduction to Feminist Biblical Interpretation in Honor of Katharine Doob Sakenfeld* (Louisville: Westminster John Knox Press, 2006).

Claussen, J., *Awakening: Challenging the Culture with Girls* (Winona: St Mary's Press, 2001).

Claussen, J., *Biblical Women: Exploring Their Stories with Girls* (Winona: St Mary's Press, 2002).

Claussen, J. with J.A. Keller, *Seeking: Doing Theology with Girls* (Winona: St Mary's Press, 2003).

Cliff, P.B., *The Rise and Development of the Sunday School Movement in England 1780–1980* (Redhill: National Christian Education Council, 1986).

Coakley, S., 'Deepening Practices: Perspectives from Ascetical and Mystical Theology', in M. Volf and D.C. Bass, *Practicing Theology: Beliefs and Practices in Christian Life* (Grand Rapids: Eerdmans, 2002).

Coakley, S., *Powers and Submissions: Spirituality, Philosophy and Gender* (Oxford: Blackwell, 2002).

Code, L., 'Naming, Naturalizing, Normalizing: "The Child" as Fact and Artifact', in P.H. Miller and E.K. Scholnick (eds), *Toward a Feminist Developmental Psychology* (New York and London: Routledge, 2000).

Coffey, A. and P. Atkinson, *Making Sense of Qualitative Data: Complementary Research Strategies* (Thousand Oaks: Sage Publications, 1996).

Coles, R., *The Spiritual Life of Children* (London: HarperCollins, 1990).

Coles, R. (ed.), *The Erik Erikson Reader* (New York: W.W. Norton, 2000).

Coles, R., 'Remembering Erik', in K. Hoover (ed.), *The Future of Identity: Centennial Reflections on the Legacy of Erik Erikson* (Maryland: Lexington Books, 2004).

Collins-Mayo, S. and P. Dandelion (eds), *Religion and Youth* (Farnham: Ashgate, 2010).

Conn, J.W. (ed.), *Women's Spirituality: Resources for Christian Development* (New York: Paulist Press, 1986).

Conn, J.W., 'Spirituality and Personal Maturity', in R.J. Wicks, R.D. Parsons and D. Capps, *Clinical Handbook of Pastoral Counselling*, Vol. 1 (New York: Paulist Press, 1992).

Consultative Group on Ministry among Children, *Unfinished Business: Children and the Church* (London: CCBI, 1994).

Contratto, S., 'A Too Hasty Marriage: Gilligan's Developmental Theory and its Application to Feminist Clinical Practice', *Feminism and Psychology*, 4.3 (1994): 367–77.

Cook, L. and B. Rothwell, *The X and Y of Leadership: How Men and Women Make a Difference at Work* (London: The Industrial Society, 2000).

Corsaro, W.A. and L. Molinari, 'Entering and Observing in Children's Worlds: A Reflection on Longitudinal Ethnography of Early Education in Italy', in P. Christensen and A. James (eds), *Research with Children* (London and New York: Routledge Falmer, 2000).

Cunningham, D.S., *These Three are One: The Practice of Trinitarian Theology* (Oxford: Blackwell, 1998).

Darling, J. and M. Van De Pijpekamp, 'Rousseau on the Education, Domination and Violation of Women', *British Journal of Educational Studies*, 42.2 (June 1994): 115–32.

Davies, E.W., *The Dissenting Reader: Feminist Approaches to the Hebrew Bible* (Aldershot: Ashgate, 2003).

Davis, J., N. Watson and S. Cunningham-Burley, 'Learning the Lives of Disabled Children', in P. Christensen and A. James (eds), *Research with Children* (London and New York: Routledge Falmer, 2000).

Davis, P.H., *Beyond Nice: The Spiritual Wisdom of Adolescent Girls* (Minneapolis: Fortress Press, 2001).

Day, L., *Esther* (Nashville: Abingdon Press, 2005).

Day, L., 'Wisdom and the Feminine in the Hebrew Bible', in L. Day and C. Pressler (eds), *Engaging the Bible in a Gendered World: An Introduction to Feminist Biblical Interpretation in Honor of Katharine Doob Sakenfeld* (Louisville: Westminster John Knox Press, 2006).

Day, L. and C. Pressler (eds), *Engaging the Bible in a Gendered World: An Introduction to Feminist Biblical Interpretation in Honor of Katharine Doob Sakenfeld* (Louisville: Westminster John Knox Press, 2006).

D'Costa, G., *Sexing the Trinity: Gender, Culture and the Divine* (London: SCM, 2000).

Dean, K.C., *Practicing Passion: Youth and the Quest for a Passionate Church* (Grand Rapids: Eerdmans, 2004).

Dell, M.L., 'She Grows in Wisdom, Stature and Favor with God: Female Development from Infancy through Menarche', in J. Stevenson-Moessner (ed.), *In Her Own Time, Women and Developmental Issues in Pastoral Care* (Minneapolis: Fortress Press, 2000).

De Troyer, K., J.A. Herbert, J.A. Johnson and A.-M. Korte (eds), *Wholly Woman, Wholly Blood: A Feminist Critique of Purity and Impurity* (Harrisburg: Trinity Press International, 2003).

Dillen, A. and D. Pollefeyt (eds), *Children's Voices: Children's Perspectives in Ethics, Theology and Religious Education* (Leuven: Peeters, 2010).

Dobbs-Allsopp, F.W., *Lamentations* (Louisville: John Knox Press, 2002).

Dockrell, J., A. Lewis and G. Lindsay, 'Researching Children's Perspectives: A Psychological Dimension', in A. Lewis and G. Lindsay (eds), *Researching Children's Perspectives* (Buckingham and Philadelphia: Open University Press, 2000).

Donaldson, M., *Children's Minds* (London: Collins, 1978).

Driscoll, C., *Girls: Feminine Adolescence in Popular Culture and Cultural Theory* (New York: Columbia University Press, 2002).

Dykstra, C., 'Youth and the Language of Faith', *Religious Education*, 81.2 (1986): 163–84.

Edwards, A., 'Education', in S. Fraser, V. Lewis, S. Ding, M. Kellett and C. Robinson (eds), *Doing Research with Children and Young People* (London: Sage in association with The Open University).

Eliot, G., *Mill on the Floss* (Harmondsworth: Penguin, 1979).

Elli, K., J. Kim and Y. Lee, *Women of Courage: Asian Women Reading the Bible* (Seoul: Asian Women's Resource Centre for Culture and Theology, 1992).

Emond, R., 'Ethnographic Research Methods with Children and Young People', in S. Greene and D. Hogan (eds), *Researching Children's Experience* (London: Sage, 2005).

Erikson, E., *Childhood and Society*, rev. edn (Middlesex: Penguin Books, 1965).

Erikson, E., *Identity: Youth and Crisis* (New York: W.W. Norton, 1968).

Erricker, C. and J. Erricker, *Reconstructing Religious, Spiritual and Moral Education* (London: Routledge Falmer, 2000).

Erricker, C., J. Erricker, C. Ota, D. Sullivan and M. Fletcher, *The Education of the Whole Child* (London: Cassell, 1997).

Erricker, J., C. Ota and C. Erricker (eds), *Spiritual Education: Cultural, Religious and Social Differences* (Brighton: Sussex Academic Press, 2001).

Fiddes, P.S., *Participating in God: A Pastoral Doctrine of the Trinity* (London: DLT, 2000).

Fiddes, P.S., *Tracks and Traces: Baptist Identity in Church and Theology* (Carlisle: Paternoster Press, 2003).

Finney, J., *Finding Faith Today: How Does it Happen?* (Swindon: British and Foreign Bible Society, 1992).

Fiorenza, E.S., *Bread not Stone: The Challenge of Feminist Biblical Interpretation* (Boston: Beacon Press, 1984).

Fiorenza, E.S., *In Memory of Her: A Feminist Theological Reconstruction of Christian Origins* (New York: Crossroad, 1989).

Fiorenza, E.S., *Wisdom Ways: Introducing Feminist Biblical Interpretation* (Maryknoll: Orbis, 2001).

Fisher, J. and E.S. Silber, *Analyzing the Different Voice* (New York: Rowman & Littlefield, 1998).

Fletcher, A., *Gender, Sex and Subordination in England 1500–1800* (New Haven and London: Yale University Press, 1995).

Flick, U., *An Introduction to Qualitative Research* (London: Sage, 2002).

Ford, D.F. and M. Higton (eds), *Jesus* (Oxford: Oxford University Press, 2002).

Foucault, M., *Discipline and Punish* (London: Tavistock, 1977).

Fowler, J., *Stages of Faith: The Psychology of Human Development and the Quest for Meaning* (San Francisco: Harper, 1981).

Fowler, J., *Becoming Adult, Becoming Christian: Adult Development and Christian Faith* (San Francisco: Harper & Row, 1984).

Fowler, J., *Faith Development and Pastoral Care* (Philadelphia: Fortress Press, 1987).

Fowler, J., 'Faith Development Theory and the Postmodern Challenges', *International Journal for the Psychology of Religion*, 11.3 (2001): 159–72.

Fowler, J., 'Faith Development at 30: Naming the Challenges of Faith in a New Millennium', *Religious Education*, 99.4 (2004): 405–21.

Fowler, J. and A. Vergote (eds), *Towards Moral and Religious Maturity* (New Jersey: Silver Burdett, 1980).

Francis, L. and J. Astley (eds), *Children, Churches and Christian Learning* (London: SPCK, 2002).

Francis, L., W.K. Kay and W.S. Campbell (eds), *Research in Religious Education* (Leominster: Gracewing, 1996).

Francis, L.J. and C. Wilcox, 'Religiosity and Femininity: Do Women Really Hold a More Positive Attitude Toward Christianity?', *Journal for the Scientific Study of Religion*, 37.3 (1998): 462–9.

Fraser, S., 'Situating Empirical Research', in S. Fraser, V. Lewis, S. Ding, M. Kellett and C. Robinson (eds), *Doing Research with Children and Young People* (London: Sage in association with The Open University, 2004).

Fraser, S., V. Lewis, S. Ding, M. Kellett and C. Robinson (eds), *Doing Research with Children and Young People* (London: Sage in association with The Open University, 2004).

Freire, P., *Pedagogy of the Oppressed*, rev. edn (London: Penguin Books, 1996).

Freire, P., *Pedagogy of Freedom* (Lanham and Oxford: Rowman & Littlefield, 1998).

Friedman, L.J., *Identity's Architect: A Biography of Erik H. Erikson* (New York: Scribner, 1999).

Frost, L., *Young Women and the Body: A Feminist Sociology* (Basingstoke: Palgrave, 2001).

Fulkerson, M.M., *Changing the Subject: Women's Discourses and Feminist Theology* (Minneapolis: Fortress Press, 1994).

Garrod, A., L. Smulyan, S. Powers and R. Kilkenny, *Adolescent Portraits: Identity, Relationships and Challenges* (Needham Heights: Allyn and Bacon, 1992).

Geertz, C., *The Interpretation of Cultures* (New York: Basic Books, 1973).

Gench, F.T., *Back to the Well: Women's Encounters with Jesus in the Gospels* (Louisville: Westminster John Knox Press, 2004).

Gerstenberger, E.H., *Yahweh the Patriarch: Ancient Images of God and Feminist Theology* (Minneapolis: Fortress Press, 1996).

Gill-Austern, B.L., 'Pedagogy under the Influence of Feminism and Womanism', in B.J. Miller-McLemore and B.L. Gill-Austern, *Feminist & Womanist Pastoral Theology* (Nashville: Abingdon Press, 1999).

Gilligan, C., *In a Different Voice: Psychological Theory and Women's Development*, rev. edn (Cambridge, MA and London: Harvard University Press, 1993).

Gilligan, C., N. Lyons and T. Hammer, *Making Connections: The Relational Worlds of Adolescent Girls at Emma Willard School* (Cambridge, MA: Harvard University Press, 1990).

Gilligan, C., A.G. Rogers and D. Tolman (eds), *Women, Girls and Psychotherapy: Reframing Resistance* (New York, London and Sydney: Harrington Park Press, 1991).

Glaz, M., 'A New Pastoral Understanding of Women', in M. Glaz and J. Stevenson-Moessner (eds), *Women in Travail and Transition* (Minneapolis: Fortress Press, 1991).

Glaz, M. and J. Stevenson Moessner (eds), *Women in Travail and Transition* (Minneapolis: Fortress Press, 1991).

Golombok, S. and R. Fivush, *Gender Development* (Cambridge: Cambridge University Press, 1994).

Graham, E.L., *Making the Difference: Gender, Personhood and Theology* (London: Mowbray, 1995).

Green, L., *Let's Do Theology: Resources for Contextual Theology* (London: Mowbray, 2009).

Green, M., *I Believe in The Holy Spirit*, rev. edn (Eastbourne: Kingsway Communications Ltd., 2004).

Greene, S., *The Psychological Development of Women and Girls: Rethinking Change in Time* (London and New York: Routledge, 2003).

Greene, S. and M. Hill, 'Researching Children's Experience', in S. Greene and D. Hogan (eds), *Researching Children's Experiences: Approaches and Methods* (London: Sage, 2005).

Greene, S. and D. Hogan (eds), *Researching Children's Experiences: Approaches and Methods* (London: Sage, 2005).

Grey, M., '"Sapiential Yearnings": The Challenge of Feminist Theology to Religious Education', in J. Astley and L. Francis (eds), *Christian Theology and Religious Education* (London: SPCK, 1996).

Grey, M., *Introducing Feminist Images of God* (Sheffield: Sheffield Academic Press, 2001).

Griffin, C., 'Good Girls, Bad Girls: Anglocentrism and Diversity in the Constitution of Contemporary Girlhood', in A. Harris (ed.), *All About the Girl: Culture, Power and Identity* (New York: Routledge, 2004).

Guenther, M., *Holy Listening: The Art of Spiritual Direction* (London: DLT, 1993).

Haag, P., *Voices of a Generation: Teenage Girls on Sex, School, and Self: A Report on Teen Girls from the American Association of University Women's Sister to Sister Summits* (Washington, DC: American Association of University Women Educational Foundation, 1999).

Hall, G.S., *Adolescence: Its Psychology and its Relation to Physiology, Anthropology, Sociology, Sex, Crime, Religion and Education* (New York: Appleton, 1904).

Hamilton, M., *The Sociology of Religion*, 2nd edn (London: Routledge, 2001).

Hammersley, M., *What's Wrong with Ethnography?* (London and New York: Routledge, 1992).

Harris, A. (ed.), *All About the Girl: Culture, Power and Identity* (New York: Routledge, 2004).

Harris, M., 'Women Teaching Girls: The Power and the Danger', *Religious Education*, 88.1 (1993): 52–66.

Harris, M. and G. Moran, *Reshaping Religious Education, Conversations on Contemporary Practice* (Louisville: Westminster John Knox Press, 1998).

Harrison, W.C. and J. Hood-Williams, *Beyond Sex and Gender* (London: Sage, 2002).

Hart, T., *The Secret Spiritual World of Children* (Makawao: Inner Ocean Publishing, 2003).

Hay, D., *Something There: The Biology of the Human Spirit* (London: DLT, 2006).

Hay, D. with R. Nye, *The Spirit of the Child*, rev. edn (London and Philadelphia: Jessica Kingsley Publishers, 2006).

Hay, D., R. Nye and R. Murphy, 'Thinking about Childhood Spirituality: Review of Research and Current Directions', in L.J. Francis, W.K. Kay and W.S. Campbell (eds), *Research in Religious Education* (Leominster: Gracewing, 1996).

Hayward, C. (ed.), *Gender Differences at Puberty* (Cambridge: Cambridge University Press, 2003).

Hendrik, H., 'The Child as Social Actor in Historical Sources: Problems of Identification and Interpretation', in P. Christensen and A. James (eds), *Research with Children* (London and New York: Routledge Falmer, 2000).

Heller, D., *The Children's God* (Chicago and London: Chicago University Press, 1986).

Hess, C. Lakey, 'Education as an Art of Getting Dirty with Dignity', in C. Cozad Neuger (ed.), *The Arts of Ministry: Feminist-Womanist Approaches* (Louisville: Westminster John Knox Press, 1996).

Hess, C. Lakey, *Caretakers of Our Common House: Women's Development in Communities of Faith* (Nashville: Abingdon Press, 1997).

Hesse-Biber, S.N. and P.L. Leavy (eds), *Feminist Research Practice: A Primer* (Thousand Oaks: Sage Publications, 2007).

Hey, V., *The Company She Keeps: An Ethnography of Girls' Friendships* (Buckingham: Open University Press, 1997).

Heynes, J., 'Engaging with Teenage Girls' Understandings of Religion and Gender', in S. Collins-Mayo and P. Dandelion (eds), *Religion and Youth* (Farnham: Ashgate, 2010).

Heyward, C., *When Boundaries Betray Us: Beyond Illusions of What is Ethical in Therapy and Life* (New York: Harper Collins, 1993).

Hinsdale, M.A., '"Infinite Openness to the Infinite": Karl Rahner's Contribution to Modern Catholic Thought on the Child', in M.J. Bunge (ed.), *The Child in Christian Thought* (Grand Rapids: Eerdmans, 2001).

Hinson, E.G., 'Ministers as Midwives and Mothers of Grace', in Robert J. Wicks (ed.), *Handbook of Spirituality for Ministers: Perspectives for the 21st Century*, Vol. 2 (New York: Paulist Press, 2000).

Hirsh, E. and G.A. Olson '"Je-Luce Irigaray": A Meeting with Luce Irigaray', *Hypatia*, 10.2 (Spring 1995): 93–114.

Holder, A. (ed.), *The Blackwell Companion to Christian Spirituality* (Oxford: Blackwell Publishing, 2005).

Hollway, W. and T. Jefferson, *Doing Qualitative Research: Free Association, Narrative and the Interview Method* (London: Sage, 2000).

Holy Bible, The New Revised Standard Version (Oxford: Oxford University Press, 1995).

Hoover, K.R. (ed.), *The Future of Identity: Centennial Reflections on the Legacy of Erik Erikson* (Maryland: Lexington Books, 2004).

Horsley, R.A., *Hearing the Whole Story: The Politics of Plot in Mark's Gospel* (Louisville: Westminster John Knox Press, 2001).

Humphreys, D., G. Koll and S. Windecker, *Daughters Arise! A Christian Retreat Resource for Girls Approaching Womanhood* (Cleveland: The Pilgrim Press, 2002).

Hyde, K., *Religion in Childhood and Adolescence: A Comprehensive View of the Research* (Birmingham, AL: Religious Education Press, 1990).

Irigaray, L., *Speculum of the Other Woman*, trans. G. Gill (New York: Cornell University Press, 1985).

Irigaray, L., 'Women-Amongst-Themselves: Creating a Woman-to-Woman Sociality', in Margaret Whitford (ed.), *The Irigaray Reader* (Oxford: Blackwell, 1991).

Irigaray, L. (ed.), *Sexes and Genealogies*, trans. C. Gill (New York: Columbia Press, 1993).

Irigaray, L. (ed.), *Luce Irigaray: Key Writings* (London and New York: Continuum, 2004).

Isherwood, L. (ed.), *The Good News of the Body: Sexual Theology and Feminism* (Sheffield: Sheffield Academic Press, 2000).

Jacobs, M., *Living Illusions: A Psychology of Belief* (London: SPCK, 1993).

James, A., C. Jenks and A. Prout, *Theorizing Childhood* (Cambridge: Polity Press, 1998).

James, A. and A. Prout (eds), *Constructing and Reconstructing Childhood: Contemporary Issues in the Sociological Study of Childhood*, 2nd edn (London: Falmer Press, 1997).

Jantzen, G., *Becoming Divine: Towards a Feminist Philosophy of Religion* (Manchester: Manchester University Press, 1998).

Jarviluoma, H., P. Moisala and A. Vikko, *Gender and Qualitative Method* (London: Sage, 2003).

Jensen, D.H., *Graced Vulnerability: A Theology of Childhood* (Cleveland: The Pilgrim Press, 2005).

Jiwani, Y., C. Steenbergen and C. Mitchell (eds), *Girlhood: Redefining the Limits* (Montreal: Black Rose Books, 2006).

Johnson, E.A., *She Who Is: The Mystery of God in Feminist Discourse* (New York: Crossroad, 1992).

Joy, M., *Divine Love: Luce Irigaray, Women, Gender and Religion* (Manchester: Manchester University Press, 2006).

Joyce, P.M., *Ezekiel: A Commentary* (New York and London: T.&T. Clark, 2007).

Kay, W.K. and L.J. Francis, *Drift from the Churches: Attitude Toward Christianity During Childhood and Adolescence* (Cardiff: University of Wales Press, 1996).

Keefe, A.A., 'Woman's Body and the Social Body in Hosea', *JSOT Supplement* 338 (Sheffield: Sheffield Academic Press, 2001).

Kegan, R., 'Where the Dance is: Religious Dimensions of a Developmental Framework', in C. Brusselmanns, J.A. O'Donohoe, J. Fowler and A. Vergote (eds), *Toward Moral and Religious Maturity* (Morristown: Silver Burdett Co., 1980).

Kegan, R., *The Evolving Self: Problem and Process in Human Development* (Cambridge, MA: Harvard University Press, 1982).

Kegan, R., *In Over Our Heads: The Mental Demands of Modern Life* (Cambridge, MA: Harvard University Press, 1994).

Keller, C., *From a Broken Web: Separation, Sexism and Self* (Boston: Beacon Press, 1986).

Keller, J.A., *Retreats: Deepening the Spirituality of Girls* (Winona: St Mary's Press, 2002).

Kidd, S.M., *Dance of the Dissident Daughter* (New York: HarperCollins, 1996).

Kidd, S.M., *The Secret Life of Bees* (Harmondsworth: Penguin, 2003).

Kielbasa, M., *Prayer: Celebrating and Reflecting with Girls* (Winona: St Mary's Press, 2002).

Killen, P. O'Connell and J. de Beer, *The Art of Theological Reflection* (New York: Crossroad, 1996).

Kim, C.W.M., S.M. St Ville and S. Simonaitis (eds), *Transfigurations: Theology and the French Feminists* (Minneapolis: Fortress Press, 1993).

King, U., *Women and Spirituality: Voices of Protest and Promise* (Basingstoke: Macmillan Education, 1989).

Kroger, J., *Identity in Adolescence: The Balance between Self and Other*, 2nd edn (London: Routledge, 1996).

Kroger, J., 'Identity in Formation', in K. Hoover (ed.), *The Future of Identity: Centennial Reflections on the Legacy of Erik Erikson* (Maryland: Lexington Books, 2004).

Lapsley, J.E., *Whispering the Word: Hearing Women's Stories in the Old Testament* (Louisville: Westminster John Knox Press, 2005).

Layard, R., J. Dunn and the panel of The Good Childhood Inquiry, *A Good Childhood, Searching for Values in a Competitive Age* (London: Penguin, 2009).

Lee, J., 'Menarche and the (Hetero)Sexualization of the Female Body', in R. Weitz (ed.), *The Politics of Women's Bodies* (Oxford: Oxford University Press, 1998).

Lee, N., *Childhood and Society. Growing up in an Age of Uncertainty* (Maidenhead: Open University Press, 2001).

Levine, A.-J. with M. Blickenstaff (eds), *A Feminist Companion to Mark* (Sheffield: Sheffield Academic Press, 2001).

Levine A.-J., with M. Blickenstaff (eds), *A Feminist Companion to Matthew* (Sheffield: Sheffield Academic Press, 2001).

Levine, A.-J. with M. Blickenstaff (eds), *A Feminist Companion to Acts of the Apostles* (London: Continuum, 2004).

Lewis, A. and G. Lindsay (eds), *Researching Children's Perspectives* (Buckingham and Philadelphia: Open University Press, 2000).

Lewis, C.S., *The Last Battle* (Harmondsworth: Penguin, 1956).

Lindner, E.W., 'Children as Theologians', in P.B. Pufall and R.P. Unsworth (eds), *Rethinking Childhood* (New Brunswick: Rutgers University Press, 2004).

Loder, J., *The Transforming Moment*, 2nd edn (Colorado Springs: Helmers and Howard, 1989).

Loder, J., *The Logic of the Spirit: Human Development in Theological Perspective* (San Francisco: Jossey-Bass, 1998).

Lykes, M.B., 'Whose Meeting at Which Crossroads? A Response to Brown and Gilligan', *Feminism and Psychology*, 4.3 (1994): 345–9.

McFague, S., *Metaphorical Theology: Models of God in Religious Language* (Philadelphia: Fortress Press, 1982).

McGinnis, C.M., 'Exodus as a "Text of Terror" for Children', in M. Bunge (ed.), *The Child in the Bible* (Grand Rapids: Eerdmans, 2008).

McIntosh, M.A., 'Trinitarian Perspectives on Christian Spirituality', in A. Holder (ed.), *The Blackwell Companion to Christian Spirituality* (Oxford: Blackwell Publishing, 2005).

McRobbie, A., *Feminism and Youth Culture*, 2nd edn (Basingstoke: Macmillan, 2000).

Malina, B. and J. Pilch, *Social Science Commentary on the Book of Acts* (Minneapolis: Fortress Press, 2008).

Marcia, J., 'Why Erikson?', in K. Hoover (ed.), *The Future of Identity* (Maryland: Lexington Books, 2004).

Marsh, C., *Christ in Focus: Radical Christocentrism in Christian Theology* (London: SCM Press, 2005).

Mayall, B., *Towards a Sociology for Childhood: Thinking from Children's Lives* (Maidenhead: Open University Press, 2002).

Menn, E.M., 'Child Characters in Biblical Narratives: The Young David (1 Samuel 16–17) and the Little Israelite Servant Girl (2 Kings 5.1–19)', in M. Bunge (ed.), *The Child in the Bible* (Grand Rapids: Eerdmans, 2008).

Mercer, J.A., *Welcoming Children: A Practical Theology of Childhood* (St Louis: Chalice Press, 2005).

Mercer, J.A., *Girl Talk, God Talk: Why Faith Matters to Teenage Girls – and their Parents* (San Francisco: Jossey-Bass, 2008).

Meyers, C., *Discovering Eve: Ancient Israelite Women in Context* (New York and Oxford: Oxford University Press, 1988).

Miles, G. and J.-J. Wright (eds), *Celebrating Children: Equipping People Working with Children and Young People Living in Difficult Circumstances Around the World* (Carlisle: Paternoster, 2003).

Miller, J.B., *Toward a New Psychology of Women* (Boston: Beacon Press, 1976).

Miller, P.H and E.K. Scholnick (eds), *Toward a Feminist Developmental Psychology* (New York and London: Routledge, 2000).

Miller-McLemore, B.J., *Let the Children Come: Reimagining Childhood from a Christian Perspective* (San Francisco: Jossey-Bass, 2003).

Miller-McLemore, B.J. and B.L. Gill-Austern (eds), *Feminist & Womanist Pastoral Theology* (Nashville: Abingdon Press, 1999).

Moi, T., *Sexual Textual Politics: Feminist Literary Theory* (London: Routledge, 1985).

Moloney, F.J., *The Gospel of Mark: A Commentary* (Peabody: Hendrikson Publishers, 2002).

Moltmann, J., 'The Motherly Father: Is Trinitarian Patripassianism Replacing Theological Patriarchalism', in E. Schillebeeckz and J. Metz (eds), *Concilium* (Edinburgh: T.&T. Clark, 1981).

Moltmann, J., 'Child and Childhood as Metaphors of Hope', *Theology Today*, 56.4 (2000): 592–603.

Moltmann, J., *In The End – The Beginning: The Life of Hope* (Minneapolis: Fortress Press, 2004).

Moore, S.H. '"Such Perfecting of Praise Out of the Mouth of a Babe": Sarah Wight as Child Prophet', in D. Wood (ed.), *The Church and Childhood* (Oxford: Blackwell for the Ecclesiastical History Society, 1994).

Morton, N., *The Journey is Home* (Boston: Beacon Press, 1985).

Nesbitt, E., 'Researching 8 to 13-Year-Olds' Perspectives and Their Experience of Religion', in A. Lewis and G. Lindsay (eds), *Researching Children's Perspectives* (Buckingham and Philadelphia: Open University Press, 2000).

Newman, A., *Winnicott's Words: A Companion to the Writings and Work of D. W. Winnicott* (London: Free Association Books, 1995).

Nolan, M., 'The Defective Male: What Aquinas Really Said', *New Blackfriars*, 75 (1994): 156–66.

Nye, R., 'Psychological Perspectives on Children's Spirituality' (unpublished PhD thesis, University of Nottingham, 1998).

Nye, R., *Children's Spirituality: What it is and Why it Matters* (London: Church House Publishing, 2009).

Oakley, A., *Experiments in Knowing: Gender and Method in Social Studies* (Cambridge: Polity Press, 2000).

Oduyoye, M.A., *Introducing African Women's Theology* (Sheffield: Sheffield Academic Press, 2001).

O'Kane, C., 'The Development of Participatory Techniques: Facilitating Children's Views about Decisions which Affect Them', in P. Christensen and A. James (eds), *Research with Children* (London and New York: Routledge Falmer, 2000).

Olson, G., *Teenage Girls: Exploring Issues Adolescent Girls Face and Strategies to Help Them* (Grand Rapids: Zondervan, 2006).

Onions, C.T. (ed.), *Oxford Dictionary of Etymology* (London: Oxford University Press, 1966).

Orenstein, P., in Association with the American Association of University Women, *Schoolgirls: Young Women, Self-Esteem and the Confidence Gap* (New York: Anchor Books, 1995).

Ormond, A., 'Beneath the Surface of Voice and Silence: Researching the Home Front', in A. Harris (ed.), *All About the Girl* (New York: Routledge, 2004).

Palmer, S., *Toxic Childhood: How the Modern World is Damaging Our Children and What We Can Do About It* (London: Orion, 2007).

Pannenberg, W., *Anthropology in Theological Perspective* (Edinburgh: T.&T. Clark, 1985).

Pattison, S. with J. Woodward, *A Vision of Pastoral Theology* (Edinburgh: Contact Pastoral, 1994).

Pazmiño, R.W., *Foundational Issues in Christian Education: An Introduction in Evangelical Perspective*, 2nd edn (Grand Rapids: Baker Books, 1997).

Pearmain, R., 'Transformational Experiences in Young People: The Meaning of a Safe Haven', *International Journal of Children's Spirituality*, 10.3 (2005): 277–90.

Pearmain, R., 'Evocative Cues and Presence: Relational Consciousness within Qualitative Research', *International Journal of Children's Spirituality*, 12.1 (2007): 75–82.

Pipher, M., *Reviving Ophelia: Saving the Selves of Adolescent Girls* (New York: Ballantine Books, 1994).

Poll, J.B. and T.B Smith, 'The Spiritual Self: Toward a Conceptualization of Spiritual Identity Development', *Journal of Psychology and Theology*, 31.2 (2003): 129–42.

Prosperi, W., *Girls Ministry 101: Ideas for Retreats, Small Groups, and Everyday Life with Teenage Girls* (Grand Rapids: Zondervan, 2006).

Pufall, P.B. and R.P. Unsworth (eds), *Rethinking Childhood* (New Brunswick: Rutgers University Press, 2004).

Punch, S., 'Research with Children: The Same or Different from Research with Adults?', *Childhood*, 9.3 (2002): 321–41.

Raby, R., 'Talking (Behind Your) Back: Young Women and Resistance', in Y. Jiwani, C. Steenbergen and C. Mitchell (eds), *Girlhood: Redefining the Limits* (Montreal: Black Rose Books, 2006).

Rahner, K., *Theological Investigations*, Vol. VIII (London: DLT, 1984).

Ramazanoglu, C., with J. Holland, *Feminist Methodology, Challenges and Choices* (London: Sage, 2002).

Raphael, M., *The Female Face of God in Auschwitz: A Jewish Feminist Theology of the Holocaust* (London: Routledge, 2003).

Ratcliff, D. (ed.), *Children's Spirituality: Christian Perspectives, Research, and Applications* (Eugene: Cascade Books, 2004).

Reinhartz, A., *'Why Ask My Name?': Anonymity and Identity in Biblical Narrative* (Oxford: Oxford University Press, 1998).

Reinharz, S., *Feminist Methods in Social Research* (New York and Oxford: Oxford University Press, 1992).

Ribbens, J. and R. Edwards (eds), *Feminist Dilemmas in Qualitative Research, Public Knowledge and Private Lives* (London: Sage, 1998).

Richards, A. and P. Privett (eds), *Through the Eyes of a Child: New Insights in Theology from a Child's Perspective* (London: Church House Publishing, 2009).

Richardson, A. and J. Bowden (eds), *A New Dictionary of Christian Theology* (London: SCM Press, 1983).

Robinson, R. and M. Kellett, 'Power', in S. Fraser, V. Lewis, S. Ding, M. Kellett and C. Robinson (eds), *Doing Research with Children and Young People* (London: Sage in association with The Open University, 2004).

Robinson, T. and J.V. Ward, '"A Belief in Self Far Greater than Anyone's Disbelief": Cultivating Resistance Among African American Female Adolescents', in C. Gilligan, A.G. Rogers and D. Tolman (eds), *Women, Girls and Psychotherapy: Reframing Resistance* (New York, London and Sydney: Harrington Park Press, 1991).

Roehlkepartain, E.C. (ed.), *The Handbook of Spiritual Development in Childhood and Adolescence* (Thousand Oaks: Sage, 2006).

Rubin, H.J. and I.S. Rubin, *Qualitative Interviewing: The Art of Hearing Data* (California, London and New Delhi: Sage Publications, 1995).

Ruether, R.R., *Sexism and God-talk* (London: SCM Press, 1983).

Rushton, K., 'The Woman in Childbirth of John 16:21, A Feminist Reading of (Pro)creative Boundary Crossing', in K. De Troyer, J.A. Herbert, J.A. Johnson and A.-M. Korte (eds), *Wholly Woman, Wholly Blood, A Feminist Critique of Purity and Impurity* (Harrisburg: Trinity Press International, 2003).

Schneiders, S.M., 'Approaches to the Study of Christian Spirituality', in A. Holder (ed.), *The Blackwell Companion to Christian Spirituality* (Oxford: Blackwell Publishing, 2005).

Schottroff, L., S. Schroer and M.-T. Wacker, *Feminist Interpretation: The Bible in Women's Perspective* (Minneapolis: Fortress Press, 1998).

Scott, D.G., 'Retrospective Spiritual Narratives: Exploring Recalled Childhood and Adolescent Experiences', *International Journal of Children's Spirituality*, 9.1 (2004): 67–79.

Scott, J., 'Children as Respondents', in P. Christensen and A. James (eds), *Research with Children* (London and New York: Routledge Falmer, 2000).

Shandler, S., *Ophelia Speaks: Adolescent Girls Write about their Search for Self* (New York: HarperCollins, 1999).

Sheldrake, P., *Spaces for the Sacred* (London: SCM Press, 2001).

Sherwood, Y., 'The Prostitute and the Prophet: Hosea's Marriage in Literary-Theoretical Perspective', *JSOT Supplement* 212 (Sheffield: Sheffield Academic Press, 1996).

Shier-Jones, A. (ed.), *Children of God: Towards a Theology of Childhood* (Peterborough: Epworth Press, 2007).

Sinats, P., D.G. Scott, S. McFerran, M. Hittos, C. Cragg, T. Leblanc and D. Brooks, 'Writing Ourselves into Being: Writing as Spiritual Self-care for Adolescent Girls', Part 1. *International Journal of Children's Spirituality*, 10.1 (2005): 17–29.

Sinats, P., D.G. Scott, S. McFerran, M. Hittos, C. Cragg, T. Leblanc and D. Brooks, 'Writing Ourselves into Being: Writing as Spiritual Self-care for Adolescent Girls', Part 2. *International Journal of Children's Spirituality*, 10.3 (2005): 263–76.

Slee, N., *Faith and Feminism: An Introduction to Christian Feminist Theology* (London: DLT, 2003).

Slee, N., *Women's Faith Development, Patterns and Processes* (Aldershot: Ashgate, 2004).

Smith, C. with M.L. Denton, *Soul Searching: The Religious and Spiritual Lives of American Teenagers* (New York: Oxford University Press, 2005).

Snell, R., *Clinical Embryology for Medical Students* (Boston: Little, Brown, 1972).

Staley, J.L., 'Changing Woman: A Postcolonial, Postfeminist Interpretation of Acts 16.6–40', in A.-J. Levine and M. Blickenstaff (eds), *A Feminist Companion to Acts* (London: Continuum, 2004).

Stanley L. and S. Wise, *Breaking Out Again: Feminist Ontology and Epistemology*, 2nd edn (London: Routledge, 1993).

Stanworth, R., *Recognizing Spiritual Needs in People Who are Dying* (Oxford: Oxford University Press, 2004).

Stark, R., 'Physiology and Faith: Addressing the "Universal" Gender Difference in Religious Commitment', *Journal for the Scientific Study of Religion*, 41.3 (2002): 495–507.

Stevenson-Moessner, J. (ed.), *In Her Own Time, Women and Developmental Issues in Pastoral Care* (Minneapolis: Fortress Press, 2000).

Stevenson-Moessner, J., 'The Practice and Theology of Adoption', *The Christian Century*, 24 January (2001): 10–13.

Stoller, R., *Presentation of Gender* (New Haven and London: Yale University Press, 1985).

Stone, H.W. and J.O. Duke, *How to Think Theologically*, 2nd edn (Minneapolis: Augsburg Fortress Press, 2006).

Strange, W.A., *Children in the Early Church: Children in the Ancient World, the New Testament and the Early Church* (Carlisle: Paternoster Press, 1996).

Strauss, A. and J. Corbin, *Basics of Qualitative Research: Techniques and Procedures for Developing Grounded Theory*, 2nd edn (Thousand Oaks: Sage Publications, 1998).

Tamminen, K., *Religious Development in Childhood and Youth* (Helsinki: Suomalainen Tiedeakatemia, 1991).

Tamminen, K., 'Gender Differences in Religiosity in Children and Adolescents', in L.J. Francis, W.K. Kay and W.S. Campbell (eds), *Research in Religious Education* (Leominster: Gracewing, 1996).

Tanner, K., *God and Creation in Christian Theology* (Oxford: Basil Blackwell, 1988).

Tillich, P., *Systematic Theology*, Vol. 3 (Chicago: University of Chicago Press, 1967).

Trible, P., *God and the Rhetoric of Sexuality* (Philadelphia: Fortress Press, 1978).

Trible, P., 'Feminist Hermeneutics and Biblical Studies', in A. Loades (ed.), *Feminist Theology: A Reader* (London: SPCK, 1990).

Veling, T., *Practical Theology: 'On Earth as it is in Heaven'* (Maryknoll: Orbis Books, 2005).

Volf, M. and D. Bass (eds), *Practicing Theology: Beliefs and Practices in Christian Life* (Grand Rapids: Eerdmans, 2002).

Walkerdine, V., *Schoolgirl Fictions* (London: Verso, 1990).

Walkerdine, V. and the Girls and Mathematics Unit, Institute of Education, *Counting Girls Out: Girls and Mathematics* (London: Virago, 1989).

Walkerdine, V., H. Lucey and J. Melody, *Growing Up Girl, Psychosocial Explorations of Gender and Class* (Basingstoke: Palgrave, 2001).

Ward, J.V. and B. Cooper Benjamin, 'Women, Girls and the Unfinished Work of Connection: A Critical Review of American Girls' Studies', in A. Harris (ed.), *All About the Girl* (New York: Routledge, 2004).

Warren, M., *Youth Gospel Liberation* (Dublin: Veritas, 1998).

Warren, S., 'Let's Do it Properly: Inviting Children to be Researchers', in A. Lewis and G. Lindsay (eds), *Researching Children's Perspectives* (Buckingham and Philadelphia: Open University Press, 2000).

Watts, F., *Theology and Psychology* (Aldershot: Ashgate, 2002).

Watts, F., R. Nye and S. Savage, *Psychology for Christian Ministry* (London and New York: Routledge, 2002)

Webb-Mitchell, B., 'Leaving Development Behind and Beginning Pilgrimage', *Religious Education*, 96.1 (2001): 136–51.

Weber, H.-R., *Jesus and the Children: Biblical Resources for Study and Preaching* (Geneva: World Council of Churches, 1979).

Weitz, R. (ed.), *The Politics of Women's Bodies* (Oxford: Oxford University Press, 1998).

West, G.O., *The Academy of the Poor: Towards a Dialogical Reading of the Bible* (Sheffield: Sheffield University Press, 1999).

West, W.M.S., *Baptists Together* (Didcot: Baptist Historical Society, 2000).

Westcott, H.L. and K.S. Littleton, 'Exploring Meaning in Interviews with Children', in S. Greene and D. Hogan (eds), *Researching Children's Experiences: Approaches and Methods* (London: Sage, 2005).

Westerhoff III, J.H., *Will Our Children Have Faith?* rev. edn (Harrisburg: Morehouse Publishing, 2000).

Whitford, M. (ed.), *The Irigaray Reader* (Oxford: Blackwell, 1991).

Wicks, R.J. (ed.), *Handbook of Spirituality for Ministers: Perspectives for the 21st Century*, Vol. 2 (New York: Paulist Press, 2000).

Wicks, R.J., R.D. Parsons and D. Capps, *Clinical Handbook of Pastoral Counselling*, Vol. 1 (New York: Paulist Press, 1992).

Wiles, M., 'Christianity without Incarnation?', in J. Hick (ed.), *The Myth of God Incarnate* (London: SCM Press, 1977).

Winnicott, D.W., 'The Location of Cultural Experience', *International Journal of Psychoanalysis*, 48 (1967): 368–72.

Winnicott, D.W., *Playing and Reality* (London: Routledge, 1971).

Witherington III, B., 'The Waters of Birth: John 3.5 and 1 John 5. 6–8', *New Testament Studies*, 35 (1989): 155–60.

Wood, D. (ed.), *The Church and Childhood* (Oxford: Blackwell for the Ecclesiastical History Society, 1994).

Woodhead, M. and D. Faulkner, 'Subjects, Objects or Participants? Dilemmas of Psychological Research with Children', in P. Christensen and A. James (eds), *Research with Children* (London and New York: Routledge Falmer, 2000).

Woodward, J. and S. Pattison (eds), *The Blackwell Reader in Pastoral and Practical Theology* (Oxford: Blackwell, 2000).

Wright, D.R. with K.C. Dean, 'Youth, Passion and Intimacy in the Context of *Koinonia*: James E. Loder's Contribution to a Practical Theology of *Imitatio Christi* for Youth Ministry', in D.R. Wright and J.D. Kuentzel (eds), *Redemptive Transformation in Practical Theology: Essays in Honor of James E. Loder Jr.* (Grand Rapids and Cambridge, UK: Eerdmans, 2004).

Wright, D.R. and J.D. Kuentzel, *Redemptive Transformation in Practical Theology: Essays in Honor of James E. Loder Jr.* (Grand Rapids: Eerdmans, 2004).

Wright, V., *Maid in God's Image: In Search of Unruly Women* (London: DLT, 2008).

Wu, K.-M., 'The Other is My Hell; The Other is My Home', *Human Studies*, 16 (1993): 193–202.

Young, I.M., *On Female Bodily Experience: 'Throwing Like a Girl' and Other Essays* (New York: Oxford University Press, 2005).

Zappone, K., *The Hope for Wholeness: A Spirituality for Feminists* (Mystic: Twenty-Third Publications, 1991).

Zimmerli, W., *Ezekiel 1, A Commentary on the Book of the Prophet Ezekiel, Chapters 1–24* (Philadelphia: Fortress Press, 1979).

Zinnbauer, B. and K. Pargament, 'Religion and Spirituality: Unfuzzying the Fuzzy', *Journal for the Scientific Study of Religion*, 36 (1997): 549–64.

Zock, H., *A Psychology of Ultimate Concern: Erik Erikson's Contribution to the Psychology of Religion* (Amsterdam: Editions Rodopi B.V., 1990).

Zohar, D. and I. Marshall, *SQ: Connecting with Our Spiritual Intelligence* (New York: Bloomsbury, 2000).

Author Index

Biblical References

Subject Index

female *see* female
formation 26–7, 31, 33, 157
gender *see* gender
girls', at puberty 30–32, 80, 85
growth 162
women's 12
independence 28–9, 169
interpersonal stage/self 29–31, 123, 126–7
Israel 1–2, 6, 46, 74, 101–2, 163

Jairus' daughter 73–4, 82, 93, 172
Jesus
    and the body 89
    as part of the trinity 112–4
    in theologies of childhood 6, 46
    maleness of 45–6
    personal understandings of 114–16,
        121, 155
jouissance 80–81

liminality 92–3
liminal places
    girls' puberty as 92, 118
    within the birthing metaphor 165–6
Lo-ruhamah/Ruhamah 1–3
loss
    of voice 17–18, 77, 133
    sense of, at leaving childhood 8, 77,
        81, 92
Lydia 164

marginalisation of girls *see* girls
masculine
    culture 80–81
    imagery, biblical 45–6
    models/values 22
masculinist
    imaginary 145–6
    imperative of research 60
    nature of RE 40
    perspectives 13
menarche 37, 81, 84
menstruation 82–5, 87–8
mentoring 49, 51, 168
midwife imagery 166–71
Miriam 139–40

mirroring 137, 156–7, 168
mystery
    children's 10, 47, 157
    of Christ 46
    of God 47
    and the interviewees 131, 155

Naaman's wife's slave girl 101–2
natality 145–7, 172
nest 151
nurturance
    by the faith community 44, 158,
        160–61, 168–9
    in the womb 141
    of holding environments 33, 142, 169
    wider contexts of 16
nurture of children 48–50

patriarchal
    animal imagery 96
    circumscription 143
    definitions of femininity 90
    discourse 22–3, 157
    images of God 122
    structures 87
patriarchy
    biblical 1, 49, 139
    in play space 153
peer groups/relationships 30–31, 124–6
placenta 80, 146–7, 158
play 48, 152–5
postmodernism 16, 25
power
    differentials 4, 51, 66, 70, 84
    female 20
    games 4
    generation and 66–7, 69
    girl 19, 21–2, 133
    of evil 120
    of God *see* God
    of Jesus 115
    of the Spirit 113, 117
    structures 3
prayer
    and care 129
    as part of church apprenticeship 169

The Interviewees